"There is no escaping the challenge represented by turning points. We can respond to these challenges by allowing them to overwhelm, defeat, and depress us, or we can approach them creatively and intelligently and turn them to our advantage. Few authors have identified these challenges before *Watersheds*."

Norman Cousins

"Easily read and full of examples of the 'sweet' but difficult uses of adversity . . . The fact that the Lauers' suggestions work—and have always worked—is what makes their book special."

San Diego Magazine

"Robert and Jeanette Lauer add to our understanding of life's turning points with case stories and suggestions for mastering change. *Watersheds* is an important work for personal growth and for helping others."

Nick Stinnett, Ph.D.
Author of *Secrets of Strong Families*

"A guided journey into mastering the art of creating a power base of joy and serenity that withstands any and all chaos that develops in our lives. . . . The Lauers shows us how our problems can be our best friend, not the enemy."

Janice Keller Phelps, M.D.
Author of *The Hidden Addiction*

WATERSHEDS

Mastering Life's Unpredictable Crises

Robert H. Lauer, Ph.D., and Jeanette C. Lauer, Ph.D.

IVY BOOKS • NEW YORK

To our children,
each a positive watershed:

Jon
Julie
Jeffrey
and the newest, Kathy

Contents

III COMMENCING

Acknowledgments

We are grateful to those who in various ways have contributed to this book:

- Our students at U.S. International University in San Diego, without whom the project could not have been completed.
- All those who willingly shared their watersheds with us, giving us a wealth of materials with which to work. We have changed their names and some of the details of their stories to protect their anonymity, but their accounts are essentially true as given.
- Mohsin Ladak, David Carson, and Susanne Wagner, who did so much of the work of tabulating and organizing materials.
- Stan Corwin, our agent and friend, who encouraged us from the start to pursue the idea of watersheds.
- Fredrica Friedman, our editor, who responded quickly to the project and gave us ample freedom and support to develop our ideas.

1
Confronting

We sail within a vast sphere, ever drifting in uncertainty, driven from end to end. When we think to attach ourselves to any point and to fasten to it, it wavers and leaves us; and if we follow it, it eludes our grasp, slips past us, and vanishes for ever.

Blaise Pascal

1

The Certainty of Uncertainty

Change is the one certainty of life. It often arrives unsought and unexpected. At some point or other we all confront the unanticipated illness, the sudden accident, the random encounter, the unexpected opportunity. And even when change is deliberately sought, the outcome may include some unanticipated consequences. Uncertainty and change are our lot in life as well as important factors in our development—sometimes for good, sometimes for ill.

In Aldous Huxley's novel *Brave New World*, the Resident Controller of the Western world says that change is a "menace." The rulers of the society abhor change. They cherish the known arrangements of stability over the uncertainties of change. Alvin Toffler presents a different though still negative view of change in his 1970 book *Future Shock*. We must, he argues, deal not only with change but with very rapid change. And that rapid change, he insists, frequently leaves people physically and emotionally traumatized. But despite these gloomy assessments, there is no avoiding change.

Such thoughts raise a number of questions. Must we, as Toffler suggests, be victims of our changing world? How much of our lives is governed by uncertainty? What are the effects of unanticipated events and experiences? Can we control the effects? How is it possible to grow into mature and fulfilled individuals in a rapidly changing world in which unexpected, unanticipated, and, in some cases, unwanted events and experiences alter our lives? To see why such questions are important,

3

we need to understand the fact that all of us have a fundamental
need to grow.

TO LIVE IS TO GROW

Most people hunger to "live deep and suck out all the marrow
of life," as Thoreau put it. We want to *live*, not merely exist.
We are not deceived into thinking that to breathe is to live. Swiss
psychiatrist Paul Tournier wrote about a man who came to him
one day and said, "I have come to see you because I am looking
for life." The man was obviously alive and rather friendly-
looking. He was a part of the fast-paced and complex diplomatic
world. But he was distressed by what he saw as the artificiality
of that world and by his own sense of emptiness. Outwardly, he
appeared to have much. Inwardly, he confessed to having little.

Of course, there are no simple prescriptions to be given to
those who come looking for life. There is no consensus on the
fundamental needs of humans. Freud said that we all need
meaningful work and love in order to be mentally healthy. But
while work and love may be necessary, they are not sufficient.
We also have physiological needs like food, drink, and rest. And
we have such psychological needs as security, self-esteem, recognition, belongingness, control, and new experiences.

Whatever else we need, however, there is consensus on the
notion that to live—that is, to experience the fullness of life—is
to grow. Many people think of paradise as a South Sea island
where they can enjoy sunshine and leisure each day, and be free
from all the cares that afflict us in modern society. Would such
a life make you happy?

Some years ago, a writer had a chance to answer the question
for himself. He lived for a number of weeks on an island in the
South Pacific. The natives were contented and friendly. The sun
shone every day. There was little work to be done. But one day
the writer became aware of something unexpected: he was incredibly bored! In the midst of his emerging discontent, he found
some old American magazines and began reading them. He
realized that the people he was reading about were engaged with
life, while he was vegetating and growing increasingly restless.
He gladly left "paradise" and returned to life.

The writer's fantasy broke apart in a blunt confrontation with reality. We all have our fantasies about paradise. It may be the small town that seems so free of crime and other urban problems. It may be the mountain hideaway that promises to insulate us from the cares of life. But the reality rarely lives up to the fantasy. We long for an escape to our particular view of paradise, only to find ourselves restless and bored when we get there. A friend told us that he spent a chunk of his time in a picturesque western town looking for a copy of *The New York Times*. For a day, he had visited the shops, viewed the historical sights, and enjoyed the feel of the Wild West. Then he was anxious to know what was going on in his world. Like the writer, he realized that a paradise somehow disconnected from the ferment of human life simply does not exist.

We do not grow without being engaged with life. And we do not experience life deeply without growing. "What's the use of having a long life," wrote the medieval mystic Thomas à Kempis, "if there's so little improvement to show for it?" Without growth, a long life can be an extended exercise in triviality. In fact, it can be worse: for some people, life is a long, weary trek punctuated by seasons of anguish and only occasionally broken up by brief moments of happiness. The alternative to this kind of weary existence is growth. There are times in most of our lives when we would like to "freeze" the process and maintain our world as it is. But that is not possible. There is no such thing as a static perfection. There is only process, movement, change, development. Those who do not advance must necessarily regress. Our only two choices are growth or decay. The individual who tries to preserve the status quo is fighting against the essence of the universe.

But exactly what does it mean to grow? What is this process that is the essence of life? Among other things, to be a growing individual means that you increasingly are able to

- relate warmly, intimately with others;
- accept yourself for what you are;
- accept others as they are;
- assume responsibility for your own behavior;
- have a realistic understanding of your world;

- express your feelings spontaneously and without embarrassment; and
- center yourself within a meaningful philosophy of life.

Growing people have a capacity for love. They can establish relationships in which others are as significant or nearly as significant as they themselves. Growing people continue to delight in both new and familiar experiences. They are capable of enjoying mystical kinds of experiences. A friend of ours attended a concert with us and sat utterly transfixed through a Sibelius symphony. Afterward he told us that he had "gotten high" on the music. And another friend told how his mother found wonder in flower gardens throughout her life. One day, when she was nearly eighty, he was driving her to visit a friend and she suddenly told him to stop the car. They had passed a garden and she wanted to get out and stroll through it.

Clearly, a growing person is someone who becomes increasingly self-fulfilled, someone who increasingly realizes his or her potential. We all strive to grow in this sense, because, as someone once put it, the human abhors incompleteness the way that nature abhors a vacuum. (In his survey of values of Americans, Daniel Yankelovich found that the search for self-fulfillment is "an authentic grass-roots phenomenon involving, in one way or another, perhaps as many as 80 percent of all adult Americans.") But we still face the question raised earlier: How is it possible to find self-fulfillment, to be engaged in that life-giving process that we call growth, when unexpected events and experiences intrude into our lives? Do we really have any control over what happens to us? Can we direct the course of our lives? Or must we always react and respond to external happenings?

In our view, it is an overstatement to claim, as a teacher did, that "life is a game of craps." People do have some control. But it is also an overstatement to insist, as William Henley did in his poem "Invictus," that we are the masters of our fate and the captains of our souls. We all face the unanticipated and, in some cases, the unwanted in our lives. The question is, how will we deal with these uncertainties? And equally important, what will be the effect of these unanticipated events and experiences?

WRESTLING WITH UNCERTAINTY

"The art of living resembles wrestling more than dancing," wrote the thoughtful Roman emperor Marcus Aurelius, "inasmuch as it stands prepared and unshaken to meet what comes and what it did not foresee." We all have to deal with uncertainties in our lives. Yet for some people, the unexpected seems to be an oppressively intrusive factor. Ivan Turgenev portrayed this kind of intrusiveness in *Spring Torrents*.

The hero, Dimitry Sanin, is a young man of twenty-three when the story opens. He is in Frankfurt, Germany, returning to Russia from a vacation in Italy. Sanin goes into a store to buy some lemonade while waiting for his train. A young woman suddenly runs from a back room and begs him to come quickly and help. In the back room, Sanin finds an unconscious boy. He administers first aid; soon the boy regains consciousness. A physician appears and indicates that Sanin acted properly in order to help the boy, who turns out to be the brother of the young woman. Sanin is quite captivated by the beauty of the woman; he cannot resist when she insists that he return in an hour so that she and her family can thank him.

Sanin's brief return visit turns into an extended stay in Frankfurt. He falls quickly and totally in love with the young woman, Gemma. Unfortunately, she is already engaged to another man. But then another unforeseen event intrudes. Sanin, Gemma, and her fiancé are at a restaurant when a drunken soldier insults her. The fiancé tries to evade the scene, urging Gemma and Sanin to leave the place quietly. But Sanin confronts the soldier, demands satisfaction, and finds himself with a duel scheduled for the next morning. Neither Sanin nor the soldier are harmed by the duel, but the effect of the whole incident is to lead Gemma to break her engagement with the man who would not protect her honor. Soon she and Sanin are engaged to be married.

Sanin is deliriously happy. He decides to sell his estate in Russia and move to Frankfurt, where Gemma will be more comfortable. He is mulling over an appropriate way to sell his property when the unanticipated intrudes yet again. He meets an old acquaintance by chance on a street in Frankfurt. The acquaintance's wife is a wealthy woman who might be interested in purchasing the property. Sanin takes a carriage to Wiesbaden to meet the wife and attempts to persuade her to buy his estate. What he meets is not simply a businesswoman but a beautiful, self-assured, and egocentric woman who does as she pleases and takes what she desires. She desires Sanin. Within a few days she has seduced him. He breaks off his engagement with Gemma and follows his new love. Ultimately, Gemma marries and moves to New York. Sanin's illicit love affair dies and he spends a good portion of his life in regretful loneliness. At the end of the story, he is preparing to leave for New York where the widowed Gemma still resides with her children.

Sanin was not a helpless victim in the face of the unexpected events that shaped his existence. But the course of his life reflected the ongoing intrusion of the unanticipated. While that may make good fiction, does it ever really happen to people? Consider the case of Felicia. She is married and the mother of three adult children. She works with her husband in their real-estate business. In some ways, Felicia appears to have everything. She had a happy childhood in an affluent home. She has a stable marriage. She has financial security. But she is a weary woman. She struggles with the feeling of being burnt out, the result of a variety of events and experiences that have intruded into her life. And they came at a time when she had very different expectations for herself.

"I've devoted years to my husband and our business," she explained, "and to my children and their lives. This is something that I had always expected to do and did willingly. But now it seems as if everything and everyone has a problem. This I didn't expect." Felicia ticked off her troubles: "My daughter has gotten a divorce and has moved back home. The business is in a slow period. My youngest son broke his neck in an automobile accident. My mother has developed problems with arthritis. And my mother-in-law has suddenly decided she needs more attention from my husband and me. And to top it off, everyone is looking to me for solutions. I don't have the answers. I'm just burnt out."

Part of the problem for Felicia is the feeling of a multitude of new responsibilities—responsibilities she had not anticipated, which deprive her of using her time for personal development.

She feels that she has to make things right for her husband, her parents, her children, her in-laws, and even her friends. She is a product of the 1950s: she was raised on the notion that a woman's main role is to nurture and please her family. But she has also been influenced by the feminist insistence of the 1960s that a woman also has a responsibility to nurture and develop herself as an individual. So Felicia keenly senses the fact that in devoting herself to those around her she has not taken sufficient time to develop herself fully as an individual. "I had always told myself, just wait until the kids are grown and then your time will come. Only it hasn't. At this point in my life, I expected that the major responsibilities would be over, and now it seems that they are beginning anew."

At the time she shared her feelings with us, Felicia was trying to detach herself from some of the unanticipated responsibilities. She was subtly encouraging her daughter to find her own apartment. She was trying to be less bothered by her mother's physical ailments. And she was encouraging her mother-in-law to find new interests and new friends. But it wasn't easy for her: "I'm not sure that detaching is right for me. Maybe I'll go back to being 'the one' for everybody. Not because they need me, but because I need them to think they do." She raised her eyebrows and asked, "Damned if I do, damned if I don't, aren't I?"

Felicia's struggle is not unlike Sanin's in one very important sense. For many years, both of them had to deal with the unexpected or with events they had not anticipated. But neither did it with much vigor. Rather, both allowed themselves to go where they were pushed. Both were unable to muster the resources necessary to take responsibility for and control over their own lives. "If I could make a change in my life," Felicia admitted, "I would start out by telling my family that my time has come. Maybe I'll go back to school and complete the degree I began before I married. And maybe I won't. Maybe I'll just vegetate for a while—walk the beach and lunch with my friends. But the choice will be mine. Allowing another person to be in charge of your destiny is a big mistake."

Of course, not everyone is buffeted around by unanticipated developments as much as Sanin and Felicia. And no one need yield to the unexpected as much as they did. But we all have a certain amount of struggling to do. And the way in which we engage in the struggle can make an enormous difference in our lives. People respond in different ways to the same kind of event. And because of their differing responses, some endure lingering emotional pain while others experience an exhilarating sense of triumph.

THE PRICE OF GROWTH

There are varying ideas about the way to deal successfully with change and uncertainty while growing into fulfilled individuals. Some people seem to hope that growth will occur if they only flow with events. Others try to avoid places, experiences, and even relationships that make them vulnerable to pain. They hope to grow by default. But we do not grow by allowing ourselves to be swept aimlessly by the winds of change, nor by trying to avoid risks and pain. To paraphrase an old saying, eternal vigilance and effort are the price of growth.

A Welsh friend once shared with us his experience of working in an armaments factory during the Second World War. The management had posted signs throughout the factory with just five letters on them: I A D O M. Everyone, he told us, knew the meaning of the letters. They stood for "It all depends on me." The management used the signs to impress upon the workers that each of them had to work as though the whole war effort depended upon what they did individually. Each daily had to think, Victory depends upon what I do this day. In a real sense, I A D O M is a metaphor for individual growth. It all depends upon what we each do this day. To some extent, we can shape the experiences of the day. And when we cannot control the events and experiences themselves, we can still control our responses. This means that our own decisions and behavior help determine whether the day's activities will be a barely remembered fragment of time, an occasion for lingering pain, or an opportunity for growth.

In other words, we grow by choosing to grow. Growth isn't just a matter of dealing properly with the changes and uncertainties that we all face. It is also a matter of deliberately initiating change as well. We grow by confronting and resisting and reaching rather than by waiting and reacting and adapting. Philip, a thirty-eight-year-old manager for a Fortune 500 company, discovered this truth for himself the hard way. For many years, Philip did not have a realistic understanding of his world. He believed the "truths" that his father taught him.

Life for my father was simple: if you work hard and keep at it, you will succeed. I grew up with the idea that people would recognize me for my achievements, that they would see how hard I worked and how competent I was and would reward me accordingly. So what I had to do was work hard and wait for the payoff.

But the payoff didn't come for Philip in his first job.

I stayed in one position for more than twelve years, working hard and doing a good job. Nothing happened in my career. I knew that other managers, some of whom didn't do as good a job as I did, were getting promoted by playing company politics. For a long time, I had to struggle with the contradiction between my belief in the payoff of good work and my observation of how people in my company were getting ahead.

I was increasingly frustrated and perplexed. I wasn't going anywhere and it was affecting the rest of my life—my marriage and my sense of self-esteem. Finally, I made the difficult decision to leave the company. It was difficult because I had a secure position there. I believe I could still be there if I had chosen to stay. I went to work for another company that didn't pay me any more at the start, didn't offer me much security, but did give me an opportunity to grow.

My life has blossomed since then. I have learned to take the initiative in getting ahead. I firmly believe that there are some people who watch things happen, some who make things happen, and some who never even know anything has happened. I used to be the watcher. Now I'm the maker.

If I have any regrets, it's only that I waited so long to make the move.

Philip has a much more realistic perspective on things now. He understands that he can't sit and wait for life to come and reward him for hard work. He has accepted the responsibility for his own growth. His decision to leave the company that stifled his development was a turning point in his life. It took twelve years of frustration, but at least he learned the invaluable lesson that we grow by acting, not by waiting and reacting.

So vigilance and effort are necessary. We don't grow simply because we survive. And we don't grow because of the nature of the event or experience. That is, what appears to be a desirable experience can turn out to be neutral or even negative in the long run. Some people let the potential helpfulness of the desirable experience slip away. Similarly, undesirable experiences and events may turn out to be positive factors in an individual's growth. Some seize the undesirable and use it for their ultimate well-being.

A seemingly desirable experience, for instance, is winning one of the state lotteries. Would a million dollars make you happier? Would it enable you to do the things necessary to grow and find fulfillment? We all think so. One midwestern couple who became millionaires through the lottery reported a number of negative experiences, however. They are happy to have the money. They like the financial security. But they have had to deal with some unexpected problems. They didn't realize how many people would want to share in their winnings. They had no idea that so many acquaintances would pressure them to change their life-style. They found themselves and other members of their family embroiled in arguments about how the money would be used. "Ironically," pointed out the wife, "one important lesson we learned was that money really isn't everything." The money took care of their financial problems but it created some other problems and it didn't fulfill all their needs.

Of course, most of us would agree in principle that money isn't everything. Henry Ford once asked an associate about his life goals. The man replied that his goal was to make a million dollars. A few days later Ford gave the man a pair of glasses made out of two silver dollars. He told the man to put them on and asked what he could see. "Nothing," the man said. "The dollars are in the way." Ford told him that he wanted to teach him a lesson: If his only goal was dollars, he would miss a host of greater opportunities in life. He should invest himself in serving others, and not simply in making money.

Few of us would disagree. At the same time, we are not altogether convinced by a lottery winner and Henry Ford telling us that money will not necessarily make us happier. Most of us will respond when we get the sweepstakes letter from Ed McMahon telling us we may have won a million dollars or more. As one man said with a shrug: "I know my chances are slim. But it's a twenty-two-cent lottery ticket. How can you go wrong?" And millions of Americans will continue to watch "Wheel of Fortune" and other televised game shows to share vicariously in the pleasure of those who have increased their fortune.

Perhaps the midwestern couple who won the lottery was wrong. Perhaps we need to listen to a greater number of people. Perhaps the experiences of other winners are much different. Three researchers who made a study of lottery winners reached conclusions that shatter our fantasies about winning. The researchers looked at 197 people who had won $50,000 or more; 7 had won $1 million. In general, the winners regarded their experience as a highly positive event that had brought about various changes in their lives (although more than three-fourths said that the winnings had not altered their life-styles). The researchers asked the winners to rate themselves on how happy they were at this stage of their lives, on how happy they expected to be in a couple of years, and on the pleasure they got from seven things: talking with a friend, watching TV, having breakfast, listening to a joke, receiving a compliment, reading a magazine, and buying new clothes. The researchers asked the same questions of a group of nonwinners who lived in the same neighborhoods as the winners.

The lottery winners were no happier than the nonwinners, nor did they expect any greater future happiness. Furthermore, they reported less pleasure from the seven activities than the nonwinners! It is probable that everyday pleasures could not compete with the thrill of winning the lottery. While the winners gained a moment of exhilaration, it appears that they lost some of their ability to enjoy the commonplace pleasures.

The point is not that money is undesirable. After all, neither Henry Ford nor any of the lottery winners gave away their money in order to gain a measure of happiness. The point is that what appears to be a desirable event can have some unexpected and undesirable results. The fantasy may be far more enjoyable than the reality. Getting more money may solve some problems and open up many opportunities. It will not end the struggles of life.

If a desirable event can turn out to have some less-than-desirable consequences, the reverse is also true. An undesirable event can have some long-term positive consequences for those who put forth the effort. Craig is fifty-three years old. He teaches physics in high school. Some fifteen years ago, he served in the navy. He was aboard an aircraft carrier, supervising the aircraft engineering wing on that ship. As he went about his work one day, he happened to notice a young sailor working on a piece of equipment. The sailor turned a turbine the wrong way. Craig knew immediately that the result could be disastrous. He shouted as he ran toward the sailor. But a fire erupted before he could reach the equipment. The fire spread rapidly, causing some bombs on an airplane to explode. The bombs, in turn, made the fire spread even faster.

Among all the personnel on deck when the accident occurred, Craig was the only survivor. But he lost a leg and suffered massive internal injuries. Doctors at the naval hospital told his wife that he would probably not live. He did live, but he spent three months in a coma, then more months in recovery. Eventually the navy transferred him to a hospital near his home so that his wife and children could see him. Nine months after the accident, Craig left the hospital.

The trauma of the experience was long-lasting. Even fifteen years later, Craig says: "I don't like to discuss my personal feelings and emotions after I came out of the coma. I got by by concentrating on one day at a time. I had a lot of nightmares." Some people might survive, as Craig did, but suffer lasting emotional damage. Among other things, survivors of disasters tend to sink into depression and struggle with guilt. In addition to coping with those reactions, Craig had to come to terms with the loss of his leg.

He used the time in the hospital to consider his situation. "I had a lot of time to think about what I would do with my life," he says. "I decided that I didn't want to get out of the navy, and I requested special permission to remain on active duty. I said I would take any job where I didn't have to go on a ship. I was assigned to instructor duty, and taught for the navy until I had twenty years of active duty and retired. When I retired, I went back to school and got my bachelor's and master's degrees so I could teach as a civilian."

We don't even like to think about such things as being in an accident where scores of people are killed and we lose a leg and spend months in a hospital. Yet Craig was able to take the experience and turn it into something positive for himself. This is not to say that his life has been easy.

Obviously, that accident changed my whole life. Losing my leg closed a lot of doors to me. It put a real strain on my marriage. Fortunately, my wife and I were able to endure the strain, and we are still happily married. But life hasn't been easy since the accident, and my health has never been as good. My leg gives me trouble, and I still have to use crutches a lot. Life just moves at a slower pace when you wear an artificial leg. I can't move as quickly as I used to, and that still bothers me.

In spite of his continuing problems, Craig is aware of having grown through the experience. The frown on his face as he speaks of his accident gives away to a gentle smile as he tells of the final outcome.

It caused me to find new meaning in life. I hadn't planned on retiring from the navy as soon as I did. I figured that I'd get a job working as a mechanic for the airlines when I retired. Obviously those plans had to change after the accident. I hadn't planned on being a teacher, but I am enjoying the work a great deal. I've become more active in community activities since the accident. I guess I feel like there must be some reason why I'm still alive, and I want to make sure that I fulfill whatever obligation I do have while I am here.

It's a tough way to grow. Perhaps Craig would have grown anyway. He certainly wouldn't say that he was happy about the accident, even if it did provide new meaning in his life. But he is a happy man. The point is not that the accident was good for him. Rather he took a negative event, refused to allow it to wring the joy of life from him, and eventually found new meaning in his life as he continued to cope with the unexpected trauma that had afflicted him.

Craig's accident, like Philip's decision to switch jobs, was a *watershed* in his life. We define a watershed as any event or experience that significantly affects the course of an individual's life. Not all watersheds involve painful or dramatic events. Sometimes a watershed can be a common situation or event that, for various reasons, is a personal turning point. Twenty-seven-year-old Natalie, for instance, is an ebullient dancer who is lithe, quick to smile, and fully engaged with life. Her watershed was her ballet lessons as a child with "Miss Catherine, a short Frenchwoman with a long, auburn ponytail." Miss Catherine was a demanding teacher who insisted that her students "walk like dancers, dress like dancers, and act like dancers. If we were late to class or did not act properly, we were dismissed for the day. If our inappropriate behavior continued, we were forever banned from her studio. She taught with a gentle but iron hand."

Natalie loved ballet. Although she is now involved in modern dance rather than ballet, her lessons with Miss Catherine were a turning point in her development: "I learned much more than how to dance. I learned discipline, how to tolerate pain, to work hard for something I love, and to get up and try again."

Thus, there are many varieties of watersheds. An individual may deal with an intrusive event like an accident or a typical experience like childhood dancing lessons in a way that turns the event or experience into a watershed. Or the individual may initiate the change that becomes his or her watershed experience, as Philip did in changing jobs. Watersheds can be positive or negative events or experiences. And their outcomes can be positive or negative.

Happily, while we cannot dictate the extent to which we will have positive or negative experiences, we *can* control the outcomes. Craig could not prevent the accident. But he could, and did, turn it into a watershed of growth for himself. Natalie could not change the gentle tyranny of Miss Catherine. But she could, and did, use it to achieve a positive watershed in her life. Sanin and Felicia allowed themselves to be controlled by events. Craig and Natalie took charge of events and experiences and shaped them into times of growth. This option is open to all of us.

A PAUSE FOR DIRECTION

All of us have a desire to find fulfillment in life, to live deeply, joyously, richly. Fulfillment requires growth. But growth is difficult when the unexpected intrudes into our lives. Like Craig, change may bring trauma that threatens to overwhelm us. Moreover, change is deceptive, for desirable events may not bring us the fulfillment we had anticipated. And even when we initiate the change, there may be unanticipated consequences with which we will have to cope. How does an individual gain control?

We have said that vigilance and effort are necessary. But that is hardly a sufficient answer. Rather, our answer will be based on the experiences of hundreds of individuals who have struggled with uncertainty and confronted opportunities. We will discuss the life-altering events and experiences that people have identified in their lives. We have collected more than six hundred such watersheds. In essence, we will show three things:

- the kinds of events and experiences—both positive and negative—that are likely to be watersheds in people's lives, including both interesting similarities and interesting differences in the watersheds reported by men and women;
- how people deal with both expected and unexpected, planned and unplanned, events and experiences (some use them to further their personal growth while others fail to use them

profitably, either missing an opportunity or emerging with lasting emotional scars); and

• how to use the information about the watersheds, along with some social-scientific principles, to initiate growth-enhancing change and turn unexpected and unanticipated events and experiences into positive watersheds.

Clearly, we are not merely providing a description of coping strategies, but are offering the kind of answers and solutions that will enable you to master the unpredictable crises of life. There are ways of coping that are not particularly helpful in the long run. One man said that he dealt with the multiple and sometimes contradictory demands that others were placing on him by "putting my mind in neutral and going where I'm pushed." That was a coping mechanism. But it was detrimental to his growth.

You need to know not merely how people cope with events and experiences, but how they use them to further their own development, and what this can mean in your life. The people we discuss have, like all of us, faced the issues of growth, change, and uncertainty. Some have come away hurt and limping. Others have emerged victorious. Why? The answers can enable you to master your own life.

2

How We Grow

It is said that there is a grave high in the mountains of Switzerland with the simple inscription "He died climbing." This is a metaphor for life. At least, it is a metaphor for the fulfilling life, which is an ongoing struggle to reach new heights. What is important is not how far you have climbed, how much you have grown, but how you got to where you are. And, most important, how you can get to where you want to go.

THE PATH OF GROWTH

Developmental psychologists have identified three basic factors in an individual's growth—those related to the person's age, those related to the particular time in which he or she lives, and those that are unpredictable. The factors related to the person's age are those that are fairly predictable because they are associated with various stages of life. That is, they tend to occur at the same time of life for each of us.

At each age, we have certain tasks, certain challenges or crises, that have to be dealt with adequately in order that we may continue to grow. And these tasks continue throughout our lives. From the challenge of infancy—learning to trust our mothers and our environments—to the crisis of later adulthood—evaluating our lives and dealing with impending death—our lives are a series of hurdles. The child in the early school years, for example, must cope with learning to become adequate and competent to deal with the world. Through interaction with peers, teachers, and parents and through their feedback, the child will, if all goes well, develop a sense of his or her personal effectiveness. There is a kind of recapitulation of that struggle in the twenties. The young adult is now likely to be out of the nest, and coping with life more or less independently. At this stage, it is important to build the foundation for one's life direction, to gain some sense of where one is going, and to do it competently.

While we are struggling with these developmental tasks, we must also deal with the varied historical influences that come to bear upon our lives. These are factors that are common to a generation of people. For example, those who grew up in the Great Depression share a unique experience that affects their path of growth. Those who experienced a war or a widespread epidemic or a major societal shift such as a revolution also share a common experience that affects their efforts to grow. It is, of course, not merely the shared experience but also the point in a person's life when the experience occurs that is important. Those who struggled through the depression as unemployed adults had a very different experience from that of their children. And their children certainly have had a quite different experience from subsequent generations, who only read about the disruptions caused by the wounded economy.

Finally, the unpredictable events, which are significant in an individual's development but are neither related to the individual's age nor to the time in which the individual lives, include such things as illness, accidents, divorce, death, a new job or the loss of a job, and moving to a new location. Such experiences are common, but they do not, like developmental tasks, occur at the same time in people's lives. And like the historical experiences, their impact varies depending upon the time they do occur. The death of a parent when a person is ten is likely to be a different experience than when one is sixty.

The way in which the three different influences come to bear in an individual's life is illustrated by Frank, a thirty-year-old management consultant who has had AT&T, General Electric, and other large corporations as clients. Initially, Frank intended to become a professional football player. Like many American boys, he had the dream of being a professional athlete. Indeed, he dreamed of being an outstanding player.

I remember when I was a boy and at home alone, I would play a game all by myself. I would get my football, pretend to be a running back, and charge through the line. Then I would be the quarterback and throw a touchdown pass while the opponents were charging down on me. I had some great games in my basement, running back and forth with the ball, dodging those imagined guys from the other team. And I was always the hero.

Frank's generation, like earlier ones, romanticizes the professional athlete. It is unlike earlier ones, however, in its perspective on work: Frank's generation holds that work should be something that brings us fulfillment, not merely a paycheck. Frank has always expected to work at something that would provide growth and ample gratification. Early on, that something appeared to be football. Because he was a strong, huskily built boy, he developed the image of himself as "tough." Athletics became an integral part of his identity. He starred on a successful high-school team. He was named to the all-state team and received a number of scholarship offers.

In college, the pattern continued. He was selected as a small-college all-American. He was voted team captain by his teammates. He was single-mindedly and successfully pursuing his goal.

I spent endless hours in the weight room and working on the fundamental skills that I saw as necessary. All other responsibilities and concerns were of little significance. I also played the part of the athlete and chose to associate only with those that fell into the same category. I overcame knee surgery and was well prepared by the time of the tryout date.

Then came the unpredictable influence, the unexpected event that intruded into this smoothly running pattern: Frank could not make the grade as a professional player. The dream of his life collapsed. The anticipated adulation of fans and glory of athletic achievement dissolved in a coach's decision.

To make a long story short, my stay at training camp lasted but a couple of days. My bubble was burst. I now had to seek new direction. I had not made any alternative plans to fall back on in case I did not succeed. Football was no longer a career possibility. I returned to work full-time at a loading dock, which had helped me financially through school.

My girlfriend, who is now my wife, had been working toward helping me see the other side of myself. It was no longer necessary to continue with the tough image that I had established for myself. There still seemed to be a vast void surrounding my life. After a few months of reflection, I decided that I wanted much more out of life than the dock could offer me, so I moved to California to continue with my education.

As I reflect back on the situation and the events that led up to this experience, I realize how much I missed by going through that period of time with a tunnel-vision approach. At first I was in a state of rage, not only at myself for failing but with the world as a whole. I wanted nothing more than to go on to the next camp and try again. They were wrong, I thought. As time went on, however, I decided that I wanted even more out of life than sports. At the time, I felt like someone had jerked me out of line when I was just getting to the front. Now I can honestly say I'm grateful it happened when it did. I really love what I'm doing. I'm good at it. And I don't have to prove it by letting somebody pummel my body.

So personal development is more like a series of abrupt shifts and stumbles and spurts than a smooth upward glide into maturity and fulfillment. "Every day, in every way, I'm getting better and better" may sound like a positive approach to life but it is completely contradictory to experience. Life is a struggle, not a slide. Some of the forces that come to bear upon us in our efforts to grow are expected and some are unexpected. Some are common occurrences and others seem to be unique to us at the moment. The outcome of them all is that we each become, as psychologist Clark Moustakas put it, "a unique and incomparable selfhood."

PERILS ALONG THE PATH

Bart is a bass-guitar player in a rock band who clearly enjoys his work. He has both an absorption in the music and a connection with his audience that suggest that he is a man whose natural talent clearly marked out a career for him. "People think I'm lucky," he says, "because I play well and love my work. They don't realize how much I practice, or how difficult it is to make a living in this business. They don't know how many times I nearly left it for something more stable, and how many years I worked at other jobs to support myself." In other words, Bart's look of contentment masks the fact that he traveled a long and difficult road to get to his destination.

In the 1980s, many people don't expect the road to be either long or difficult. "Life's a beach," says a bumper sticker. "I guarantee you will stop smoking after one day," promises the ad of a therapist. Instant relief for headaches and indigestion is the offer of commercials. And a host of ads and seminars offer us a quick road to wealth through everything from real estate to mail-order schemes. Bart scoffs at the whole notion of instant gratification.

> Younger musicians ask me to help them. They want success and they want it quickly. But I try to get them to see that they have to pay their dues. They have to play wherever and whenever they can. And while they're trying to get gigs, they have to find other things to support themselves. They have to be willing to work as a waiter or a truck driver or whatever. They look at me like I betrayed them. Then I tell them all the things I worked at, like a temporary with Manpower, a salesman in a shoe store, and a waiter for a hash joint. Half the time, they don't believe me. They don't want to scratch and climb their way to the top. They want somebody to drive them up there in a limo.

There are hazards along the path to growth. As Bart puts it, we don't drive there in a limo. We get there by struggling with the obstacles. We need to be aware of them and to refuse to be deflected. In particular, let us look at three perils that can cause us to stumble or lose our way: adversity, ignorance, and inappropriate responses.

Can adverse experiences lead to growth? Some have stressed the point that we grow primarily through so-called peak experiences, those high moments when our whole beings are caught up in exquisite fulfillment. Unquestionably, adversity can be detrimental to both our physical and our emotional well-being. Such things as loss of a job, marital problems, divorce, illness of a child, and problems with parents can lead to anxiety and depression. They also can result in a lowered sense of effectiveness, control, satisfaction with life, and personal optimism.

On the other hand, adversity need not be an insurmountable barrier to growth. A number of psychologists have argued that suffering is a door to growth, not a blockage. There is generally, of course, short-term trauma. But the long-term consequences can be positive. Divorce, for example, virtually always involves considerable short-term, and sometimes long-term, emotional problems. Yet a study of divorced women reported that in retrospect fully 80 percent saw the divorce as a positive turning point in their lives. They learned to seize the adverse situation and use it to further their own growth by a fresh experience of freedom and the sense of getting a new start in their lives.

Both men and women who report positive outcomes from divorce talk about the stimulation of the new experiences. Women do things they had never done before: keep their own financial records; make minor repairs around the house or apartment; experience the freedom of not being accountable to someone else for things done or not done in the home; and know the gratification of being financially self-sufficient. Similarly, men find pleasure in new challenges and new freedom. As one man told us: "The divorce was painful, but I really enjoyed coming home and not having to account for my behavior or worry about being late or feeling I had to eat at a particular time. I felt free for the first time in years."

Another peril is ignorance. We refer here to general misconceptions and misinformation about ourselves, other people, and the world in which we live. It is perilous to believe that whether or not you find fulfillment in life is essentially a matter of luck or fate. It is perilous to assume that you ought to be free of adversity. It is perilous to be blind to the fact that growth means a call to struggle, commitment, and perseverance. And it is perilous to ignore the fact that men and women follow somewhat different paths of growth.

For example, a good deal of the research done on development has focused on males, sometimes with the assumption that the resulting portrait has been one of human rather than male development. But we know now that men and women do not develop along the same paths. Some of the challenges and crises are the same for both, but some are different.

One important difference between male and female development involves the so-called midlife crisis. For men, the crisis usually develops in the forties. It involves a sense of mortality, a recognition of doors being closed and options being reduced, a sense of dreams being unfulfilled and perhaps unfulfillable, a fear of the decline or loss of sexual potency, and questions about the meaning of life. For women, however, there does not appear to be a major transition around age forty. As Gail Sheehy points out in *Passages*, women tend to reach a critical time a bit earlier than men, around the age of thirty-five. At that point, a woman may feel that she faces her last opportunity to accomplish certain things in her life. She may also experience important changes, such as her last child going to school and the prospective end of her childbearing years. But women in their forties do not seem to have the same concerns as men about mortality, and they have an increasing sense of sexual interest and satisfaction. Women report greater uncertainty and dissatisfaction in their twenties than in their forties. In fact, during their late forties and fifties they tend to experience increasing satisfaction with their lives and their marriages and such positive developments in personality as mellowing, assertiveness, and patience. We do not yet have a comprehensive portrait of female development, but it is clear that influences related to age differ in some very important ways for men and women.

The third peril is related to the other two. If we do not positively deal with adversity, or if we respond inappropriately to events and experiences because of ignorance, we imperil our growth. The important point to keep in mind here is that there are always alternative ways of responding to anything. The feeling of being trapped, of there being "nothing else I can do," is rarely, if ever, realistic. The peril is always there, of course, but so is the opportunity.

Recall the story of Craig and his encounter with disaster. Was Craig just an unusual person? Could an accident have the same sort of result in someone else's life? The answer is yes, but not necessarily yes. The point is that it all depends on how we respond to the event. Negative events can have positive outcomes. When a group of college students was asked to report both a very negative and a very positive experience in their lives, and to discuss the long-lasting effects of each, about 40 percent reported positive outcomes resulting from the negative events.

Obviously, this means that more than half did not report positive outcomes. We do not want to promote a simplistic, "you-can-do-it-if-you-try" philosophy. Some people suffer permanent scars from adversity. When 80 percent of women report long-term, positive outcomes from divorce, we should not forget about the 20 percent who did not see divorce as positive. A ten-year follow-up study of sixty divorced families reported that in two-thirds of the families only one of the spouses used the divorce to improve life significantly. In only six of the families did both spouses significantly improve their lives. And women who were over forty at the time of the divorce had a much harder time coping than did those in their twenties and thirties. Many of these older women continued to feel angry and lonely even after ten years.

Not everyone recovers well from a crisis. "Time heals all wounds," the old adage assures us. But researchers at the Institute for Social Research at the University of Michigan reported that between 20 percent and 40 percent of people do not fully recover from a crisis despite the promised healing of time. It is important, then, to learn how to deal with adversity and to gain the knowledge that will enable us to grow through all kinds of situations and experiences.

WATERSHEDS

Watersheds, as we have seen, are events and experiences that significantly affect the course of our lives. They are usually unpredictable events, though some of the age-related and history-related experiences may also be watersheds. For some people, like Craig, an accident may be a watershed. For others, the watershed may be a childhood incident, a religious experience, a crucial decision, an encounter with another person, or a new experience of some fundamental kind. The watershed event or experience may be either negative or positive. It may involve a great deal of trauma or intense pleasure or minimal emotion. Its short-term and long-term consequences may be negative or positive. It may leave the individual emotionally scarred. Or it may be a springboard for growth.

A watershed experience may occur over an extended period, as it did with Craig's accident and months of hospitalization or Natalie's years of ballet lessons with Miss Catherine. Or it may occur in a matter of a few moments, as it did with Paul, a newspaper reporter who covers sports in a large eastern city. Paul came to this country as a refugee in the 1950s. He was six years old at the time. His initial experiences as a schoolboy who could speak no English were painful. He found himself either fighting over or running from the taunts of his classmates a good deal of the time. He developed what he calls a "refugee mentality," which "manifested itself in the following typical sentiments: 'Don't make waves.' 'Be thankful you're here.' 'It's not your turn.' " He particularly held to the latter notion through the first nine years he was in America.

Then came June of 1967 and my job at a summer camp. It so happened that the most prestigious job at the camp, the position of waterfront director, became available. The position was offered to me since I had the necessary licenses and qualifications. Then I heard this voice in my head dutifully saying: "It's not your turn to win. You're not on the first string. Let someone else do it. Maybe someday . . ." Then quite unexpectedly, like a light being turned on, it all fell into place. "Someday" was now. It was my turn. I needed to be the "someone else." So I said yes.

Paul isn't sure why he got that flash of insight. But that moment changed his life. It was like cutting the umbilical cord with his refugee past.

This decision freed me to be myself in what had become my world and at the same time allowed me to respect and appreciate the gravity of the sacrifice my parents had made on my behalf. This single event changed a reluctant and frustrated observer into a player who enjoys being on the starting team. I have since taken many risks. Whether for good or ill, I have come to recognize that at each step the greatest freedom and greatest joy comes in the ability to choose.

Paul's decision may appear to be relatively trivial. It was only a question of whether a young man would accept a position at summer camp. But to Paul, the moment was life-changing, a positive watershed that opened up a new world of growth to him. There was no drama, no extended agonizing over the choice, only a sudden, inexplicable insight that led him to say yes to a new direction.

In spite of their importance in our lives, very little time and effort have been devoted to the study of watersheds. In our own attempt to gain insights into them, we have gathered watershed experiences from 632 individuals over the past few years. We asked each person not only to tell us about a watershed, but also to describe how he or she responded and to assess the short-term and long-term impact of the watershed. The responses were almost equally divided between males and females—315 males and 317 females. Their ages ranged from nineteen to ninety, with an average age of thirty-seven.

What kinds of events or experiences did people consider to be watersheds? The accompanying table gives our breakdown of the percentage of responses in each of seven categories. *Interpersonal problems* involved such things as divorce (including the divorce of a person's parents), death or illness of a significant

KINDS OF WATERSHEDS

	Men	Women	All Respondents
Interpersonal problems	19.8%	34.5%	27.0%
Crucial decisions	29.7	16.7	23.2
Social transitions	19.3	25.2	22.4
Meaningful relationships	12.0	11.4	11.7
Personal problems	12.5	8.4	10.5
Changes of philosophy	2.9	1.3	2.1
Others	3.8	2.5	3.1

other, violence, humiliation, and problems in a love relationship. *Crucial decisions* were mostly about education and work or career. Other kinds of decisions ranged from the woman who made the decision as a girl never to be dependent on a man (a decision prompted by observing her mother's behavior with her father) to a man's decision to stop smoking. *Social transitions* were moves to a different social world: travel, change of residence, involvement in a small group, and religious conversion.

Meaningful relationships were positive ones formed with friends, lovers, a spouse, and children (including the birth of a child). *Personal problems* involved accidents, physical and emotional illness, and unwanted behavioral patterns such as overeating or drug abuse. *Changes of philosophy* occurred when people were exposed to, and influenced by, certain nonreligious writings (Freud and Marx, for instance) or when frustrating situations forced them to reassess a philosophy of life. And the *Others*, the 3.1 percent that could not be placed in any of the above categories, ranged from a discovery by a woman that her legal name was different from what she had thought to another person's recurring, frustrating dream.

While the range of experiences that people defined as watersheds in their lives was considerable, nearly three-fourths fell into one of three categories: an interpersonal problem, a crucial decision, or an experience of social transition. Freud wrote about the importance of work and love in maintaining emotional health. Obviously, these two elements are important in the life course of the individual, and changes in either can become watershed experiences that alter the individual's direction of development.

William I. Thomas, a sociologist, was one of many who tried to identify the basic needs of all humans. Early in this century, he wrote about our common desire for security, response, recognition, and new experience. New experience fits into our category of social transitions. The idea of a universal desire for new experience runs counter to the folk wisdom that people tend to resist change and that you can't teach an old dog new tricks. But it is consistent with the very idea of lifelong development.

Robert Seidenberg, a psychiatrist, has written about the "trauma of eventlessness," a situation in which the absence of sufficient stimuli results in trauma to the individual. He treated a female patient who suffered a breakdown when she realized that without some significant change in her life, the future would be a duplication of her dreary past. The woman suffered from a lack of change. Thus, new experiences that involve the move into a new social world are factors in maintaining our mental well-being and, like interpersonal and career experiences, can become watersheds.

Men and women differed in the kinds of watersheds they reported. As our table shows, women were far more likely than men to select interpersonal problems as watersheds, while men were far more likely than women to select experiences related to education and career. This is not surprising in view of the fact that women tend to be more oriented to the needs of those around them. Women often are more emotionally involved in the lives of others, so that watersheds are more likely to involve interpersonal relationships. Indeed, nearly half the women in our study identified an interpersonal experience (either a problem or a meaningful relationship) as a watershed in their lives.

Women are also more likely than men to name a social transition as a watershed experience. The most common experience cited was a move to a new location that resulted in a greater sense of autonomy and independence. For example, one woman told us she moved across the country, found a job, and decided to stay in her new location. Her initial fears gave way to a new sense of confidence: "I learned to be on my own. To manage my money and maintain a home. It left me mentally stronger and more aggressive. I feel that I am better equipped to handle any obstacles. It gave me an opportunity to mature and become totally independent.''

Women may have "come a long way," but it seems that they are still more prone than men are to doubt their ability to be independent and autonomous. They frequently identified watersheds as those experiences that forced them to be independent. The sense that a woman could make it on her own as a competent individual was an exhilarating one that many women defined as a giant step forward in their development.

When do watersheds occur? They can occur at any age, including very young ones. In his autobiography Lee Iacocca tells about an incident that occurred when he was in the sixth grade and that was one of the three episodes in his childhood that impressed upon him the nature of the adult world. The incident involved the election of the captain of the student patrol—a job he really wanted. He lost by two votes. The next day one of his classmates pointed out to him that the total number of votes was greater than the number of students in the class. But when Iacocca told his teacher, she simply advised him to let the matter rest. It was, he recalls, his first lesson in the fact that life would not always be fair.

Bonnie, a buyer of jewelry for a department store, had a watershed experience at an even earlier age. She recalls making a decision when she was seven that she would never be dependent on a man. She had watched her mother relate in a very subservient manner to her father. No matter what her mother was doing, she had to be home in time to have dinner ready by six o'clock. Her mother always made plans according to Bonnie's father's desires, never around what she or the children wanted. The families of Bonnie's friends seemed to operate in a similar way. But she found the arrangement obnoxious and decided that she would not repeat the pattern.

In order not to repeat her mother's experience, Bonnie learned to be assertive. "Sometimes it is hard and I am not comfortable with it. Ladies don't do that. I'll sound bitchy, but after you do that you feel good. You don't just lie there and get a good swift kick. You don't have to be a screamer or yeller. You just get to know yourself better and like yourself better.'' Bonnie's decision at age seven has affected the pattern of her life.

For most people, of course, watersheds occur a little later. About 41 percent described watersheds that occurred in their twenties. Twenty-five percent of the watersheds happened in the teens, 21 percent in the thirties, and 7 percent in the forties. The rest took place either in the preteen years (4 percent) or the fifties or sixties (2 percent).

The age at which an event occurs is important. Some developmental psychologists have argued that events like the death of a parent are likely to have their greatest impact when they do not occur at the typical time in an individual's life. That conclusion may be too simplistic. It is not only age that is important, but the nature of the relationship and the circumstances. In our sample, 40 people mentioned the death of someone as a watershed, and 22 of those identified the death of a parent. But 14 of the 22 were adults (over twenty-one) when the parent died. Ed is a successful stockbroker and has an aggressive confidence that belies the first three decades of his life. Ed was thirty when his mother died. He explained why it was a watershed in his life.

I had a very strict upbringing. My father would not allow any of his children to smoke, drink, swear, or gamble. I would get a long lecture every time I used improper grammar or misspent my money. I would constantly receive messages that I would never amount to anything and that no one would hire me unless I learned better work habits. His was a constant inner voice within my mind.

When I was twenty-four and still living at home, my mom developed kidney disease. Her illness and subsequent death transformed my life. It began by changing my relationship with my father. When Mom first became ill, I was afraid of getting into a yelling fight with him because of the fear that she might die afterward. I was afraid my father would hold me responsible for her death, and I didn't think I could live with the guilt if that happened.

And at the same time I was experiencing burnout at my job. The market was down and I was working twice as hard for half the money. I was seriously thinking about quitting.

I felt like that character in the comics who walked around with a black cloud over his head. Everything that could go wrong, did.

My mom died a month after my brother and I arranged to have the whole family come home for our parents' fortieth wedding anniversary. But my fears were not realized. After she passed away, my father and I developed a much closer relationship. We both realized how much we needed each other, and he was appreciative of what my brother and I had done for Mom. He told me that he didn't realize how mature and responsible I was until he saw how I handled everything. It wasn't just the anniversary party. I took care of all the funeral arrangements and helped him deal with the paperwork and get all his affairs in order. I stopped receiving the sermons from him. We started having conversations like you would expect from a man and his adult son. We talked about things man to man for the first time in my life. We talked about everything from his feelings of being alone to my aspirations. I started to feel a tremendous freedom to become the person I wanted to be.

The market got better about the same time. But the success I had at that time was more than market conditions. I realize now that my self-confidence took off because I was finally free of my father's domination. And that made me tremendously effective in my work. It's ironic that my mom had to die to get me out from under my father's thumb. But that's what happened. Her death saved my life and gave me a new sense of freedom. The experience was like a rebirth, where the errors of the past are wiped out and you're given a new lease on life.

Like Ed, many people discover that adverse experiences can have beneficial outcomes. We have a remarkable drive and capacity for using adversity to further our own growth. We have the creativity and imagination necessary to turn the trivial and the commonplace into positive watersheds. Neither the unexpected nor the ordinary is an enemy to our development. Rather, all of life is an opportunity.

II

Conquering

For the greatest suffering, so long as it does not cause fainting, does not touch the part of the soul which consents to a right direction.

Simone Weil

3

Personal Problems
The Whirlwinds of Life

Four men that we know respond quite differently to our question, "How are you?" Each consistently gives the same answer, but each gives a different answer: "Terrific." "Fine." "Better." "Terrible." Each has had his share of what we call the "whirlwinds of life," problems such as illness that inevitably afflict all of us. But the problems have affected each of them differently. And for one of them, the whirlwinds have nearly destroyed his well-being.

At the very least, personal problems do to us what a minor health problem did to an acquaintance. He answered the question of how he felt with one word: "Vulnerable." It is disquieting when you first face up to your vulnerability. It is disturbing to recognize the fact that afflictions come to all of us at one time or another. It is unsettling to realize that some of us will crumble in the face of those afflictions and may even live long years of quiet desperation. Physical and mental afflictions break into the lives of the rich and famous as well as the nameless. No one is exempt. Beethoven, raging in vain against an encroaching deafness; van Gogh, tormented by demons of the mind; Jack London, wracked by his failing struggle with alcoholism; Roy Campanella, suddenly thrust from a highly successful career as a major-league catcher to the confines of a wheelchair; Betty Ford, struggling to fulfill her responsibilities as the wife of a political leader while slowly succumbing to the power of alcohol; and the nameless millions who have confronted the same problems in their own lives—all attest to the fact that we are a vulnerable species.

We are, of course, in some ways better off than we were in the past. Life expectancy has increased dramatically. At the turn of the century, people lived, on the average, about forty-seven years; today, they can expect to live into their mid-seventies. The difference is due in good part to the progress made against infectious diseases. But we still battle against the chronic diseases. On the average, each American will face about twenty days of reduced activity each year because of illness or accident, and about one out of every seven will have some limitation of activity because of a chronic condition such as heart disease, arthritis, or hypertension. Mental problems and disorders are also widespread. In fact, one noted study of Manhattan residents reported that only about 18.5 percent were completely free of any psychiatric symptoms. Conservatively, we could say that one out of seven Americans has some degree of mental disorder and as many as eight out of every ten have at least mild psychiatric symptoms.

But even if we accept the fact that we are a vulnerable species, most of us do not expect to be personally vulnerable. The whirlwinds are things that happen to other people. Astronaut James Irwin, who served on the Apollo 15 mission and drove the Lunar Rover on the moon, suffered a heart attack some years later. He reported that one of the problems he had was the sense that such a thing could not happen to him. He was not afraid, only embarrassed and somewhat stunned that he was stricken. His reaction is typical; few of us expect to confront the physical and mental afflictions that come our way.

The whirlwinds of life, then, are a threat to us all. But a threat is not a defeat. Vulnerability does not mean collapse. Fortunately, mental and physical ills can have positive outcomes. Growth does not depend on avoiding the ills, but on dealing with them appropriately. When singer Pearl Bailey was hospitalized with a heart ailment, she had a lot of time to think. She also had some painful experiences in the hospital. Her physical condition was aggravated by an angry encounter with a young intern. He came into her room one day and asked why she did not walk the halls as her attending physician had advised her.

She told him her doctor had not given her a specific time to
begin walking; he only told her that it should be done at some
point. At that time, she was still trying to sit up in a chair without
tiring rapidly. The intern began to shout at her about not following orders. He accused her of being devious and resistant.

Miss Bailey responded that she simply could not walk the
halls until she regained her strength. The people would tire her
too much. "What people?" He screamed the question at her.
He didn't realize that since she was a well-known performer,
other patients would want to talk to her, and that her physician
had told her to minimize talking.

The incident upset her greatly. And she relived the upset when
she related it to her own physician. It was nearly a disaster for
her. She was so emotionally upset by it that she had a relapse.
But she slowly recovered and learned a great deal in the process.
She had what she called a "rebirth" of her ability to accept
other people. Her illness was a watershed-type experience with
a positive outcome for her. A great many people have had a
similar experience. We will look at the varied outcomes of physical and mental afflictions. Subsequently, we will discuss how
people can transform these afflictions into positive growth experiences.

BROKEN BODIES, UNBROKEN SPIRITS

Few people emerge unscathed from an illness or an accident.
Some find, as Norman Cousins did, that even a life-threatening
illness cannot conquer their spirits. In his memoir *Anatomy of
an Illness*, Cousins described in detail the way in which he used
a combination of physicians, his own medical knowledge, and
old episodes of the "Candid Camera" television show to recover from an illness that could have been fatal. For other people, the outcome is less happy. A number of those who shared
their watershed experiences with us talked about the long-term
negative consequences of a physical illness or an accident: depression, anxiety, a loss of interest in life, anger and bitterness,
a sense of isolation, confusion, and a sense of helplessness and
insecurity. And in some cases these negative emotions were
intensified by financial difficulties and strained relationships.

Physical and mental problems are not entirely separate experiences. They frequently occur together and, in fact, each may contribute to the development of the other. For instance, the long-term negative consequences of an accident may take the form of a mild neurosis. Brandon, a twenty-six-year-old financial planner, noted that he is deathly afraid of drowning and that he will never go into water over his head. This stems, he said, from an accident when he was six years old in which he nearly drowned. He has dreaded the possibility ever since.

Accidents particularly impress us with the fragile nature of our lives and our vulnerability to the unexpected. Mark is a thirty-seven-year-old literary agent who deals mainly with plays and movie scripts. Soft-spoken but intense, he has a different view of life than he had before his watershed experience, which had occurred just four months before he related his story to us. He had a near-fatal automobile accident when a speeding car going in the opposite direction went out of control, crossed the median, and headed straight for his car. His wife, who was driving, was able to avoid the car, but a construction truck in another lane rammed into them as it also tried to avoid the car. A third car then hit the truck. Mark and his wife came within five feet of being pushed into a deep ravine. Both were severely injured. Mark sustained lower back and hip injuries. His wife had neck, shoulder, and back injuries. Four months later, they were both still in physical therapy. But the physical trauma was not the worst part of the incident.

One of the most frightening aspects of the accident was that there were no alternatives or options. I was helpless and powerless to make any changes before or during the event. It was a sunny, bright, clear morning. We were driving within the speed limit. We didn't do anything wrong. The feeling of being helpless and powerless is frustrating and frightening. The realization that my life and the life of someone I love can be drastically and irreversibly affected in a matter of seconds is overwhelming.

My initial reaction right after the event was one of thankfulness and relief that we were alive. I felt fortunate that we could walk away. But my injuries began to affect my life more and more. I get anxious whenever I have to drive. I have some pain and some limitations of activity. My feeling of being fortunate has given way to apprehension and a sense of my mortality. I'm angry that we were hurt and are suffering pain and discomfort. I'm worried that we may have some permanent disabilities that may change our lifestyle and the things we like to do. And I resent feeling all of these things.

Mark may eventually come to terms with his situation. He might find the resources someday to turn his trauma into positive growth. Many people do. In fact, 85 percent of those who identified an illness or accident as a watershed also indicated positive, long-term effects. Typically, there is an initial feeling that the event or experience is very negative. But that initial feeling is replaced by acceptance and action that brings about a beneficial outcome.

Some people use an accident or illness to restructure their lives. Julio Iglesias was a professional soccer player in Madrid when he was involved in an automobile accident that left him paralyzed for a year and a half. His soccer career was obviously at an end. A sympathetic nurse gave him a guitar to play to help pass the long hours in the hospital. Iglesias subsequently became a phenomenal success in the pop music field. He had no musical aspirations—or even any sense of his ability—prior to that time.

Accidents do not usually produce such spectacular results, but for many people positive outcomes—new perspectives, and new and desirable personal qualities—have occurred from unexpected trauma. The illness or accident literally jars them into a new direction of development, a direction that enables them to become more mature and fulfilled. As one woman put it: "I like the kind of person I have become, and I don't think I would ever be the way I am if it were not for my time of illness."

When an illness or accident forces the issue, when it leads to growth that might otherwise not have occurred, there may be a sense of gratitude for the incident. Stan, for example, began his watershed experience under 405 pounds of weights. He was only nineteen, and he was on his way to competition in the Olympics. He had already won his place on the team. He decided to try for a new record in his weight class: a 405-pound squat. He placed the bar across his shoulders with relative ease, confident of his powers as he dipped down. The judge nodded at him, and he thrust his body upward. As he surged up, he felt an intense burning in his left knee. The weights came crashing to the floor as the pain left Stan helpless.

Stan's career as a weight lifter and athlete had come to an abrupt end. As he lay in the hospital with a cast on his leg, the words of the doctors burned in him with an intensity that matched that in his knee on the day of the competition. He recalls that he ''felt as if a part of me had died.'' He went through the same phases as someone who is bereaved.

First denial. Thinking it was all a dream or not as serious as the doctors indicated. I attempted to work harder than ever at physical therapy, yet the ligaments and tendons failed to respond as I wanted them to. Then I tried bargaining with the doctors. I would do whatever they said, undergo any kinds of operation or extended treatment, if only they could assure me that my withered knee would be whole again. When this brought no results, I felt despair and sorrow for myself and my dismal future.

Months later, Stan sat gloomily watching the Olympic weight-lifting trials near his home, his burly body crumpled into a soft chair. His coach, who had competed in the Olympics himself, earlier had asked Stan about his plans for the future. Now Stan had no plans. Before the injury, he had hoped to compete and eventually be a coach himself. But as he watched and reflected, some new thoughts wedged themselves into his consciousness, thougths that would not have been allowed entry prior to the accident.

I finally realized this was not the end for me. At nineteen, weight lifting appeared so glamorous. Yet all those around me seemed stuck in life. My coach had hundreds of medals, yet lacked a steady job and always complained about the condition of his life. I began to think about alternatives. I thought about past work I enjoyed. My perspective was changing. Life now seemed full of possibilities. It was then that I made a conscious decision to let go of the lifting and pursue another love, working with people.

Stan accepted his loss and moved on with his life. He had been a camp counselor and a coach for retarded children. He knew he loved working with people. He also loved competition. And he had an idea how he could combine his loves. When he returned to college in the fall, he shifted out of a physical-education major and into political science. He went to work in his father's business, but immediately plunged into the world of politics as well. Today he is a city councilman, enjoying both working with people and the thrill of competition in political campaigns. Eventually, he hopes to run for national office.

Looking back, Stan sees the injury as an important step in his personal growth.

Although painful, confusing, and frustrating at the time, it forced me to step back and take a very close look at my life, and to evaluate my future. Prior to the accident I was simply taking the course of least resistance. I never questioned the direction I was going in. The injury proved to be a time-out period of introspection. I was forced to adapt to the injury, and that meant I had to pursue a new life direction.

In addition, weight lifting may have been a defense, a means of protection. Letting go of the bodybuilding and competitive weight lifting allowed me to soften and develop some qualities that I had been suppressing. I no longer had to keep up the appearance of being a tough guy, a jock. When I gave up lifting, it took a great weight off my shoulders, both figuratively and literally.

Like Stan, David was also jarred into a new direction as a result of both physical and emotional trauma. He had to deal with an unusual illness and then had to face painful humiliation. David is a tall, redheaded man who was raised in Pasadena. His father, a surgeon, was very conservative and very traditional in his views. His mother was a nurse, but stopped working after she began having children. Although he never aspired to be a surgeon like his father, David's ambition was boundless. And it ran into a wall when he was a twenty-five-year-old newly appointed manager in a firm engaged in medical technology.

This was early 1972, and I was thrilled and thought I was headed for the big time. It was a great opportunity for me. I was on top of the world. I went to work in March. In June I had to go for my annual two-week summer military reserve camp in southern California. My wife flew down and we spent a weekend in Mexico.

On the way back, I developed a very high fever. She drove home. I was incapacitated. I thought it was a severe flu. I went to my physician and he thought the same. Soon after—I remember it was the night that Richard Nixon was nominated—I watched the nomination on TV and my hands and my joints started to hurt as if they were on fire. It got so severe that my wife took me to the hospital. My hands were all contorted like I had arthritis.

David spent a week in the hospital. He could not even bend his legs. The doctors were uncertain about the cause of his problems but felt it was a form of arthritis. The attending physician ordered David to stay at home in bed for six to eight weeks. David's immediate concern was his job. He had not worked long enough to have the necessary sick leave. But his superior arranged for him to take a leave and hired a woman to do his work on a temporary basis.

A woman. For David, it was humiliating. At the time, he was an admitted chauvinist. The news about his replacement seemed to turn his world inside out.

I felt very threatened about my job. I was incapacitated. I was only twenty-five years old. And I had been replaced by a woman! I had no idea what my future held. Up to that point, my life had been a lark—no problems, no sweat, no sense of my own mortality.

For the first time, I realized that life and good health were very tenuous things. I had heard that one develops a sense of his own mortality when one hits his thirties and here I was all of a sudden in my twenties, a kid who had never even had a stitch taken, not knowing if I was going to spend the rest of my days as an arthritic person. And I had been replaced by a woman in my office. That was the last straw. I knew my boss was very supportive, but I didn't know what the future held for me there.

David tried to go back to work part-time after eight weeks, but he became ill again and had to return to the hospital. After another extended stay in bed, he was fully recovered. He returned to work and has been working full-time ever since. But he is not the same as the twenty-five-year-old carefree man who began the job.

The experience gave me a real appreciation that a woman could do my job as well as I could, and I feel that gave me real insight. It led me to believe that nothing is particularly special about me just because I am a man.

Reflecting on the experience, David feels that he has grown in two ways.

Before, I just assumed that I would live to be a ripe old age with no health problems. Health problems and disabilities were a very abstract concept. Now I realize that good health is a very tenuous thing and that one should appreciate life on a day-to-day basis. And up to this time I had viewed women as nurses, secretaries, spouses, and support persons. My being away from the office and being replaced very adequately by a woman gave me a much greater appreciation for the fact that women could be strong managers and creative people and assertive people. Since that time, I feel that I have always had a very good working relationship with women in professional positions. I think that has made me a better manager in my area than I might have been otherwise. I deal with women differently because of that. I work with a woman as I would with any male.

My marriage is better, too. My wife is now working in

public relations. There was a time when I would not have wanted her to have a career. That would have led to serious conflict between us. I shudder to think of what would have happened to our marriage if my attitude hadn't changed.

An accident or illness may do more than force us in a new direction. It may save us from pursuing a destructive course. Stan could have very well found competing and coaching a satisfying life. But he believes it would have been second-best to what he is doing now. And David would certainly have been an inept manager had he not learned to deal with women as equals. Claire, on the other hand, a teacher at a private school for handicapped children, feels that her watershed rescued her from a terrible mistake.

Claire's watershed began with an unexpected wedding present. It was during her second year of college. The wedding was only a week away. Brushing her long hair back from her eyes, Claire related her watershed with a faraway look in her eyes, as though she were intimately reliving the entire experience. "The invitations had long been sent out, the cake was ordered, the catering arrangements had been made, my dress was on order, honeymoon plans had been finalized, and the apartment of my dreams was ready and waiting for us to move in." Her fiancé had a good job with an excellent income. She was preparing to be a teacher. Life was basically good.

Then she got her unexpected "present": a sudden and serious problem with her back. She awoke one morning and noticed that she could not walk very well. When she drove her car, she found that she couldn't sit against the seat because it pained her lower back. By the end of the day she could not even stand up.

My boyfriend rushed me to a doctor and his plan was to prop me up for the wedding and worry about what was wrong after the wedding. That didn't go over so well with my parents. The next day they took me to an orthopedic hospital where I had been taken as a baby for a foot disorder. Now, twenty years later, the same doctor treated me. He discovered that I had two deteriorated disks that had to be removed immediately if I was to walk again.

The day before my wedding I was scheduled for surgery. The morning before the surgery my fiancé came in and announced that he couldn't handle what was going on. He said that he needed to get away. So he was going to go camping—to all the places we had planned to go on our honeymoon! Of course that sent me into the pits of depression. And my parents hit the roof. They had the hospital psychiatrist come see me because the doctor was afraid to operate with me in that frame of mind and the operation couldn't be put off any longer.

Claire assured everyone that she could handle the surgery. As the orderlies wheeled her into surgery, she saw her fiancé's parents. They were crying. "He just can't handle this," they told her. "Don't blame him." Claire stared at them with disbelief. All she could think of to say was, "It's a good thing one of us can handle it or there wouldn't be anyone here for the operation."

It was four days after the surgery before Claire became lucid again. She had to stay in bed for a week. Her parents insisted that she never see her fiancé again. She debated the issue with them. She really didn't want to talk about it or think about it at the time. She only wanted to get well, and then she would worry about what, if anything, to say to him.

As it turned out, her feelings for her fiancé shifted dramatically during her time in the hospital, along with her perspective on her own life. One day she saw some children who made her cry. "They would never walk; and I would. Maybe that was the start of my dedication to special-ed kids." At the same time, she quickly came to the conclusion that her fiancé no longer meant anything to her. "I didn't feel any bitterness toward him, nor any love. I was actually glad that the experience had saved me from a terrible mistake." Looking back, Claire realized that she had doubts and fears that she had refused to acknowledge, or that she had dismissed as typical wedding jitters. Now she saw that they represented her own struggle against the direction she was pursuing.

Admittedly, it was a difficult way to learn: "I kept thinking that it wasn't supposed to happen like this. I couldn't remember who or when someone had told me that you grow up, you go to college and meet the perfect young man, get a degree, get married, and have perfect children. There was no room for crisis, and I had trouble putting this one into perspective.''

Actually, it took Claire ten years and a series of events that "weren't supposed to be that way" to come to terms with her life. She got her degree, married someone else, and today is teaching handicapped children and is deeply satisfied with both her work and her marriage. On balance, she is content with her life and grateful for the fact that she never pursued what would have been a destructive marriage.

> My life certainly is not the storybook type that someone— whomever and whenever—promised it should be. But I am happy and fulfilled and no longer allow this experience to hurt me. The biggest hurt was that my illness prevented me from having children, which once was all I had wanted out of life. But I have found a life with my kids at school. I love them and I offer them something they don't get anywhere else. We have a very special relationship.

EMOTIONAL WHIRLWINDS

Clearly, physical ills are usually attended by emotional trauma. For some people, however, the basic problem begins and ends at the emotional level. They struggle with depression, anxiety, midlife crisis, chemical dependency, and other problems. Interestingly, everyone who identified an emotional struggle as a watershed declared that the ultimate consequences were positive. The experiences were not without their costs, however.

Emotional whirlwinds are often long as well as painful. To the individual and those who care about and interact with that individual, the process may seem endless and, at times, hopeless. We live in an age of quick solutions and short-term therapies. We expect instant answers. We get frustrated and even angry with those who seem to plod on mired in their problems or who seem to get better momentarily only to regress time and again.

But there are no quick solutions to emotional pain. And our

lives are not tales of ceaseless progress. Nevertheless, it is important to keep in mind that people can overcome emotional as well as physical problems. Even those who seem to be "hopeless" can break free of their shroud of dark emotions and destructive behavior. Gina, for instance, was thirty-nine years old when she entered an alcohol treatment program for the third time in three years. By that point her drinking problem had become a matter of life and death for her. At the time, she was a divorcée living in a midwestern city and was trying to raise three children on what she earned as a purchasing agent for a small retailer.

"Alcoholic" conjures up images of bleary-eyed, drawn, and listless people. But Gina is attractive and outgoing. She has escaped some of the costs of addiction. She was in her early thirties when she began to have trouble controlling her drinking, the result of a combination of marital problems and a group of friends that tended to drink to excess at social functions. A number of times she attempted to stop on her own, but she never abstained longer than two weeks.

> I was drinking a quart and a half a day, pouring it into my coffee cup at work. I couldn't go more than three or four hours without a drink before I started to shake. During the few times I went cold turkey, I didn't realize how dangerous it was. The chances were good that I could have gone into a seizure from the abruptness of stopping after steadily drinking that quantity.

Gina says that she was unaware of any kind of help available to her. But finally her employer forced the issue. He told her she would either have to go to a treatment center or lose her job. She chose the former.

> I got into treatment that first time without having to actually say "help me," something I would not do back then. The biggest impact that this first treatment had on me was finding out that many other quite normal people had the same problem. The enormous relief from this knowledge is still a sharp memory. But after four weeks of inpatient treat-

ment, I left feeling that I had the problem licked and I said no thanks to aftercare and Alcoholics Anonymous.

Gina soon relapsed into her destructive drinking patterns. Her marital and drinking problems fed on each other. The more she drank, the worse her marriage became. And the more her marriage deteriorated, the more she drank. She finally divorced her husband. But she continued to drink heavily, and two years after her discharge from the treatment center, she entered another treatment program. She was sober for eight months, then once again resumed her drinking. The behavior was stressful not only to her but to those around her. "By this time my children had pretty much given up on me," she recalls. "I was looked upon as a loser, and my last drunk, covering most of a week, was bad enough for me to realize that I no longer could play with this subject of sobriety." Gina feels that she nearly killed herself.

Once again her employer gave her the ultimatum: treatment or loss of her job. But this time, she reacted differently. She welcomed it. Her brush with death was frightening enough to cause her to be willing to go to any lengths to stay sober. She was finally willing to give up on the idea that she could help herself. "This time I could openly reach out for help. I decided to try it their way."

This third time, Gina stayed in treatment for six weeks. She also committed herself to three months in a halfway house and to involvement—for the first time—with Alcoholics Anonymous.

My alternatives as I saw them were to die, go insane, or sober up. I still see these same alternatives. I had gone too far in alcoholism for there to be any other way out. I made the choice for sobriety because I wanted to live. So when someone compliments me on being so strong or wonderful in resisting alcohol, I don't accept it as praise.

Choosing to live is quite easy when you appreciate life as I do. That has been one of the most satisfying things about my sobriety, and one of the most shameful aspects of my alcoholism—that in letting alcohol get a hold on me, I gave up the principle of appreciating each and every day.

It came back through sobriety and has stayed back. I look at the time since my first treatment, almost nine years ago, as a bonus life.

Gina's children had decided she was hopeless. Many employers would have given up on her by the third time. Fortunately, she had a boss who didn't believe she was a hopeless case. The result is that she had a second chance at life. One valuable lesson she gained from her bout with alcoholism and her treatment programs is how to handle the stresses of life without resorting to mood-altering chemicals.

I have a built-in warning system for telling me when I am way off track in the way I am conducting my life. And that is the desire to drink. I'm not talking here about the occasional sad regret when the champagne is opened and I wish I could drink like everyone else, or the occasional wish to enjoy the taste of a good wine with a gourmet meal. I'm talking about a desire to drink in order to gain the comfort and lessening of pain that alcohol can bring. Not fighting this desire but feeling it and learning from it was one of the most important things I learned that last time around. After several years of sobriety, this desire is a red flag. I've discovered, slowly and painfully, that this particular desire only comes when I am feeling terrible about myself as a person, when my self-esteem is dragging on the ground.

There are likely to be some irretrievable losses in going through an emotional problem. Gina acknowledges that as she reflects on her ''lost'' years with regret, even though she is grateful for what she learned through being an alcoholic. At least Gina feels that she is now headed in a more fulfilling direction. She presently does purchasing for a large industrial company, and is enjoying both her work and her sobriety.

For Scott, on the other hand, drug abuse has meant a direction that he considers second-best. At one time, Scott was a medical student. He still has the energy and bedside manner necessary for the life of a physician, but he will never pursue that career. He recalls with a slight grimace that he had only five months to go to finish earning his medical degree when he was asked to withdraw from school because of alcohol and drug abuse. It was a difficult time for him.

"My immediate response to this dismissal was to further withdraw into my addiction," he explains. "I was devastated, to say the least, at what had occurred. The realization that I was not going to be a physician after the many years of hard work made me extremely depressed. Subsequently, my use of alcohol and pills escalated, which served to fuel and deepen the depression."

Eventually, Scott sought help and learned to overcome his addiction. He went into business for himself, and now owns a small chain of fast-food restaurants. He can see some positive as well as negative outcomes from the experience. "My initial depression and increase in drug use were eventually replaced by a healthy response: seeking treatment and confronting and dealing with my anger. I had been on a self-destructive pathway, and was slowly killing myself with drugs. My rehabilitation has restored my health as well as provided me with a respect and concern for my body that I previously did not have." Scott also faced a huge debt because of student loans—easily granted to a medical student but difficult to pay back without the earnings of a physician.

Scott knows that it was necessary for him to change, to deal with the forces that were driving him into self-destructive dependence on drugs. He laments the fact that it cost him so much, however: "I believe that change of any kind is difficult to accomplish. Major life changes often occur only as a result of great pain and suffering, for pain is a strong motivating factor in human behavior. In my case, I had to lose a great deal—a career, physical health, and my self-respect—before I was willing to seek the help required to change." Scott is not unhappy with his life now, but there is a tinge of regret in his words as he describes his experience. His loss is irretrievable.

Still, something can always be salvaged. Scott has regained his health, his self-respect, and his sense of humor. "I did at least have one experience of being a physician," he says. "I had to pay back the money I borrowed to go to med school." And, like Gina, he has gained the insight into himself necessary to pull away from and avoid the life-destroying quicksands of drug abuse. Self-insight and self-control are no small gains in life.

Another positive outcome commonly associated with illness or accidents is a posture of questioning the meaning of life. Holly is an executive assistant to the president of a furniture manufacturing firm. When she was a teenager, she had ongoing and intense conflict with her mother. Finally, Holly moved into her own apartment. Before the move, however, she experienced a period of deep depression. In her struggle to be free of the depression, she began to question all things.

> For the first time in my life, I asked myself whether I really had an obligation to stay at home as my mother insisted or move out as my instincts told me I should. I asked what my life was all about, and whether I should just accept the answers my mother had been giving me. My mother was trying to control my thinking, my beliefs, my behavior, and even my feelings. She couldn't accept the fact that I was raising questions about her beliefs and values. And I probably wouldn't have done it if I hadn't gotten so depressed. I just didn't care if it upset her or not.

Holly's questioning stance was the beginning of her growth. "What is a life without questioning?" she asks now. She agrees with Socrates that the unexamined life is not worth living. "You have to be willing to challenge people's ideas. Otherwise, you will just be a pawn, moved around by others to suit their purposes."

Questioning does not mean cynicism. It does not mean being what psychologists call an oppositional person (like the man who said that as long as he was a member of the group there would be no unanimous decisions). Rather, a questioning posture means that you take nothing for granted. You avoid unquestioning obedience to anyone. You are willing to change your opinion about any matter. You do not blithely accept things at face value. Holly struggled a great deal with her decision to move out of her home. But after the move, she gradually established a much better relationship with her mother. She gained a sense of her own independence and automony as a person. She no longer agonized in the clutches of an oppressive depression. And she determined to be a questioning person for the rest of her life.

For Holly, learning to question things was the one important tool she gained from her period of depression and conflict. Others talk of multiple benefits from their times of distress. Charles's watershed experience began at around the age of thirty—a time when most people get restless with what they are doing in life. They have struggled to establish themselves as functioning adults only to find a certain dissatisfaction about what they have done creeping into their lives. They want to do more, to be more, to set off in some new direction. Many people wind up scrapping what they achieved in their twenties and start off on a different pathway in their thirties.

Charles ended a love relationship in which he had been involved, decided to change careers, and moved to a different area, thereby breaking off with friends he had had for six years. He even changed his appearance, letting his close-cropped hair grow long and buying elevator shoes to add to his 5′9″ height. The broken relationship, abandoned career, and lost friends were very painful for him. But his life prior to the changes had also been painful. Having achieved certain career goals in his twenties, he found himself at age thirty with a sense of disquiet rather than of satisfaction. He had risen to an executive position in an advertising firm. But instead of the glow of triumph, he struggled with feelings of depression and emptiness. He decided to reshuffle his life and strike out in a new direction in the hope that he would find the fulfillment that had eluded him.

But Charles could not deal with his situation on his own. He went into therapy, seeking to understand why he had decided to change his life so drastically. He gained the understanding for which he hungered. The psychotherapy was a watershed experience for him. He can list a virtual catalog of benefits that he got from it.

I gained personal power and learned how I had kept myself helpless. I don't ask so much anymore, ''What is going to happen?'' but struggle instead with ''What do I *want* to happen?''

I had to accept the fact that my family and I are separate and different. After a period of grieving about this, I felt much freer and less responsible for them. Also less guilty.

I learned that there are alternative ways of viewing and then approaching most situations in life. There is an abundance of possibilities in life. Through this I also gained more power as life seemed to become less predetermined.

Instead of allowing myself to fall into relationships, I began to form images of those qualities I wanted in a mate. Instead of settling for less, I began to meet people who fit my newly developing images.

In general, there has been an increase in my quality of life in both personal and interpersonal areas.

Charles's battle is not over. The depression and disquiet that haunted him at age thirty may well return at some point in the future. A number of psychologists agree that we live in an age of melancholy. W. H. Auden wrote *The Age of Anxiety* in 1947. And indeed, anxiety was widespread at the time, in part because of the new fear of massive self-destruction through atomic weapons. Today, however, Auden might have written instead about melancholy, which includes everything from a mild feeling of the blues to serious depression. It is true, at any rate, that depression is one of the most common complaints and that there have been an increasing number of people diagnosed as depressed in recent years.

Even depression can be mastered, however. People have confronted and overcome the effects of every kind of illness and accident. Charles found the help he needed in therapy. Other people have used various tools and resources to meet the challenge. If the bad news is that we can't avoid the whirlwinds of life, the good news is that we can surmount them and even use them to enhance the quality of our lives.

4

Working Through Personal Problems

In the play *Rossum's Universal Robots*, the makers of the robots decide that they have to introduce pain because otherwise the robots have no way of knowing when they have suffered injury or are in danger. Similarly, there are those who argue that suffering and pain are important to humans because they not only alert us to danger but also mark times of challenge and growth.

Even rats seem to need some adversity in order to develop their skills. One psychologist raised rats in his laboratory in two different environments. In one, the rats had ample food, water, and opportunity for exercise but no problems to solve or barriers to overcome. In the other, they faced obstacles, blind alleys, and other rats with whom they had to get along. The rats reared in the problem-free environment were never able to develop the skills in problem-solving that the other rats learned from an early age.

But even if we agree that some adversity and suffering can be important stimulants to growth, we also are aware that they can thrust people into despair rather than onto the path of growth. Growth isn't automatic because we have problems. There is an enormous amount of human wreckage in the world. We have seen a number of examples of people who were scarred rather than stimulated by their encounter with adversity. What makes the difference? What are the tactics used by those who struggle through the morass of pain and emerge stronger and more mature?

DEVELOP A NEW PERSPECTIVE

An illness or accident frequently results in your having an abundance of something that is generally very scarce: available time. An illness or accident may require confinement, release from normal responsibilities, or both. This allows more time than usual to be wrapped up in your own thoughts. There are various ways to respond to this extended encounter with your own stream of consciousness. Some people simply engage in a long period of feeling sorry for themselves. Some squander the time in pursuing trivia or unrealistic fantasies. And others use the time constructively and creatively to have fun, to pursue new or old interests, or to rethink their lives and develop new perspectives.

A woman who was confined to bed with a cast on the lower half of her body told us she decided to try oil painting. She has pursued it avidly as a hobby ever since. A man recovering from mononucleosis used his time to read joke books and write down his favorites. "It's my smile book now," he says. "Whenever I feel harried or down, I pull it out and read some of them. Did you ever try to keep your gloom and laugh at the same time?"

Others use the time to change their perspective on life. Michael is a boyish-looking pilot in his early thirties. His father was also a pilot, so he spent a good part of his life at airports and in airplanes. He relished it. "I ate, slept, and breathed flying." He became a bush pilot for a time. One day as he took off with a planeload of passengers, something happened that changed his life: the plane flipped over. Fortunately, no one was killed. But several people, including Michael himself, were injured. For a number of weeks, Michael was unable to fly while he recovered.

"I made a startling discovery," he recalls. "Airplanes were the only thing I knew. They were my profession and my hobby. Now what? I realized that in my eagerness to fly, I had ignored every other facet of my life. I really hadn't lived yet." Michael determined that he would never again give himself totally to one thing. "Flying will always be my first love, but now it will never again be my only love."

Michael developed a new perspective as he reflected on what his life had been before the accident. He came to the conclusion that no one should invest his or her whole life in one thing. He decided that a person should at least taste a wide variety of the delectable offerings of life.

Similarly, Brett, a slender, young psychotherapist who looks too fragile to withstand a gusty wind, talks about an incident that was "the best and worst thing that ever happened to me." The incident occurred a few years ago when Brett came down with fever and severe diarrhea. He lost thirty pounds from his spare frame in a few months. He got so weak that he could only work a few hours at a time. Finally, he went to a physician, who diagnosed his condition as inflammatory bowel disease. The physician told him that the disease was incurable. The only therapy he would prescribe was a restricted diet and repeated surgery to remove portions of the bowel that had been damaged by prolonged inflammation.

In the ensuing weeks, Brett continued a kind of mechanical existence. He tried to keep working, though he had to minimize the time spent with patients. He became socially withdrawn because of his inability to talk with people comfortably, his restricted diet, and his embarrassment over his haggard appearance. Sexual encounters with his new wife were difficult and infrequent. "I was limp from one end of me to the other. I was afraid that I would not be able to maintain either my practice or my marriage. And that made me depressed."

Gradually, however, Brett began to improve. There were relapses, but he seemed generally to be making progress. A part of his progress was the rethinking of his life. "I began to reevaluate my life and where I was going," he explains. "What did I want? I had always been happy-go-lucky in my approach to life. But now I felt insecure and afraid of what the future held. I had to find out how to lessen this insecurity. I also came to value highly some things I had taken for granted, like relationships and just waking up in the morning and feeling halfway decent."

Like Michael, Brett has a new sense of what is important, of where he wants to go with his life. Both of them used the time granted them by their problems to reexamine and reorder their perspectives. It isn't necessary for the entire convalescence to be given over to productive thinking, of course. Brett spent a good deal of his time in the early days of his illness worrying and pondering the worst scenarios. A period of worry and grieving is common. The point is not to get stuck there. And that may require a conscious decision to use at least a portion of the time available to develop a new perspective on life.

USE THE NEW PERSPECTIVE TO REDIRECT YOUR LIFE

A new perspective is useless unless it produces new patterns of behavior. Like the deathbed promise that is retracted when the patient unexpectedly recovers, a reordering of values and priorities is meaningless if it is nothing more than an intellectual exercise. People who grow do not play such intellectual games. They do not make promises or establish new priorities only to discard them in the rush of life following their recovery. They develop new perspectives and then use them to reorder their lives.

Sometimes the reordering involves a commitment to something the individual believes to be important in his or her life. The illness or accident gives a person the courage to make a commitment. Lisa is a young actress who studied acting part-time and performed in some amateur productions while working as an office manager. An automobile accident left her unable to work or even walk for four months. Her devastation was obvious as she poured out the story.

The first two weeks, I cried. Constantly. It had to be the worst thing that could possibly have happened to me. I felt helpless, hopeless, totally miserable. But then I started to think. And I realized that this single event was forcing me to a reevaluation of everything in my life. I took stock of what I was doing and really had an opportunity to look at the direction my life was taking.

Until that time, I had always treated acting as something

I *might* be able to do. I was too terrified of failing to really commit to it, and so I worked at a job I heartily disliked, but which made me feel safe. But lying there in bed, scared and hurting, with nothing to do but recuperate, I realized that life was much too precious to while away, and that it was time to make a decision. I either had to commit to developing as a professional actress, or move on to something else. I chose acting, and I have never regretted it. Never!

Lisa wasn't sure whether she would have had the courage to make the commitment apart from the accident and the time to reflect on her life. Of course, as with Brett, the time immediately after the accident was painful: "Those first few weeks, when I could not find a meaning for the accident, were absolutely awful, something I would never want to repeat." But when she used her recovery time to gain a new perspective, the accident finally took on a positive meaning. She not only gained the courage to commit herself to an acting career, but also learned some invaluable lessons that are useful in her work.

It taught me that commitment is the opposite of fear, because commitment enables one to confront fear, and deal with it. It also taught me to look for the flip side of any situation or event. For every negative, there is a positive. This has been critically important to me, because an actress's life is *filled* with apparently negative events, which must be dealt with. And now I'm helping other actresses by coaching them and helping them deal with *their* negative experiences.

Lisa not only gained personal benefits but also learned how to help others. This is a common outcome. That is, when people redirect their lives, they usually do one or both of two things: they determine not to get so involved in various responsibilities that they miss out on things they enjoy, and they commit themselves to helping others in some way. Confronted with their own vulnerability and mortality, they decide not to miss out on the important things, and the important things include both some personal enjoyment and some giving of themselves to others.

Thus, one woman was hospitalized for two and a half months after an automobile accident. At first, she wanted to die because of the pain. But she recovered, and committed herself to a "more fulfilling life" by getting involved in community groups such as the Girl Scouts. And Daniel, a quiet, serious-looking accountant, supports a local boys' club. That is his way of getting more involved in helping others. Daniel wants to help others because he nearly died when he was a teenager. In fact, at one point he heard the paramedics say that he *had* died. And he probably would have died had it not been for two strangers.

Daniel's watershed began on a night that started as a time of fun. He and a friend were driving to a party on a nippy autumn afternoon. They drove near a lake, which could be seen through the vibrant colors of the changing leaves. Daniel felt great. Life was good. His friend noted that another car of partygoers was coming up behind them. "I don't want them to beat us," the friend said as he pressed down on the accelerator.

Soon they were hurtling down the road at eighty miles per hour. At a bend, the car lurched out of control. There were a few crazy seconds of blurred images, then an eerie quiet after the impact. Daniel heard his friend groaning. He jumped out of the car to try to find help. The young men in the other car had stopped and were coming toward him. One of them grabbed him and said he was bleeding badly. It was the first time he even realized he had been hurt.

I reached for my head and felt the warm blood. I brought my hand down and it was bright red. I felt no pain and had no real concern for myself. My concern was for my friend, who by now was out of the car and only suffering from a small cut on the head.

At that point, the occupants of the other car panicked and decided to leave.

We were left with a ruined car, my friend's minor injury, and me bleeding to death with each beat of my heart. And we were miles from a phone.

My friend had the presence of mind to get us to the side of the road; fortunately, a young couple saw us and stopped. The woman took one look at me and literally ripped the coat off her boyfriend's back. She tried to use it as a bandage. She wrapped my head and kept pressure on the wound. Then they placed me in their car, my head in her lap while she held the wound, and raced for the ranger station.

I was aware of little except the pool of blood forming in her lap and on the backseat of the car. At the ranger station, the telephone was out of order and the rangers were out on patrol. My friend and the woman's boyfriend ran to find the rangers or a phone.

I have no idea how much time passed, but it couldn't have been long. The woman tried to keep me talking while she maintained pressure on the wound. When the ambulance arrived I was quickly placed into it and rushed off. My last glimpse of that couple was as the door closed.

Somewhere en route to the hospital, they said that I died. I didn't have the experiences most people talk about—you know, the out-of-body stuff where you're looking at yourself from up above. All I remember is watching them frantically working on me and listening to their talk. I was very unemotional and detached. At the hospital, I was rushed into emergency surgery.

I don't remember anything else until I woke up at home in bed. It was almost a week later. My first thoughts were that it had been a bad dream, until I realized I was in a hospital-type bed with tubes in my body. It seems that I had believed that the hospital was trying to kill me. I fought the drugs and the restraints. So a minihospital was created at home.

Daniel underwent a series of five operations. He has one more to go. But he is, he says, "almost as good as before." He reflects back on the experience and realizes how many things happened in an almost miraculous fashion: "The car doors should have been impossible to open, yet I managed to open one easily. My head injuries should have been immediately fatal. My bleeding should have caused death. The pressure applied to my wounds should have caused bone fragments to be pushed into my brain. None of the 'shoulds' happened.''

Daniel thought about all of the ''shoulds'' that didn't happen while he lay in bed recovering. He also thought about the young man and woman who helped. ''We never discovered the identity of the young couple who saved my life. But their great kindness remains with me. The accident, the couple, and my parents' love taught me that there was something more to life than beer parties.'' He still enjoys parties. But he wants his life to be something more than that. That's why he willingly gives some time each week as a counselor at the boys' club.

TAKE RESPONSIBILITY FOR YOUR LIFE

One of the interesting things about Daniel's account is that he never spoke bitterly about the friend whose foolish driving caused the accident. Instead of blaming his friend, as understandable as that would have been, Daniel focused on how he himself could deal with his situation.

Not everyone is as wise as Daniel. For instance, Jessica—a computer specialist who identified an automobile accident as her watershed. Her initial reaction was one of trying to assign blame. She was on her way to church when the accident occurred, so she blamed God. ''I had attended church every Sunday. But I didn't go after the accident, thinking that I should have been saved from it since I was going to church.'' She finally sought help from a psychiatrist, who assured her that her feelings were normal and that eventually she would be able to return to church and feel the same about it as she once had. She did, but now she is bitter about the justice system and the way things work. ''I really feel sorry for people who are involved in accidents and it is no way their fault,'' says Jessica. ''You're really put through the mill. To me, there is no justice. Because I wasn't actually hospitalized, it is hard to get a settlement even though I have all the bills to back up the damage and treatments. You have to be bleeding to death to even start a case.''

Jessica blamed God, then blamed the legal system. But blaming others is nonproductive. In the end, as former first lady Betty Ford said with respect to her alcohol problem, it all comes down to the fact that you must take responsibility for your own life. You may not be responsible for what happens to you, but you are responsible for how you respond.

A number of professional athletes have undergone suspension or dismissal for drug abuse. In some cases, they attempted to minimize or justify their behavior. But a self-righteous response is avoiding responsibility. In contrast, when Dwight Gooden, star pitcher for the New York Mets, was suspended for cocaine use, he went into a rehabilitation program and eventually came back to pitch for the Mets. On his return, he acknowledged his own responsibility both for getting involved in drug abuse and for breaking the habit.

Taking responsibility means refusing to retreat into a life of self-pity, of blaming anyone or anything for your situation. It means refusing to give way to feelings of helplessness and despair. It means positive action, such as Dwight Gooden took, to get back on the path to growth. It means doing something with your life even if you have permanent limitations.

Susan, who is in her thirties, cannot do some of the things that most of us can. But she does a great deal, including her work as an interior designer. She loves to transform people's homes and workplaces into "havens of cheer." The ever-present smile on her face is a reflection of her aim in life, an aim that emerged in spite of a debilitating illness that permanently limits her physically.

Susan was a healthy and active child until the age of fifteen. Then she noticed a loss of strength in her arms and legs plus discomfort and pain at the back of her neck. A neurosurgeon diagnosed the problem: a benign tumor growing near her spinal cord in the neck area. The tumor had to be removed, but that required a cutting of the spinal-cord nerves. The particular nerves that were cut do not regenerate. Susan was left with a partial paralysis and a lessening of her body strength. For the next six years, she spent periods of time in a rehabilitation hospital, learning how to function with her limitations. Those limitations still cause her some brief moments of distress.

I can no longer run, play baseball, go skating or waterski-
ing, or engage in the other physical activities that I was
once able to do. Sometimes I feel down when I see all my
friends doing the things I can no longer do. But then I give
myself a little pep talk and get on with life.

Susan does not allow herself to sink into self-pity. She takes
the responsibility for finding meaning and fulfillment in her life.
She has done this through a career that not only brings her in-
trinsic satisfaction but also enlivens the existence of others. At
the same time, she knows that the progress she has made in
overcoming her disability was not completely her own. Taking
responsibility for yourself does not mean a solo effort. Susan
found others a great source of help, both physically and emotionally.

The impact that the disability had on me was not as traumatic as it might have been. My family and friends were
always there for me whenever I reached out for help. I feel
that I am very fortunate, because I know I am cared about.
I am not alone in this world.

MAKE USE OF THE RESOURCES AVAILABLE

There are always alternatives, because there are always sources
of help that are available. Without the support of relatives and
friends, Susan's outcome might have been quite different. Former professional baseball player Roy Campanella, confined to
a wheelchair following an accident, found an important resource
in his faith. He felt only anguish and despair when he first became aware of his plight. He spent many nights crying until he
sank into the unknowing bliss of sleep. One day his physician
came in and talked frankly with him. He told Campanella that
he was disappointed in his progress. The physician declared
flatly that Campanella himself would have to be responsible for
a good part of the healing process.

Roy Campanella feared he would never leave his wheelchair.
He would never play ball again. He would never walk. What
good was he to anyone? he thought to himself. But he knew the

physician was right. He knew also where to turn for help. All of his life he had found help in his faith. He asked the nurse to take the Bible out of the drawer on his night table and read him the Twenty-third Psalm. From that moment on, Campanella improved. He remains in his wheelchair. But he says that he knows that God is on his side. He once yearned for death. He now affirms that it is great to be alive.

Among the numerous resources we have, other people are one of the most important. Americans tend to value the self-reliant individual. But that can be a detriment to our growth when we refuse to make use of the resources available to us. Blaming others is a form of irresponsibility; refusing to allow others to help is a different kind of irresponsibility. The growing individual does not get mired in blaming or in isolation.

Other people can be invaluable to us in dealing with all kinds of problems. For Angela, the problem was one that torments millions of Americans: excess weight. She tipped the scales at well over two hundred pounds. Off and on, she tried various ways to lose—diet pills, exercise, and even fasting. Fasting made her ill, but did not significantly change her weight. Like many who are overweight, she would lose for a while, then regain the pounds. The whole process was more difficult because it was easy for her to rationalize her size: as the manager of a nice restaurant, she was virtually a living advertisement for the appeal of the food her establishment served.

Angela's ambivalence about her weight changed abruptly, however. Her watershed began one night at a party when a woman asked her when her baby was due. Angela was not pregnant. She left the place in an agony of embarrassment. But what could she do? Everything she had tried before had failed. Nevertheless, the next day, Angela began a low-calorie diet. She also began attending an exercise class. She enlisted the help of her husband and children. They became a crucial part of her progress by both admiring and encouraging her efforts. "It took a year," she says, "but I lost nearly ninety pounds. And now I'm a different person—on the inside as well as the outside. I feel better. I have more energy. And most important, I have become more outgoing, more confident. I have finally discovered who I really am."

In addition to family and friends and even strangers like the one who spurred Angela to act, a trained therapist may be an important source of help. Kathleen was fifty-one, an active and very successful real-estate broker, when she heard what she, and many other women, might consider a death sentence. "My surgeon was telling me I had breast cancer and needed to make a decision regarding treatment as soon as possible. I was numb, but knew the choice I needed to make concerning the type of surgery which would be in my best interests."

Kathleen had no choice but to submit to the mastectomy. But that raised many fears, some of which she knew were not totally rational. Would her husband find her sexually unattractive? Would she lose some of the feminine qualities that she prized? Would her customers and the salespeople who worked for her sense that she was no longer the robust and self-confident woman who forged an enormous success in a male-dominated world?

After the surgery, Kathleen dealt with her situation the way she had always handled problems: she tried to talk herself into treating the matter lightly, without emotion, and with no negative thoughts. "Stay high and positive," she kept telling herself. "You need not worry. The cancer is gone. Forget about it. You are going to have to take care of yourself because no one else will. You don't need anyone. Not your family, not your friends. Only yourself. Because no one else can be depended on." Kathleen had never felt as though she could look to other people for support in times of personal crisis. She had to deal with her problems on her own. But this time it didn't work. She couldn't suppress the powerful anxiety and fear that welled up in her. And she couldn't completely hide those feelings, hard as she tried to do so. She said nothing to others, but a sensitive friend suggested one day that she talk to a psychotherapist.

"As I look back on my state of mind at the time," Kathleen muses, "I believe the decision to enter into therapy saved my life physically as well as emotionally." Kathleen kept a written record of her experience in therapy. She wrote the following a few months after she had begun:

I had a serious operation a few months ago. Four or five days I waited for the pathology report. I did not know whether I would live or die within a few years. I have never been as vulnerable as I was at that time. Just waiting. There were things that started happening. Emotional processes that I knew were occurring, but I did not know what they were all about. Did it involve the uncertainty of life? The loving care and support of my family and friends? I need help in understanding. Why did the fact of having my family and friends show support and care create anxiety? Do I feel unworthy of their caring and concern? Am I afraid of the risk and possibility of loss if I allow others to get close to me?

I was different when I came out of the hospital. Not just the surgery, but inside. A crack in the inner wall was beginning. The barrier to my inner self, my emotional self, had been penetrated. Keeping everyone away from me, on a superficial level, had been my approach to life. It was safer that way. But in the hospital, I was not in control. Others were. I came out okay. What began the crack in the wall? Support, care, love, and not being in control? I knew that in order to survive physically and emotionally, I needed to understand what I was feeling. Me! Who never would allow myself to show my feelings. I am afraid. Afraid of what? What might be there? Under all those layers of pushing back and back, afraid of allowing another to see inside. What is there? What might be there? Can I take the risk? I must. Else I will die. I'm convinced of that. What are my fears? Fear of others, death, loss. That is why I have to understand and be aware of myself, not to stuff my emotional self into a tight package. I can't keep pushing that part of me away any longer. She needs to come out, to be heard, to heal, to live.

What will happen to me if I undertake this journey to myself. Will I come out okay? Who will be there if it becomes overwhelming? Will you, my therapist? Can I trust you? Will I let myself trust you to see me through the pain of self awareness? I will let you in and then you will leave me, and I will be left alone again. How can I let you in? But I cannot be as I have been. It will kill me. So, I have to do this for my life. I'm very much afraid, emotionally

fearful. I need help. I can't do it by myself. I need to know.
I need to be reassured.

Kathleen did open herself to help from others. She took the
journey she needed in order to live. Today, Kathleen looks back
and sees the cancer and her resulting psychotherapy as steps to
becoming "a more complete person." She knows that the cancer could appear again; it has only been three years. But for her
the disease of death became a doorway to life: "Cancer, a disease that means death in the eyes of many, has given me life
which is more complete, whole, and genuine. My relationships
with family, friends, and my world reflect my emerging confidence in allowing my total self to be experienced. I am continually changing and understanding who I am in my world and
how I want to relate to that world. The growth will continue as
long as I live."

Through her therapist, Kathleen was finally able to reach out
to a resource that is immensely important in dealing with personal problems: relatives and friends. For a good part of her
life, Kathleen had cut herself off from this powerful tool for
growth. Social scientists have found increasing evidence of the
importance of close relationships for our mental and physical
well-being. In times of crisis, those who have supportive relatives or friends fare much better than those who do not. For
example, the people who lived near the Three Mile Island nu-
clear power plant in Pennsylvania suffered from stress following
the accident at the facility. The higher stress levels lasted for
more than a year after the accident. But those with a greater
amount of social support from friends and relatives had fewer
psychological and behavioral symptoms of stress than others.

The accumulating research on the value of having supportive
people around us is so impressive that the California Department of Mental Health put on a campaign with the slogan
"Friends can be good medicine." Among the findings that led
to the campaign are the following:

- If you isolate yourself from other people, you are two to
  three times more likely to die an early death. This is true

independently of whether you take good care of yourself
by exercising and refraining from smoking.

- If you isolate yourself from others, you are more likely
  to contract terminal cancer.
- If you are divorced, separated, or widowed, you have a
  five to ten times greater chance of being hospitalized for
  a mental disorder than if you are married.
- If you are a pregnant woman without good personal relationships, your chances of having some kind of com-
  plication are three times as great as those with strong
  relationships, even given the same amount of stress.

Clearly, friends and relatives can be good medicine. They can
help insulate us from the full negative impact of stress and they
can give us the support we need to overcome our problems.

Alan, now in his forties, illustrates the importance of social
support. Alan is a large man with a penetrating voice and a quick
grin. He virtually glowed as he told his story in his Texas drawl.
The last thing anyone would suspect about him is that he ever
had any problems with his self-confidence. But it has only been
a few years since he was "crawling with my nose in the dust."

Alan was a successful sales manager in Houston. But he had
dreams—dreams that went beyond "hawking filters to industry." Alan loved the sea. With his wife and three children, he
rented a small yacht at every opportunity and went cruising in
the Gulf of Mexico. He fantasized about all of them taking off
and sailing around the world together. It would be a sensational
family adventure.

One day it occurred to Alan that he could come closer to his
dream by quitting his job and setting up his own boat business.
After all, he knew as much about seagoing vessels as anyone,
so he should be able to run the business effectively.

My family was enthusiastic. We agreed that it would be a
business in which we would all get involved. And we
thought that somehow it just might lead to that trip around
the world. So you know what I did? I flat out quit my job,
got a loan, and opened up my new business.

Initially, the decision appeared to be a wise one. The business flourished. Alan's exuberance enabled him to make sales as quickly as people came in. It was soon time to expand. It was then that his lack of experience in this particular business got Alan into trouble. He overexpanded and began to have serious cash-flow problems. He tried to compensate by selling some of the boats at large discounts to increase volume, but that left him too little profit margin. He came to the edge of bankruptcy. But Alan had to cope with more than the failing business.

For the first time I could ever remember, I lost faith in myself. I saw our dreams going down the drain. I had trouble getting to sleep at night, because I felt I had failed my family. I began to think of myself as a big pile of trash. My wife kept trying to cheer me up, but I guess I went around looking like a man already dead. So one day she sat me down and talked with me. I can remember nearly every word of that talk.

"Honey," she said, "let's discuss what's troubling you."

"What's the point?" I mumbled. "We both know what's wrong."

"No," she said, "I don't think you really do."

That surprised me. In fact, it bowled me over. I exploded. I started hollering at her. "The business is going down the tubes. I've screwed it all up. What do you mean I don't know what's wrong?"

Alan's voice grew softer as he related the rest of their conversation.

Usually if I holler at her, she'll holler right back, and we fight it out. But this time, she stayed real calm and told me that the reason I didn't know what was wrong was that I had forgotten what was really important in our lives. It wasn't the business that was wrong. It was my attitude. I was down on myself and down on the world.

"We can deal with the business failing," she told me. "But you have to stop feeling guilty about it. You're a great husband and a great father. And I don't want you to forget that for a minute. Just remember that a great husband and a great father can never be a failure. In the long run, it doesn't matter if you lose the money we put into the business. But it would matter if we lost you. So you just stop feeling so sorry for yourself, remind yourself every day that we love you, and don't ever think anything except that Big Al is one hell of a great guy.''

"You know," Alan said very quietly, "I've never stopped believing that about myself since that day. Maybe that's what changed the business around. Maybe even my customers and creditors had realized that I didn't believe in myself anymore. But they did after that day. And even if the business hadn't turned around, I got a gift from my wife that day that will keep me rich for the rest of my life.''

LEARN TO ENJOY WHAT YOU HAVE INSTEAD OF GRIEVING FOR WHAT YOU DON'T HAVE

In the movie *It's a Wonderful Life*, George becomes despondent when he is on the verge of losing the bank his father established. In spite of a good family and loyal friends, George feels that his life is meaningless. He goes to a bridge to end his life. Clarence, an angel, stops him and takes him back to the town to show him what the town would be like if he had never been born. George sees a much different town, an undesirable town with numerous problems. He is appalled at the sordid scenes that Clarence shows him, and he now realizes what a difference his life has made. George's sense of self-worth returns and he goes back to his wife and family with gratitude for what he has.

In the end, George didn't lose the bank. But that didn't matter. Whether or not the bank survived, George was a happy man. It isn't only in the movies that such things happen. We were sitting in a city park one evening waiting for an outdoor concert to begin. Two men walked by arm in arm. One was blind. His friend asked him, "Where do you want to sit?" The blind man replied, "Let's sit near the front." And then he chuckled as he said, "We can see better from there." The blind man was obviously enjoying what he had—his sense of hearing and his sense of humor—rather than grieving for what he lacked.

People who overcome personal problems learn to appreciate and enjoy what they have. They don't waste themselves by perpetually grieving for what they don't have. They don't keep running into a cul-de-sac of self-pity. As a part of developing a new perspective and taking responsibility for their lives, they set out once again to discover and experience some of the basic joys of living.

Alan pointed out that he gained a new direction for his life after his wife rescued him from being down on himself.

> It took a while for our boating business to finally start prospering again. For a few months, I was sure that we would be bankrupt. But after that talk, I could handle it. I knew I had a family that loved me and would support me no matter what happened to the business. It didn't matter if I had to go back to selling filters. We were enjoying life. We were enjoying just being together. It would be sad to lose the business. But we weren't going to sit around and cry about it. No sir, we have too much to enjoy.

The family still hasn't taken the trip around the world. And the business, while prospering, is still somewhat precarious. But it was a confident and happy Alan with whom we talked. He had learned to enjoy what he had instead of grieving for what he did not, or might not, have.

When Alan talks about his experience, you don't get the sense that he's trying to sell you on anything. And you don't get the sense, as you do with some people, that he's trying to sell himself on anything. Alan's watershed was a genuine turning point in his life.

You get the same sense in talking with Darlene, whose eyes sparkle and whose quick wit charms listeners. Darlene is a reporter for a major urban newspaper. Her charm is important in getting people to open up to her, but the charm is real and not fabricated for public consumption. She is the kind of person who makes friends quickly and easily. She is a woman that others like to be around. She makes them feel good. It seems

odd that there was a time in her life when she was very lonely.
It was then that her watershed occurred.

"When I graduated from college, I got an offer to write for a
small-city newspaper. I was ecstatic, because I would get to
write about all kinds of things. The paper didn't have a large
staff, so I would get experience in almost every kind of report-
ing." Darlene paused and smiled warmly. "I had no idea
just how much experience I would get. I reviewed books regularly. I wrote columns for colleagues who went on vacation.
I wrote some local news stories. I learned every aspect of the
business."

Darlene had always lived in a large metropolitan area before
moving to the small city. She missed her friends and family but
expected to make a new set of friends quickly. Her expectations
quickly dissolved in a combination of long working hours and
the age of her co-workers: Everyone in her office liked her, but
everyone was at least twenty years older than she was. And in
her determination to do an outstanding job on every assignment,
Darlene had no time to join community organizations or to find
friends outside of the newspaper staff.

It was late one night while she was putting her notes together
for a story that she realized what was happening to her. She felt
weary and decided to wait until the next day to finish the piece.

I looked up from my desk and thought, What shall I do
now? I need to have a little fun. And then it hit me. I had
no one to have fun with. I called one of my best friends
back home. I knew she would commiserate with me. She
was out. I called another old friend. She was away on a
trip. I put the phone down and stared at the wall. I suddenly
felt an overwhelming sense of loneliness. And I began to
get depressed. I called home. It helped to talk with Mom
and Dad, but when I hung up I was still in that room that
was barren of all human life except my own.

When Darlene went to work the next day, her face lacked its
usual luster. After a few hours, several of her co-workers noticed.

One of the men told me I needed to stop working such long hours. One of the women asked me if I was coming down with something. I felt too embarrassed to tell them about my loneliness. It would be like inviting yourself to go to someone's party. So there I was. They didn't know what was bothering me and I couldn't tell them. I felt trapped. My mood began to swing between depression over my loneliness and panic over being trapped in a depressing situation. I wonder now what would have happened to me if I hadn't met Ben.

Ben was a blind repairman who had recently moved to the city. Blinded in the Vietnam War, he had learned to everyone's surprise how to repair lawn mowers. He came to the city because it was near the area where he had grown up. A blind repairman is news. Darlene was assigned to interview him.

I was stunned when I found out that he had been a photographer. That meant that sight was particularly important to him. Yet here he was, apparently happy and satisfied. The interview turned into more of a therapy session for me. I had to find out his secret. How had he adjusted? He told me a lot, but he said one thing that has been glued to my mind ever since: "I can't change it. But I can use it." He *used* his blindness to develop his other senses and learn a skill that most of us wouldn't think possible for a blind person.

When I went home, I kept thinking about that one phrase. I couldn't change my loneliness. Maybe I could use it. But how can you use loneliness? And then I would think about how much more difficult it would be to have to use something like blindness. If Ben could use a disability, I could surely use loneliness and make something creative out of it.

For the next few days, Darlene set herself to the task of turning her loneliness into a creative time of growth. She decided to read some books that she had not had time for before. She started a plan for her career, working out a time line and some goals. She allocated some time to writing children's fiction, something that she had always wanted to do. And she began to think about various ways that she might meet some people and make some friends, including the suggestion to her editor that she write a story on singles' groups and the life of singles in the city.

Darlene soon found herself less lonely. She was enthusiastic again about her life and particularly about the plans she had formulated. She was still alone, but she had learned to enjoy her aloneness instead of grieving over her lack of friendships. And she used her aloneness creatively. In time she began to develop some friendships with people her own age—the story on singles had opened the doors. "It was an invaluable lesson for me. Ever since, I've tried to make use of my circumstances instead of moping over them." It's a good way to approach life. Don't grieve over what might have been or what you wanted but didn't get. Take what you have and ask yourself, How can I use this?

Enjoying what you have instead of grieving for what you don't have is not merely a problem for people like Alan and Darlene, of course. Throughout history, humans have bewailed the holes and gaps in their lives. The biblical king Ahab had a kingdom. But he coveted the vineyard of one of his subjects, Naboth, and he sulked until his queen had Naboth killed and the vineyard became his. The Ahabs of the world will always be with us. They will envy. They will sulk. They will try to exploit us. At times, they may take advantage of us. But they will never be satisfied. They will never find fulfillment. For growing people learn to enjoy what they have; they don't waste their time grieving for what others have that they lack. To enjoy what you have is to transcend the vicissitudes of an uncertain world.

5

Relationships That Enhance

What do you want out of life? Whatever you put on your list, you undoubtedly place it there because you believe it will add to your well-being. Most of us want those things that will increase our happiness, our pride of achievement, our feeling that things are going well. Conversely, most of us prefer to avoid feeling depressed, lonely, or anxious. But what will bring us the former kinds of things and help us minimize the latter? Two researchers at the California university set out to find the answers among people living in London, Los Angeles, and Sydney, Australia. They found that the quality of an individual's relationships is crucial to his or her well-being. Intimacy with friends, good relations with kin, and marital companionship contribute heavily to our well-being.

THE WEB OF LIFE

Relationships are the web of life. They are the matrix within which we learn to think, to feel, to behave. They are the influences that come to bear on us as we construct our dreams and our aspirations. They are the arena within which we find our deepest satisfactions, the fulfillment of our innermost yearnings.

All kinds of relationships affect the course of our lives. For some people, it is a relative who is a crucial factor. Barbara Jordan, the charismatic former congresswoman from Texas, gives considerable credit for her achievements to her grandfather. She always carries three photographs of him with her. She recalls that he didn't want her to be like other kids. Over and over again, he instilled in her a desire to be her own person, to be something more than ordinary, to pursue her own course. She lives out his philosophy and remembers him fondly as one of the major influences in her life.

But it isn't only our intimates who influence us. A teacher, a casual acquaintance, or even a stranger may have a deep impact on our lives. Norman Mailer entered Harvard as an engineering student. He did so because his mother, who had experienced the ravages of the Great Depression, wanted her son to have a marketable degree. In his freshman year, Mailer took English A, a basic course in which students were expected to learn how to write well. A number of well-known writers taught at Harvard at the time. Mailer found the atmosphere stimulating. Although he was an engineering student, he spent many hours reading and writing fiction.

For the final exam in English A, the students had to write a novella. Mailer received an A+, a grade seldom given and one that made his name known on campus. His roommate later said that Mailer owed a debt of gratitude to the teacher who gave him the grade, because it was the real beginning of his career as a writer, giving him both the self-confidence and the recognition that he needed. To please his mother, Mailer finished his degree in engineering. But from his freshman days, influenced by the Harvard writers and his classroom experiences, Mailer pursued a life of writing.

Relationships are important in all aspects of our lives. We have seen that close relationships with others are one of the most important resources we have for dealing with personal problems. Good relationships are not only healing, however, but also protective and nurturing. They facilitate our growth. Perhaps this is why there has been a striking increase in the number of Americans searching for closer ties with others. The increasing emphasis on "me" and the continuing mobility that disrupts relationships have combined to touch a panic button within millions who became aware of a deep void in their lives.

Long ago, the famed American psychologist William James wrote that "no more fiendish punishment" could be devised for us than to be in society and yet treated as though we were nonexistent. To be "unworthy of attention at all" is the worst plight for humans, worse than even bodily torture. A popular song asserts that "people who need people" are the luckiest of all humans. That isn't true. We all need others. The lucky ones are those who recognize their need and develop enriching relationships. Such relationships are found in friendships, in marriage, in children, and in that occasional, more casual relationship that resembles a visit from "an angel in disguise."

FRIENDSHIPS: GIVING AND RECEIVING

Relationships are demanding. Friendships require us to give, to invest time and energy, to compromise sometimes on our preferences, to overlook or work through annoyances, and to offer various kinds of support when needed. But friendship is more than giving. We tend to receive some invaluable gifts from friendships, including a general sense of well-being, a higher level of self-esteem, and a ready source of support (people are as likely to turn to friends as to family during troubled times). For some, the gifts received from friendships are so important that the experience is a watershed.

Seni is a young scientist who came to this country in his early twenties to study for two years. When he first attended the university in his own country he gradually made a disturbing discovery about himself: he felt sexually aroused by men rather than by women. During that first year at the university, he had a number of homosexual encounters. His friends soon became aware of his homosexuality and reacted negatively to it. Some scorned him and some joked about him. His response was predictable.

I began to withdraw, to minimize my interaction with others. But that did not solve my problem. The thought of suicide came to me a number of times. That frightened me. I decided to see a psychiatrist. I wanted two things: to stop thinking about suicide and to change my homosexual nature.

Seni worked with the psychiatrist for a period of time, and was able to get beyond any desire to commit suicide. But there was no change in his homosexual orientation. Finally, he decided that he must accept his homosexuality and live with it. For him this meant that he would have to continue to minimize any relationships with others and concentrate on his studies. He still had his family, but he could not risk letting them know of his sexual orientation. They thought of him only as a hardworking student who was more concerned with succeeding at school than with developing any romantic interests.

Seni graduated with honors and did so well at his job that the company he worked for decided to send him to America for advanced training. In preparation for this venture, he enrolled in an English-language institute. There he found a more tolerant group of people.

> For the first time since I accepted my homosexuality, I felt confident in relating to people. I learned that there is always some place that we can be accepted by someone without being judged or criticized. At the institute I met a group of friends who accepted me the way I am. I became less withdrawn. I could be happy again.

Seni experienced one of the important gifts of friendship: acceptance. That experience rescued him from his self-imposed isolation and set him back on the pathway of growth. Another gift of friendship that can be a watershed experience is direction. Friends can see things in us that we ourselves miss and set us on a different direction than we otherwise would have taken. Friends can give generously of their time and energy to help us take that different direction. Some people find a whole new way of life because of the caring and persistence of a friend.

Friends who are willing to do so much for us and believe in us so strongly are not common, of course. But they do exist. And when we need help, they seem ready to go to almost any length to do what is necessary to enhance our well-being or to divert us from a self-destructive course of action. Eric is a television producer who found this in a friend whom he previously had alienated. When Eric reached out for help to his estranged friend, he found himself in the grasp of a hand that would not let go until Eric was free of the peril that threatened him.

Eric grew up in an affluent home. His parents gave him everything he wanted that could be purchased with money. But they fell short in giving time and love. Eric felt neglected by them. He tried various ways to get his parents' attention, including overeating and getting fat. They didn't consciously deprive him of anything, but they couldn't seem to give him the one thing he wanted most: their time and interest in what he was doing. In his search for love and security, Eric started using drugs while he was still a high-school student. He started spending time with a group of students who also used drugs. Eric's longtime friend Aaron refused to get involved. As Eric's attachment to the drug-using group grew, he saw less and less of Aaron.

By the time he was a high-school senior, Eric was hooked. His parents, detached as always, were unaware of his habit and supported it by supplying him with whatever money he needed. Eric also became a dealer in order to increase his income. One morning he came face to face with the perils of his addiction.

I got out of bed and fell flat on my face. I broke out in a cold sweat and couldn't move. I needed a hit. I needed it badly. This scared me so much that I decided to quit right there and then. I had fooled myself into thinking that I wasn't hooked because I never used the stuff at home, only when I was with my friends.

I really intended to stop, but I knew it would be tough. I called Aaron and asked him to help me. He said he would. For a while I would stop for a few days, then go back to it. Aaron spent a lot of time with me, trying to encourage me. But I didn't seem to be making progress.

Christmas vacation was coming up. A lot of us went skiing for the week every year. I knew there would be the usual amount of drug use, but I thought I could just refuse to participate. Aaron asked me to drive up with him. We would stay together, he said, so he could keep me from going and just getting high for a week. I agreed.

Aaron came by and picked me up. After we drove for an hour or so, I asked Aaron if he knew where he was going. I knew he wasn't going the right way. He told me he had taken the keys to his parents' mountain cabin. We would stay there and ski on the local slopes so that I wouldn't be tempted to get in with the same crowd from school.

I wasn't too thrilled with that. I insisted that we go with the others. Aaron refused. I lost the argument. We stayed in the cabin for a week. It was tough. It was hell sometimes. But Aaron gave me a few snow baths and we had a lot of good skiing. At the end of the week, we called our parents and told them we were going to stay two more days. When we got home, Aaron watched me while I flushed what remained of my stash down the toilet. It was the last time I used drugs.

MARRIAGE: METAPHOR FOR LOVE

Someone has called marriage a metaphor for love. It can, of course, also be a crucible of pain. But at its best, marriage enables us to discover all the benefits of an intimate relationship. Actress Candace Bergen feared that marriage would somehow restrict and constrain her. Instead, after a few years of marriage, she declared that the relationship had expanded and enriched her existence. She had thought that marriage would be an end point; instead, she discovered that it was an initiation into a new life of adventure and fulfillment. Similarly, Willard Scott, the exuberant television weatherman, likens marriage to a retirement plan. You invest your all in it and discover that it turns "from silver to gold to platinum."

Most people will be married at some point in their lives. Not everyone will have the experience of Candace Bergen or Willard Scott. But some will. The experience will be so transforming, so enriching, that they will define the marriage as a watershed event. Those who do identify marriage as a positive watershed talk about the wealth of benefits they have received: personal growth, less self-centeredness, happiness, love, and purpose in life.

For instance, Grant, a recruiter for a private university, has been married forty years. Grant is a retired military man in his late fifties. Although he still holds himself erect like a General Patton, there is a softness and warmth in his face. Grant met his future wife when he was a teenager; he was already in military service and, in fact, had decided to make the military a career. He also decided to get married at an early age—five months after he and Cindy first met. Teenage marriages are vulnerable. The chances of a breakup are much higher than they are for those who marry somewhat later.

Not surprisingly, Grant's marriage has had some rocky moments. He and his wife had a good deal to learn and a lot of adjustments to make as each of them changed over the years.

> Among other things, moving around a lot in the military puts a strain on your marriage. There were times when Cindy told me she didn't think she could stand one more move. Making friends and then leaving after a few years is tough. At first, the strain drove us apart instead of drawing us closer together. But in time we learned to help each other through the difficulties. We learned how to deal with things as a couple instead of fighting each other along with the problems we faced.

Despite the rough times, Grant sees his marriage as a warm and loving relationship that has endured for four decades. And the decision to get married was a watershed for him.

> It changed my life. I grew less selfish. I learned how to give of myself. I learned the real benefits of loving, caring, and nurturing a relationship over a lifetime.

Grant shared with us a number of ways in which his marriage changed him.

> As an officer, I expected men to follow orders. For a while, I expected the same of Cindy. I expected her to take care of my home and my personal needs, and to do so without raising questions. Cindy would complain that I was behaving like a drill sergeant, but I didn't pay much attention. Then one day I came home and saw her packing a suitcase. I asked her what was going on. She said she was leaving me.

It was like one of my men bluntly telling me he had decided to go AWOL. I told her to unpack and she refused. It seemed the officer had met his match. I decided to treat her like a wife instead of a private, and asked her to talk about our problems. She did, and we had a long discussion about my attitudes and behaviors. She let me know that I had to stop being an officer and be a husband when I came home. That I had to give as well as take from the marriage. That I had to care as well as be cared for. It was quite a discussion, but in the end I promised to do my best and she unpacked.

Startled and shaken by his wife's ultimatum, Grant determined to change. He admitted to himself, grudgingly at first, that he had been insensitive to her needs. He vowed that he would do whatever was necessary to keep his marriage intact. In the process, he became a more caring person in all of his relationships. In essence, it was by working out the problem with his wife that he evolved into the kind of person he really wanted to be. But his marriage was a watershed for another reason. Not only dealing with problems between them but coping together with outside problems helped Grant to see the richness of a stable relationship.

On one of my assignments, we had a couple with whom we became best friends. They got a little bored with their marriage and started swinging with other couples. They tried to get us to join them, but we're not into that kind of thing. Pretty soon it got to the point where we either had to go along with them or end the friendship. Cindy always hated leaving or losing friends. It was a crisis for us. Only that time it didn't become a crisis between us. It brought us closer together.

We decided we would let the friendship go and find other ways to have fun. Both of us spent time thinking about how to make the other happy. It was like dating again, doing things to please and making a real effort to help each other have a good time. We both learned how much we could enrich our relationship by caring about each other and putting the effort into making each other feel good.

As Grant discovered, the marital relationship can make significant changes in us. Folk wisdom has it that a person should not marry someone with the intent of changing that person. That is only partially true. Those who think that marriage will bring sobriety to a problem drinker or responsibility to someone with sociopathic tendencies will be bitterly disappointed. But there is a process of mutual education in marriage in which each spouse is both a teacher and a student. A man may teach his wife to be more assertive. A woman may teach her husband to be more sensitive. In good marriages, this happens by gentle reminders and by modeling the behavior. Thus, there is a certain amount of "re-forming" of one's spouse that is both possible and essential if the marriage is to endure and be fulfilling. As one man told us: "I'm not what I ought to be. And I'm not what I could be. But, thanks to my wife, I'm not what I was, either." All of us change over time. The point of mutual education is to help each other change in a way that the spouses become more rather than less compatible.

The changes that marriage brings may be sweeping. One man, married for five years, told us:

It would be difficult to specify how my life was changed because no part of my life has remained the same. From the simplest things like eating, sleeping, and dressing to the most complex things like thinking, believing, and imagining, I am no longer the same. The quality of my life is greatly improved. I feel better about myself in many ways. I feel better about my relationships with others. I feel better about myself in the area of self-worth, improved health and fitness, and increased enjoyment from recreation and leisure time. I do more living now than I have ever done before. I find that I can handle more of everything with less anxiety. In this profound sharing, I feel that I have grown as a person and as a human being.

Whether the changes are wide-ranging or few, the process is

never a smooth one. Those who see their marriage as a watershed do not talk about a problem-free relationship. Marriage does not mean that they have taken off on one long exhilarating flight to fulfillment. Rather, they see their marriage as one of the most significant experiences of their lives—one that, on balance, has proved to be a crucial factor in their growth and in the quality of their existence.

Julie, a loan officer for an urban mortgage corporation, is in her thirties. She has been married for seven years. Like Grant, the odds were somewhat against her having a successful marriage, but for a different reason. Julie grew up in a traditional family in which females waited on males. She learned at an early age that women should be subservient to men. She played the traditional female role for the first two decades of her life. In high school, she was a cheerleader and a member of the home economics club. But in college she was introduced to the sport of crew and became a member of the women's racing team. She grew proud of being a strong woman, both physically and mentally. She listened to fellow students who were feminists. She saw, for the first time, some of the inequities between males and females in our society. She determined to fight for women's rights. And that meant, among other things, that she would never be a traditional wife.

Julie's views on the female role created some problems when she first married. "I was so used to doing things my own way and in my own time. We had to get acclimated to each other and sort out what marriage would mean to each of us."

Julie and her husband are still working at it, but they feel that they have a strong and meaningful marriage. Julie sees an analogy between crew and marriage: both involve a grueling task and demand serious commitment, but can result in fulfillment and even fun. She is completely committed to her husband, but says that she is also a strong and independent woman. She has managed to retain her autonomy while committing herself with "total enthusiasm" to the relationship. "My life," she says, "seems more stable and full and meaningful. The impact is incredible. And very hard to express in words."

One incident that illustrates both the stormy and the bright side of the marriage occurred in their first few months together when Julie and her husband were negotiating the division of labor around the house. They negotiated most things in the early days because of Julie's antitraditional attitude. Her husband got angry one day because she had not washed his clothes that week.

> I told him that I didn't have time and, besides, why was it my responsibility to do the washing? He said that most wives did the washing. I told him I wasn't like most wives. I would take care of the lawn and he could do the washing. I didn't like washing. He shouted that I was just being bull-headed as usual to make the point that I was as good as any man. We argued vigorously for a while, then suddenly he stopped and looked at me.
>
> "Would you really prefer to cut the grass than do the washing?"
>
> "I sure would," I said.
>
> Then he took all of the fight out of me. "If you'll just tell me what to do, I'll take over the washing." I asked him if he really meant it, and he assured me that he did. "I knew you weren't an ordinary woman when I married you, but sometimes I forget and expect you to be like my mother. Our relationship is more important to me than who does the washing."
>
> About thirty minutes after that we were making mad love. And as I lay in bed thinking about the incident, I realized that this man really loves me. That he is thoughtful and sensitive. That he is willing to let me be myself and pursue my own interests and yet still love me. That he'll never try to force me to be like other wives. I thought to myself, What a treasure of a husband I have! You see why I'm enthusiastic about our marriage?

Julie's experience underscores the fact that, for some people at least, marriage contributes to physical health, mental health, and general well-being. Marriage places more demands on people than friendship, but the rewards are enormous for those who are able to work through the differences and annoyances and maintain a growing relationship. For some, the rewards are so immense that marriage is a watershed in their lives.

CHILDREN: TEACHING AND LEARNING

Like marriage, having children has differing consequences for different people. Like marriage, becoming parents puts heavy demands on us. One father told us:

> I remember taking turns with my wife getting up at night to feed our third child. And I remember thinking to myself, I'm getting too old for this sort of thing. I was twenty-eight at the time. I wouldn't trade our family for anything. But three is enough. It takes an incredible amount of energy to be a parent.

Parents are teachers, caretakers, nurturers, and friends. But the relationship is not one-way. Children can also teach parents. And sometimes those lessons are so significant that they become watersheds. The birth of a child may lead to personal growth and general happiness. Being a parent provides a newfound capacity for caring and loving, an increased sense of responsibility, and a new purpose in life.

In part, the impact of children depends on timing. Pregnancies occur by accident as well as by design. Children may be born at a difficult time in a parent's career. An interesting aspect of timing is the middle-aged man with children who divorces, marries a younger woman who has never had children, and starts a second family. Unlike the father above who said three is enough, a number of these men talked about the thrill of the event.

> The first time around, I didn't participate in the birth. At that time, the man stayed in the waiting room until someone came and told you that you had a baby. This time, I was there with my wife and helped in the birth. It was fantastic! I never realized how much I would enjoy being a father again. I missed a lot with the first two. This time, I'm a partner with my wife. I don't intend to miss anything.

The birth experience itself is a memorable event. A fifty-four-year-old banker recalled the birth of her first child as the watershed in her life. A neat, accomplished professional woman, she declared that ''the most thrilling experience in my life was seeing a new human being, a part of myself, for the first time. It was a beautiful and touching moment and continues to be a most wonderful and rewarding experience.'' Her son is now in his twenties, married, and is pursuing a career. She still places the moment of his birth as a high point of her life and one that continues to enrich her.

Interestingly, more men than women said that the birth of a child was their watershed. For example, Khiet, a Buddhist who is a software engineer for an electronics firm, wanted to participate fully in the process of his child's conception and development. He remembers the birth of his first child vividly.

From the time the pregnancy was announced until her birth, I often sat looking through medical books which pictured the development of the child at different time periods. As I have always had a habit of arising very early in the morning, I would get up and sit for an hour or more examining the pictures and wondering what this child of ours would be like.

As my wife's body became larger, I would often listen and touch, to experience this growth in a more personal way. During the term of her pregnancy, I rubbed her stomach seven times in a circular motion and recited the seven names of the Buddha to ensure the development of a healthy child.

When the time came for his wife to deliver, Khiet faced an unexpected obstacle. He was supposed to be in the delivery room with his wife, but he was instructed to go to the waiting room. He sat there for hours, waiting fearfully. The doctor finally came and informed him that they would have to deliver the baby by cesarean section.

This meant that I could not be with my wife during the birth of our baby, an event which we had planned and discussed all during her pregnancy. I signed the consent forms for the operation. I waited outside the operating room, all the while trying my best to see what was taking place through the small windows in the door.

When the operation was over, I went to the room where our daughter was brought. Looking through the large window, I gazed and followed the doctor's movements as he methodically prepared her for life. With tears of joy, I counted toes and fingers and gave her a visual examination to ensure myself that everything a child should have was there and in its proper place.

Two years later, Khiet had a son. Both children are teenagers now. Khiet speaks fondly of them.

My daughter has become a charming young girl and a very close friend. Her growth and development are a continuing concern to me, and will remain so for the rest of my life. My son is a source of endless pleasure. Both of my children have changed my life, in that they have given me a father's responsibility to care for and nurture the growth and development of two other persons.

Clearly, Khiet's children have given him a purpose for living. For many people, children thus redefine the goals of life. Indeed, the birth of a child can revolutionize every aspect of life. Richard, an architect, makes a career out of being creative. When asked to identify a watershed in his life, his usually serious face erupted into a bright smile. He named the most creative act of his life: the conception and birth of his son. That birth, which occurred some thirty years ago, totally transformed Richard's existence.

Some of the changes were ones we expected, and some were not. I expected to change diapers. I didn't expect to have our entire life-style change. We couldn't go out on a moment's notice anymore. I was just starting out, working for a firm, and my income was barely enough for us without the expense of baby-sitting and eating out.

But more than that changed. I changed, too. I became aware of my own mortality. I realized that one day I would die, but that my son would still be here. And I didn't like that—not because I would die, but because he and I would be separated. But the most profound impact was a new feeling of self-worth and a responsibility for the life I had helped to create. My son gave me a higher purpose in life and a new sense of direction.

Childbirth forces a lot of people to confront larger issues. Faced with larger issues, they work through them and emerge as changed creatures. In the midst of the ecstasy of a child's emergence into the world, they suddenly find themselves caught up in the tangles of their own world view. They rethink and rework their philosophy of life, and find themselves taking a somewhat different course than they had been following.

Consider Michelle, a genial, attractive woman who is now a lawyer. Michelle began her domestic duties early and her career late. She married when she was a teenager. She finally went to college when she was thirty, completed her degree, and then went to law school.

In the early years of her marriage, Michelle played the role of a traditional wife. While her husband worked, she stayed home and had children—three of them in three years. The children were a watershed experience for Michelle, but in a different way from that of Richard or Khiet.

I was very inexperienced. I had never even seen a newborn baby until I was in the hospital having my own firstborn. All of this forced me to adjust to a different reality. It was a difficult part of my life. I was forced to mature quickly to take care of my children. I realized that I needed to be more secure myself in order to be strong enough to care for the children.

I survived. And I learned. I gained an incredible amount of knowledge that I might not have gotten otherwise. I feel that I have greater empathy for others—that helps me with my clients—and a better understanding of myself. I can tell

my two daughters with confidence that they can do anything
they want if they work at it.

THE ANGEL IN DISGUISE

There are some relationships that contribute mightily to our well-
being even though they are not intimate ones. It may be a
stranger, a casual acquaintance, or someone such as a teacher
or mentor with whom we have a more or less formal relationship
who turns out to be an angel in disguise in our lives. That is, an
encounter with the person becomes a transforming experience.

We talked earlier about baseball great Roy Campanella and
his battle with paralysis. One of the prominent memories he has
about the first years after his accident was an encounter with an
elderly woman in Florida. Campanella was sitting in his wheelchair at a ballpark when he noticed a crippled, elderly woman
working her way up a steep ramp. The woman had braces on
both her legs. Walking with the aid of a crutch, she struggled
until she reached Campanella. Panting from the exertion, she
looked at him for a moment, then took his helpless hand in hers.
With a voice weak from suffering and age, she thanked him for
giving her the courage to continue the effort to live.

She had been a patient in the same New York hospital he had.
A stroke had left her paralyzed on one side of her entire body.
She lost her will to live. But the doctors at the hospital talked
about Campanella as an example of courage and faith in the face
of overwhelming adversity. The woman was so inspired by the
story of Roy Campanella that she determined to make the effort
to live. And she traveled over a thousand miles to meet him in
person and thank him. A stranger was an angel in disguise,
giving back to Campanella some of the inspiration and courage
that he had instilled in her.

For Jeb Magruder, one of those convicted in the Watergate
scandal, the angel was William Sloane Coffin, who wrote about
Magruder's ''moral dilemma'' in *The New York Times*. The article was not a flattering one, but it did show some sympathy.
Magruder called Coffin and thanked him. Coffin responded by
inviting Magruder and his wife to his home for dinner. The night
of the dinner, Coffin advised Magruder to see his situation as

one in which there was an opportunity for reworking his moral structure. He said that Magruder could grow as a result of his experience or he could be destroyed by it. The choice was Magruder's. Coffin was an important source of support at a time when most people were bent on punishment.

Although help can come from a stranger, it is more likely to come from an acquaintance or friend. Some people have the good fortune to have a watershed experience through a mentor. A literary agent pointed out that she continues to get guidance from an older agent who helped her avoid some of the pitfalls of the business when she first began. A professor told us about one of his college instructors who guided him through his dissertation and then got him his first teaching job. A professional football player talked about the college coach who still comes to the pro games and calls him afterward to offer helpful and encouraging observations. Successful people—whatever their field—frequently have had mentors who guided them into and through the early years of their careers. The relationship may be so crucial to their success that they view it as a watershed in their lives.

For many people, a teacher or school counselor is the angel who gives them some kind of redirection in their lives. Laura, a sales manager for a pharmaceutical firm, is now in her late thirties. She has a presence and a drive today that must have been missing at the time of her watershed. It occurred when she was in the ninth grade and an obstinate school counselor wouldn't let her make her own decision, a decision strongly supported by her mother and her friends. The counselor insisted that everyone, including Laura herself, was wrong. The incident began when he asked Laura to come into his office.

His extremely serious tone and manner confused me. It was the first time I had been asked to visit the counseling center. I squirmed with discomfort as he began addressing the subject of my future plans. I had no plans, other than to graduate from high school and work, like all my friends planned to do.

Laura's counselor, however, had other ideas. He took his job seriously and was determined to push his students to their highest levels of ability.

He opened my eyes. He insisted that I plan to attend college and he refused to let me out of his office until we had worked out a complete schedule of college preparatory courses. The fact that I would be self-supporting, and that my mother didn't want me to continue my education—she felt college a complete waste of time—didn't matter to him.

"Laura," he said to me, "I'm married, supporting a wife and five children, and I worked and went to college. So don't tell me it can't be done. You need to go, and that's all there is to it. Your test scores show that you have the potential, and if you don't make the most of it, you will be cheating yourself as well as all the rest of us."

I was surprised by the counseling session. My grades and school performance, to my teenage mind, were a reflection of the personality of the teacher in each subject. If the teacher presented the material in an interesting and comprehensible way, I excelled. If the teacher was boring or unclear, my performance was average. My mother never pressured me to study, either. And she despised homework and would never help me with problems. So overall I was a very average student.

This gentleman changed my life in less than two hours. He provided me with a new direction that I wouldn't otherwise have considered. My close friends were not college-bound, and my mother never encouraged it. In fact, I became alienated from both my mother and my friends when I began seriously studying. My mother was hostile and angry for a time, and my friends scoffed at what I was doing. I think they felt threatened by the new, studious me. They thought I was slipping away from them.

Spurred on by the counselor, however, Laura finished her college prep course at high school, majored in biology in college, then completed a master's degree in business. She is grateful for the path she has taken. "It is difficult to imagine what life would be like without an education," she says. "My understanding of life, problems, and day-to-day events is far more expansive because of my education. I feel that I am much happier and more secure than most of my old friends.''

Laura has worked in sales for a number of years, but now she is returning to college to pursue a doctorate in business administration. She thinks her high-school counselor is still affecting her: ''Somehow he touched my essence, igniting a smoldering spark within me. There is a little voice within me that reminds me that my education isn't complete yet. Could that little voice be my old counselor?''

We heard a number of similar stories of encouragement and support by counselors and teachers. Such people are in a position to be particularly influential, of course. Students tend to view them as authority figures who can make correct judgments. If a counselor or teacher tells a student that he or she has real potential, the student is likely to gain a new sense of self-confidence. Janet, a magazine editor, told us that when she was in the eighth grade her teacher gave her an invaluable gift: an appreciation of her own ability. The teacher noticed Janet reading a novel one day and talked to her about her interest in reading.

> I told him that I loved to read more than anything else. He said that reading was important for many things, including writing. I hadn't thought about writing before, but he told me that he was very impressed with some essays I had written. He said I should try to write some stories.
>
> I wrote one the next weekend and brought it to him. He critiqued it and urged me to write more. The rest of that year, I wrote stories, brought them to him, and rewrote them under his direction. Because of him I began to feel special, to feel that I had a unique talent. My self-confidence grew enormously. I've always held on to that feeling of being special that he gave me.

It isn't always the student with the obvious potential that teachers encourage. Some teachers are able to reach through the tangles of adolescent apathy or resistance or even hostility and turn a life around. Travis is an insurance broker in his early thirties. Everything about his life, with one exception, suggests that he should not have succeeded. The one exception was a high-school English teacher.

Travis grew up in a blue-collar community in the Midwest. His father worked in a steel mill. Both parents had quit school after the eighth grade. Travis was the third boy in the family. When he was born, his older brothers were already ten and thirteen. By the time Travis was five, his oldest brother had quit high school, gotten married, and joined the army. Two years later, the other brother did the same. Over the next few years, it appeared that Travis would be the third to follow the same pattern.

> My school grades were terrible and my attitude toward education even worse. Of course, looking back on this now, my school problems made perfect sense considering education had never been reinforced in my family as a meaningful endeavor. In fact, when I talked to my brothers, they told me that their only regret was not getting out of school sooner. And why not? They each owned a car, made fairly good money as auto mechanics—a skill they had learned in the army—and were starting their own families. And all that before the age of twenty-one.
>
> So there it was, the recipe for a happy life laid out before me. All I had to do was tolerate school until I was seventeen, old enough to join the army with parental consent. While the six years I had to wait seemed insurmountable, I was consoled by the fact that I wouldn't have to put any energy into schoolwork. As a result of this attitude, I became a major discipline problem in the classroom. I'm sure there are still some old teachers there who occasionally take my name in vain. My behavior was limited only by how far I thought my father could be pushed. From time to time I would miscalculate the limits, making it necessary for my father to redefine them with the back of his hand.

Travis's world fell apart within a year, however. He came home from school one day and learned that his father had had a heart attack. The doctors were hopeful, his mother reassured him. But later that evening the hospital called and said that his father had died. The days ahead were filled with a mixture of grief and fear.

> My father had not much life insurance, which meant that our—myself and my mother's—lives would have to change drastically. My mother would have to work, and I would have to do without many things. In addition to all the emotional changes that occurred during this time, the death of my father meant that there were no longer any constraints on my behavior. My behavior became progressively worse, resulting in numerous disciplinary actions by the school and minor encounters with the law.
>
> At the age of fourteen, my freshman year in high school, another event occurred that would set my life on a totally different course: my chance assignment to a ninth-grade English teacher, Fred Langley. It was immediately apparent to me that he was different from any teacher I had encountered before. He accepted me unconditionally, yet with an added dimension of certainty about the emotional and intellectual potential he felt I possessed. He challenged my mind with issues, not just with facts. He forced me to think by gaining first my interest, and then my trust. And most importantly, he took time with me.
>
> Of course, my perspectives and behavior did not change overnight. It isn't possible to pinpoint the exact moment when I began to reevaluate myself and establish new goals. But I was lucky enough to have his class for two years, so I had plenty of time to change.

Fred Langley helped Travis in two important ways. One was his total acceptance of Travis as he was. And the second was his reinforcement of even the slightest effort that Travis made in his schoolwork.

> The result of this complete acceptance and systematic reinforcement was that I began to explore different options as possible to achieve. . . . I'm quite sure that without this

experience I would have continued on the same course as my father and brothers.

The story of Travis, like all of those previously described, underscores the importance of human relationships to our well-being and growth. The practical application is clear: we should cultivate good relationships and should look on each person we meet as an opportunity. This does not mean that we should crassly use other people for personal ends, of course. Growing people do not exploit others. Relationships involve giving as well as receiving. Sometimes a stranger is an angel in disguise, but at other times we may be the angel in disguise for someone else. In either case, we grow. Every relationship, every encounter with another, becomes an opportunity for mutual development.

6

Relationships That Hurt

Bjorn Borg was known for his coolness on the tennis court when he was one of the top-ranked players in the world. Unlike many of his contemporaries, he never exploded in anger over what he regarded as a bad call. He learned to control himself through a humiliating experience that occurred when he was twelve. At the time, he typically had temper tantrums on the court. His parents had become so ashamed of his behavior that they refused to come to any more matches. And the Swedish Association suspended him for six months. People began to call him the "bad boy" of Swedish tennis. He was so humiliated by the experience that he resolved never again to act badly in public. He succeeded admirably.

It is difficult to deal with the humiliation of having your parents ashamed of your behavior. It is difficult to have those whose respect and friendship you want label you as bad. Borg's experience illustrates the fact that interpersonal relationships can be two-edged swords. When they go well, they help you cut through the growth-retarding entanglements of life. When they go badly, they can be a bitter and painful experience. Relationships that hurt vary from those involving humiliation to those that break up involuntarily to those in which there is violence. Some people are permanently traumatized by such relationships. Others are able to turn even an abusive relationship into a positive watershed.

WHEN THE SUPPORT FAILS

When Jennifer was nineteen, she looked like a young woman out of the sixties: long, straight hair, ever-present jeans, and a cavalier approach to life. She met a man she found attractive— Jonathan, a travel agent. He had a good sense of humor and had traveled throughout the world. For a year, they had a close friendship. Then the friendship turned into a romantic relationship. She remembers that it was Friday the thirteenth when the romance began. She never thought about it at the time, but later she would remember the date and think of it as a sign of what was to follow. Over the next year, Jennifer's love for Jonathan was alternatively nourished and rebuffed.

> I got many mixed messages from him. There were occasions when we shared our most intimate thoughts and desires, and I felt closer to him than I had felt to anyone in my life. All the barriers and walls that generally separate people seemed to crumble, and our intimacy seemed complete. Yet every time this happened, he would pull away from me. I could feel it. He would clam up, or he would not respond when I tried to share my feelings with him.
>
> This was hard to take. In fact, one time, after a particularly delightful evening together, he didn't call me for over a week. I felt very confused. I knew at some level that the relationship was not working. It was obvious that he was uncomfortable with the new level of our intimacy. Maybe I was too clinging. Or maybe I got boring to him after we spent too much time together. I just couldn't figure it out. At one point, I decided to leave him. But I couldn't. Finally, he left me for another woman. Soon after that I met the man I ultimately married.

But this is not the story of going through the tortuous paths of dating and courtship, finally to emerge with the ''right'' mate and to live happily ever after. Five years have elapsed since Jennifer's early love left her. She loves her present husband, and is happy with her marriage. Nevertheless, there is a residue of pain.

I don't like to say it, but I know that I haven't really finished with that relationship. I haven't seen him for many years now. But that was the closest time I ever came to feeling crazy. I lost a friend and a lover, and I'm still not sure why. It made me distrustful of people, especially men. Now I really appreciate people who don't give me mixed messages.

Jennifer's watershed experience left her with some bitterness and distrust. Her story is more than one person's experience; it is a parable of the relationship that hurts. We expect such a relationship to be a source of support, but find ourselves betrayed by it instead. We expect it to add to the richness of our lives, but find that it brings us pain. It is understandable, then, that such experiences hurt so much and are particularly difficult to understand. It isn't just that the relationship falls short of our expectations. Rather, it yields the very opposite of what we had expected.

Abusive relationships epitomize this process. There are, however, different kinds of abuse. Quite a few people endure the psychological abuse of a boss, as witnessed by the popularity of the song "Take This Job and Shove It." Shawn is a geophysicist who works for a major oil company in the Southwest. Lean, tall, and tanned, he looks like a man in control. But for a number of years, he endured an abusive boss. He worked for a man like the one comedian Henny Youngman talked about, a man of even temperament—always miserable.

Shawn's boss believed in the haranguing method of management. He belittled people, harassed them, and pressed them to meet deadlines that he had set.

I found out later that he set deadlines that were weeks in advance of those requested by the top executives. So he gave us extremely difficult work schedules, growled and shouted at us to meet them, and then took credit at the top level for being a good manager. The guys at the top didn't know how unhappy we all were.

The boss also reacted strongly to any errors, even those that had no adverse consequences. He would get enraged and publicly humiliate the employee. Shawn decided to take action.

> I went to him one day and told him flatly that there was a lot of discontent. He looked surprised. I tried to be diplomatic, so I told him we appreciated his efforts to get top-quality work and to do it with maximum efficiency, but that people need some strokes as well as prodding. I said we needed to know from him when we were doing a good job and that we hoped he would understand that we regretted mistakes and delays as much as he did. We were professionals, too. We were as anxious as he was to have a first-rate department.
>
> I was sort of surprised that he seemed to understand what I had said and indicated that he would keep it in mind. I left his office thinking I had won—that I had converted that SOB with my brilliant but gentle arguments. About three hours later, he came charging out of the office and shouted at one of my colleagues who was late with a report. I just stared at him. It was like I hadn't said a word.

It was then that Shawn made a decision that altered his life. He vowed that he would not work for a man who treated others so badly. He stalked into his boss's office and confronted him a second time. In contrast to the first meeting, they got into a loud argument.

> I had no choice now. I went to a VP and told him I was resigning. He had hired me, and he appreciated my work. I knew the shock value of what I was doing. He asked me why and I gave him a long list of grievances. The upshot was that in two weeks my boss was gone and I was offered his job. I felt guilty about that. But my colleagues eased my guilt by telling me how grateful they were for my action.

The incident was a watershed for Shawn not only because he got out from an oppressive situation and advanced in the firm, but also because he learned to take a different approach to life.

I'll never be a doormat for anyone again. When I look back and realize that I spent four years working for that guy . . . I'm willing now to do something that I never even thought about before: take responsibility for changing a situation where people are being hurt.

In addition to the kind of abuse Shawn endured, there is physical abuse in relationships. It is difficult to know exactly how much. A national crime survey reported 3.8 million incidents of violence among intimates (relatives, friends, neighbors, or work associates) in one four-year period. Both the wealthy and the poor experienced violence. About 40 percent of the incidents resulted in injury. It is also estimated that about 4 percent of the elderly of the nation are subjected to physical or verbal abuse, or both; that at least 16 percent of married people commit an act of violence against a spouse during any given year; and that over half of all parents use some kind of violence against their children.

Even dating and courtship relationships, normally thought of as a high time of sweetness and consideration, frequently involve abuse. In one sample of single people, more than 60 percent reported that they have been abused or abusive while dating, or that they had engaged in aggressive behavior during courtship. And a study of high-school students reported that 12 percent admitted to abusive behavior in a heterosexual relationship (including pushing, grabbing, shoving, slapping, kicking, biting, or hitting with the fist).

Some people find it hard to recover from an experience of abuse. Marie is a young computer programmer in an aircraft manufacturing firm. When you first meet her, you wouldn't think that she's been abused—she's pretty and cheerful. But it doesn't take long to recognize the tinge of distrust that keeps flitting across her eyes. Her first experience of physical abuse occurred when she was a child and her father started to hit her. As a result, she felt unloved and unaccepted by him. Wittingly or not, he abused her both physically and emotionally. As a young woman of twenty, Marie again experienced abuse at the hands of men. This time it was severe physical abuse.

My boyfriend attempted to beat me up by hitting me in public. He felt that I had insulted him somehow. I was in shock, and just took it. I didn't fight back. Finally, another man interceded and stopped it. No bruises. No broken bones. I was just emotionally upset.

I thought about pressing charges, but with no physical evidence and nobody willing to testify, I gave up. I phoned some hot lines for help, but I didn't get any. I was really shaken up. In spite of his abuse, I missed the stability of the relationship that we had had. I felt alone. I almost went back to him.

Marie eventually started dating again. She dated one man who felt strongly about her, but she broke off the relationship when he confronted her with a gun.

He was going to shoot me. I told him if he wanted me dead that bad, to go ahead and kill me. He just started crying. Then he started to hit me. He broke one of his fingers in the fight. I didn't press charges against him. But I decided to get some counseling and find out what I was doing wrong.

Marie thinks she has some insights now that will help her avoid future abusive relationships. She realizes that she has spent her life seeking acceptance from men, the acceptance she never got from her father. At the same time, she has set herself up to be rejected, repeating the pattern of her relationship with her father. After several years in therapy, she thinks she can now deal with the problem.

I now ask a man I date if he has ever, or would, hit a woman. I can tell from his response if he would or has. And I tell him why I'm asking. I still have scars. But I'm starting to feel bolder in my relationships and to make my needs and feelings known.

Marie has done something else to protect herself. She has had no long-term relationships since the former abusive ones. She doesn't get deeply involved with any man. Instead, she devotes herself to her career and her personal development. She admits that she tends to "castrate" men by cracking jokes about them being "only good for one thing." But she herself has largely avoided even that "one thing," choosing to remain celibate for long periods in order to cultivate her own strengths. Marie's story is not yet finished. She readily acknowledges that she still has not developed a satisfying mode of relating to men and that she still must work on this part of her personal life.

One of the more insidious forms of abuse is incest. Perhaps as many as one out of five females under the age of eighteen are the victims of incestuous abuse. The experience is particularly painful if the perpetrator is the victim's father, the person who is supposed to protect and support her. For many victims, it is difficult even to discuss the experience without generating intense feelings. That is the case of an editor of corporate publications, Becky, who says that she is "overwhelmed by feelings" as she discusses her childhood.

What do I remember that can possibly make sense out of this watershed? There was an atmosphere of tension in my home—volatile arguments between my parents which frightened me terribly. Even now, a raised voice causes me to freeze until laughter accompanies it. No one I knew could effectively stand up to my father. Arguing may have been a way of life for him, as I know it was for his parents. My mother took the brunt of his wrath, and I was extremely protective of her.

I never saw my parents resolve an argument. As far as I knew, they ended when either my mother left or I became hysterical. Later, it seemed, it was my mother who began yelling at us kids. But then she went away to a hospital and when she returned she was calm again. My feeling is that the incest began before she left, but I don't actually remember. I think I was about eleven at the time.

Some people have suggested that youthful seduction is the basis for incest. Recent studies indicate that this is rarely, if ever, the case. Becky recalls the incest beginning in the context of youthful innocence.

Sex at that age was not even the subject for jokes with my circle of friends. I hardly thought about it. I didn't react to the incest as a sexual act, but as a way to keep the family together. I know now how much I felt responsible for my parents' feelings and well-being. I desperately wanted harmony in my family and every other need became subordinate to that. Except in times of crisis, when I lost control of my emotions.

When my father wanted to use me for sexual gratification, I was passive. Without giving away the secret, I was able to gather that other fathers did not behave this way with their daughters. But it didn't occur to me that I could do anything about it, because my father *wanted* to treat me the way he did. In fact, when he asked me if I wanted him to return to my bedroom, without hesitation I said no. But I was not the least bit surprised when he showed up again. . . . That he didn't want my mother to know meant to me that it would be bad for her if she knew, so I didn't tell her. I saw myself as the buffer between my parents and the protector of my brothers and sisters as well as my mother when she was being hurt by my father. And I could not imagine having behaved otherwise.

Why could she not imagine behaving any other way? Why did she not consider alternatives? For Becky, her choice was clear and unavoidable.

To consider other alternatives is to suggest that I would have been willing to jeopardize the entire family structure for the sake of a better world for me, which I could not envision anyway. So the only choice available was to maintain the delicate equilibrium which existed. At least that was a world I knew; and what seemed fortunate then but now seems shameful, I had the self-control to pull it off.

Does it sound as if I had the power to make or break the family unit? I rarely felt powerful as a child in terms of directing my own fate. Yet I very definitely sensed and quietly accepted my role as balancer, as if that was what it meant to be the oldest child.

The intensity of Becky's pain is somewhat masked by her almost clinical discussion of her situation. One needs, however, to pay close attention to her words—to the fact that she saw herself as an "object," that she became "invisible" to herself, and that she assumed the burdens of the parental role as a child. Her pain becomes more evident as she talks about the subsequent effects on her life.

> My self-image has probably suffered the most damage, because I have tended to ignore my own needs whenever I'm with someone I feel is more powerful than I am. This leaves me with little self-respect because it repeats my childhood experience. Also, as an adult I have replayed my mother's behavior. This has carried over into the sexual area. With my ex-husband, who gave up his own control in our relationship, I became emotionally abusive because I had no respect for him. He behaved like the helpless female my mother was. That caused me even more self-hatred because it put me in the role of my father, the controller.
>
> I am also still burdened with a self-abusive voice telling me I was responsible for the incest by my acquiescence. So I tend to either be overresponsible for things beyond my control or I become helpless and want to relinquish any responsibility.
>
> Most importantly, I am concerned about the impact I have had on my children. Learning to say to my crying five-year-old daughter when appropriate, "It's all right, honey, it's not your fault—I made a mistake," is such a cleansing statement for us both to hear. Yet it is so difficult to say, never having heard it as a child.

Becky feels that she is slowly working through the problem: "Though its impact is indelible, at least I now know what I'm dealing with so that I no longer have to feel so helpless and alone." Her struggle has continued for more than twenty years. She dramatizes the enormity of the pain that people endure when betrayed by someone expected to be a source of support.

CAN YOU RECOVER?

The hurt of the betrayed is illustrated by the numbers of those hospitalized for mental illness who endured some kind of abuse in their past. One study of psychiatric patients discharged over an eighteen-month period from a teaching hospital reported that 43 percent had a history of abuse, physical or sexual or both. In spite of the intense hurt endured, there are those who turn the hurt inside out. That is, they take painful relationships, work through them, and emerge as stronger and more mature individuals. The answer to the question of whether you can recover, therefore, is not merely yes. It is yes, you can not only recover but grow in the process.

Consider, for instance, the problem of childhood humiliation. Even though the abuse is only verbal and emotional, a single instance of humiliation can remain as a shudder in your memory. What if a significant part of your childhood was a series of humiliating experiences? That is what happened to a physician, Matthew, who recalls his watershed when he was eleven years old. Matthew speaks with the rapidity of a busy professional, but with a gentleness that is in stark contrast to the harshness of his experience. He lived in Philadelphia, and attended school where he was labeled as the "kike jewboy." He remembers walking to school and being accosted by groups of boys who would call out: "Hey, jewboy. Got a dime?" Often he would give the dime, depending upon how many boys there were and how big they were. The boys would then call out, "See you later, kike."

His watershed experience began when he was working on a tie rack for his father in his woodshop class. Suddenly he felt pain in his head. Someone had hit him with a plane.

As I fell to the floor, bleeding, all I can remember hearing was some slurs about Jews. I was taken down to the nurse's office. I was suspended from school, along with the student who hit me, for what the principal called "contributory school violence." When I arrived home with a bandaged head and a suspension note in my hand, my grandmother looked at me in disbelief. When I explained to her my situation, she looked at me with hurt in her eyes and said that those who had hit me wouldn't be happy until they had made us all suffer.

I was very angry and hurt. But worst of all, I was afraid to return to school. I can remember crying to my parents that I could not go back, that I needed to change schools. My father told me that once you run from anti-Semitism you'll spend your entire life in fear. He suggested that I take up boxing. So I joined the YMHA and took up boxing and weight lifting.

There was no dramatic follow-up, with Matthew using his boxing skills to defeat the bully. This is not another version of the movie *Rocky.* "In fact," Matthew says wryly, "I don't know if I could have actually hit anyone. I just hoped they would see my new muscles, know that I could box, and leave me alone." His training did give him the confidence he needed to return to school. One of the things that he learned from the experience was the fact that "the world is not a fair place." If that had been the only thing he learned, he could have turned into a hostile cynic. But Matthew gained more.

I also learned that we cannot limit our lives, based on the ignorance of a few who can only accept themselves by degrading others. And I have learned to value the use of language rather than force to convey my thoughts and feelings. As a physician, I have had plenty of opportunity to put this into practice. Medicine is filled with prima donnas who are adept at humiliating others. I have made a concerted effort to avoid such behavior myself, and I get extremely irritated when I am confronted with arrogant colleagues. But I have found that a few well-chosen words are far more effective than a well-placed fist in combating haughtiness. I have made it a mission in life to use words—along with my medical skills—as instruments of healing.

Matthew had one great advantage in his struggle: the support of his family. Those without a supportive family are handicapped in their efforts to deal with problematic relationships.

Those for whom the family not only is nonsupportive but constitutes the problem itself are doubly handicapped. Yet even they can sometimes demonstrate a remarkable capacity to overcome.

Carrie is the executive director of a social-service agency. She is a vibrant woman in her late forties. Talking to her now, you would not suspect that she had endured years of verbal and physical abuse from those she had expected to protect and nurture her. Her watershed comprised two experiences about ten years apart. The first occurred when she was eighteen.

You've heard of jumping from the frying pan into the fire? Well, I jumped from the swimming pool into the fire. I fell madly in love with a guy. My parents were totally opposed to any relationship with him. Unlike me, they suspected the kind of person he was. To their horror, I ran off with him and got married. It was one of the dumbest things I ever did.

In the first year of our marriage, I found out that my husband was going out with other women. It took me a long time to build up enough courage to confront him about finding lipstick on his shirt collars and condoms in his wallet. I was six months pregnant at the time.

All hell broke loose when I confronted him. He struck me for the first time. Scenes of violence, yelling, and throwing things became commonplace over the next eight-and-a-half years. After a particularly violent scene in which our housekeeper was shot in the shoulder trying to protect me, my father-in-law intervened and removed my husband at gunpoint. He told my husband that he would answer to him if he ever returned.

Carrie feels she had few alternatives during those years.

At that time, there was no such thing as women's hostels, where the woman and her children could seek refuge. Support groups were unheard of. Discussing wife abuse was a taboo. There was little or no empathy with the plight of the battered woman. I found the police unsupportive of my plea for help.

She is also contemptuous of theories that blame the woman in such a situation.

> Somewhere I read that Sigmund Freud one time said, "It is better to be abused than ignored." I guess a psychiatrist would say that I was guilty and needed to be abused, or that my self-esteem was low, so I was willing to accept anything. But common sense tells me that I had no economic resources. I had not finished high school. I had no skills. I was too proud to go back to my parents and admit I had totally screwed up. So I was dependent on my husband for everything.

The second part of Carrie's watershed experience occurred when, at the age of twenty-eight, she ran away to another part of the country, taking her four children with her. A short time earlier, Carrie had developed a friendship with a woman who convinced her that she did not have to endure abuse and told her about groups that would help and support her. Carrie's own instincts had been telling her for years to get away from her abusive husband. She only needed someone—anyone—to say that it was all right for her to leave.

Carrie went to Arizona, linked up with a feminist group, and helped them make a videotape about wife abuse. She went to work and also returned to school. She is aware of the tendency of abused people to become abusers themselves, and is determined that she will not perpetuate the abuse that she endured.

> I have worked very hard to avoid making the same mistakes with my children. I made a promise to myself that I would never strike my children in anger as first my mother and then my husband did to me. My experiences have made me a more compassionate and understanding person.

TURNING HURT INTO HEALTH

Clearly, people can use hurtful relationships as stepping-stones to growth. The steps are precarious, covered with hazards and sure to cause pain, but they are not insurmountable. Some of those who surmount them do so only with the help of therapy. Others find support in friends or relatives. All use one or more of the following techniques for turning the hurt into health.

1. Listen to your instincts.   If each of us has a fundamental need to grow, then there should be urges and desires and impulses that prod us on to new levels. That is, within each of us there are drives that resist the notions that we are incompetent, unlovable, or rightful objects of abuse. It is important to attend to those inner proddings and not allow them to be stilled by the clamor of external directives and demands. We noted that Carrie felt her instincts telling her to leave her abusive husband for many years before she finally found the courage to do so. A number of people spoke about their watershed experiences crystallizing around a sudden inner voice that seemed to tell them to stop, to change directions. It was as if something inside suddenly welled up and insisted on being heard. They listened. And they changed their lives for the better.

Stacy, a forty-three-year-old floral designer who now owns her own shop, listened to her instincts when she was a child, then suppressed them through thirty years of difficulty, and finally listened once again.

My dad was a salesman and gone most of the time. And my mother was withdrawn, sad, and mean. I was raised being told that I was no good, dumb, ugly, and worthless. For some reason I didn't believe it. I fought the idea that I was bad. I would go outside, where she could not hear me, and I would scream at her: "I am not bad. You're the dumb, stupid, ugly one." I know now that I was probably losing the battle.

The event that really sealed my fate happened when I was about nine. I hated school and I hated being at home. The only pleasant memories are of the weekends, when I was allowed to go to my girlfriend's house and even stay over occasionally. Since my dad was rarely home anyway, my mom started going out with her girlfriends on the weekend. She would leave me with her friend's little baby all weekend, so I could no longer go to my girlfriend's house. Now I even hated the weekends.

My hatred and anger grew and grew until one weekend while I was baby-sitting and couldn't stand it any longer. I spanked the crying, eighteen-month-old little girl I was watching and I couldn't stop. I hit her repeatedly. She was not hurt badly, but that event proved to me what my mother said all along. She was right. I was bad, stupid, ugly, and even mean, just like mom. It was like I gave up my fight to be accepted as good and okay. I now felt that I could no longer even accept myself that way.

Stacy began to act like the kind of person she now believed herself to be. She was willing to do the kinds of things that "bad and stupid" people do. She was willing to act out the role that had been assigned to her and that she had finally accepted. The inner urge to resist had faded. As she grew older, she engaged in all kinds of self-destructive behavior.

My life led me through drugs, alcohol, three marriages, and many poor relationships. For nearly thirty years, I was that worthless child. Can you believe it? Thirty years! Then in one of these relationships I was beaten badly.

It was at that point that the inner urges once again reared up.

I had been beaten before. But for some reason, this time I got in touch with a very deeply hidden feeling that I didn't deserve such abuse. I somehow still believed that I was better than that. But I was at the lowest point of my life. I didn't know where to go or what to do.

I decided to call a psychologist. . . . Before I had my first appointment, I had started again to blame myself for what had happened. The thought that I deserved the abuse I had gotten kept gnawing at me. I thought about canceling my appointment, but somehow I knew it was my last chance.

I went to see the psychologist. I went to him for over a year. Since that first appointment, I've been creating a new person and building a new world. I have gotten in touch with what I feel and why. I am no longer that bad and stupid child.

2. Refuse to play the victim game.   In numberless small ways, we are victimized by others. An out-of-towner driving in Manhattan came to a stop sign and called to a man standing on the corner, "Excuse me, where is Forty-second Street?" The man shrugged and said: "I'm a pedestrian. I don't help automobiles." The out-of-towner just grinned and drove on. He could have gotten angry. He could have felt sorry for himself for being a victim of someone's rudeness. He chose not to define himself as a victim.

Those who are betrayed by abuse are unquestionably victims. They live in a splintered world. Like other kinds of victims, they tend to find that the assumptions on which they based their lives are no longer valid, including the assumptions of their own invulnerability, of the world as a meaningful place, and of their own worth as persons. In addition, children who are incest victims are likely to feel an intense sense of insignificance, hopelessness, and guilt. Like Becky, the child may feel abandoned and unprotected because she has assumed the role of parent and become responsible for family harmony. Her own needs are of no consequence; she is insignificant. And to compound the matter, she is likely to feel guilty, blaming herself for her parents' behavior.

Abused wives tend to remain in the relationship, as Carrie did for many years, because they see no viable alternative, and because a sexist society may suppress their feelings of betrayal. They may come to see themselves as bad individuals, as meriting the abuse they are receiving. They may develop what psychologists call "learned helplessness," a perception on their part that they are unable to control events or solve problems. The perception arises from experiences in which they can't solve a problem. The inability may have been rooted in the situation itself or in their lack of resources at the time. But they reach the unfortunate conclusion that they are generally not capable of dealing with problematic situations. As a result, they stop trying, they accept their impotence, and they slump into depression.

Those who continue to define themselves in these terms are playing the victim game. They continue to be victims, not because—as Carrie rightly pointed out—they have some masochistic need to be brutalized, but because they are unable to find their way out of the tangled maze of assumptions and circumstances that bind them to their misery. Those who turn hurt to health, on the other hand, are those who refuse to play the victim game. No matter how seriously they have been victimized, they will not submit to an ongoing victim role.

The point is that we tend to perpetuate problems unless we make a conscious decision and effort to do otherwise. We can unthinkingly slip into the victim role in the midst of a troubled time and continue to play the part for years or even a lifetime. But growth only begins when we reject the victim game, repudiating the idea that we are doomed to remain helpless victims in a situation that is beyond our control.

3. *Work to change the conditions that produce hurtful relationships.* People who grow not only refuse to continue in the victim role, but take the next step and turn the hurt on its head by attacking the conditions that produce and help perpetuate hurtful relationships. When the Reverend Jesse Jackson was a young boy, he ran into a store in his town and whistled at the white grocer to get his attention. He was in a hurry, he told the grocer, and he needed to get some candy. The grocer responded by pulling a pistol from under the counter, holding it against the boy's face, and telling him not to whistle at a white man ever again. That was but one of a series of humiliating events that Jackson suffered as a black in a southern community. But he refused to fall into the victim role. Instead of becoming bitter and hostile, he has devoted his life to changing the conditions that produce prejudice and discrimination.

It's not easy to respond in a positive way when we have been bruised by others. Ironically, the tendency is to hurt others in return. Those who were abused as children, for example, are more likely than others to abuse their own children. It requires insight and a conscious decision to break out of the pattern; otherwise, the victim may become a victimizer. A number of people told us that they were determined not to abuse their children as their parents had abused them, or to have a hurtful marriage like that of their parents. They realized that there is a tendency to perpetuate abuse and were making a conscious effort to avoid doing so.

There are various ways to try to eliminate hurtful relationships. Carrie, for example, has spent a number of years working with abused women. Another woman told us that she was hurt by the prejudice she encountered because she is Hispanic. At first she felt resentful and hostile towards non-Hispanics. She returned their prejudice with her anger and contempt. It was one day while she was watching a group of children playing in the park that she realized how she, the victim, had become a victimizer. There were white, Hispanic, and black children playing happily together. It was a watershed in her life. With misty eyes, she watched the children enjoying themselves, oblivious of the racial distinctions between them. She now works for the government in an Equal Opportunity office and volunteers time to participate in a minority children's program.

4. Affirm your own worth. One of the common results of victimization is self-doubt. People begin to question their worth as humans. They begin to think of themselves as less deserving, less competent, less powerful, and less lovable than others. Self-esteem is a fragile possession at best. Those who are betrayed are particularly vulnerable to losing it.

Affirming your own worth in the face of betrayal can be a difficult and painful process. But it can be done. Brian, a certified public accountant who is in his fifties, happily married, and enjoying his work, made a decision to assert his own worth after an unsettling dream.

I didn't realize it at the time, but I was verbally abused as a child. I thought it was natural that I should be criticized and demeaned. My stepmother had convinced me that I was a difficult and irresponsible child. The severity of the tongue-lashings was just proof of my unworthiness. The constant put-downs reinforced my low self-esteem. Comparisons with a genius half-brother didn't help either. He rarely got criticized. And worse, he was often praised.

By the time I was a teenager, however, I began to receive a different message from some relatives—especially my

Aunt Helen—and other caring adults. According to them, I did have a few good traits. Of course, I knew, as my stepmother was quick to point out, that these other people were mistaken. I had pulled the wool over their eyes. And I don't regret it. In a way, I was playing at being two different kinds of people. Eventually, I would choose which one to be. I didn't intend to stay Jekyll and Hyde all my life.

By the time I was in high school, I knew I had the potential to become someone of greatness, just as long as nobody found out what the real me was like. And that would be no problem, for I had learned to become two different people—quiet but winsome, playful, intelligently creative, and considerate while away from home, and silent, smoldering, sarcastic, and defensively rebellious at home. Away from home I felt free, sometimes appreciated and even loved.

Brian was in his second year of high school when his watershed experience occurred. He had, for the first time in his life, discovered something in school that really excited him: ancient history.

I couldn't get my hands on enough books and even got permission to go to the Library of Congress in Washington, which was near to my Virginia home, for further research. How ancient civilizations struggled and rose to glorious heights was heady stuff. Perhaps I related these rising cultures to my own growth, overcoming environmental obstacles, barbarous enemies, internal politics, and countless other obstacles to eventually triumph.

But no study of ancient civilizations is complete without the decline and even utter disappearance of those people that fought so valiantly to create for themselves a better world. It saddened me. Why must there be a fall within every rise? Our study of the subject was to learn from these ancient civilizations so we would not repeat the same mistakes. Yet the same mistakes were recorded there, over and over again. Was there no hope? I began to think not.

The stage was now set for my watershed. It was a dream. During that week there was a new international crisis that seemed very threatening to me. Apparently, I took my anxiety to bed with me, because I had a nightmare. In that dream, the world was divided into two contentious sides. No resolution occurred. Disaster struck. The planet literally shattered into two jagged halves just before I awoke in horror.

There was no relief in realizing it was only a dream. The feelings of despair, utter futility, and horror lingered. I believe it was that week that I came to a conclusion that has become a primary motivation for my life: that life is fragile and that we must take advantage of what we have to be the best we can. If the world does fall apart, it won't be because I haven't given life my best shot.

Brian embarked on a personal quest for growth. He studied math, science, and philosophy. He got his college degree in accounting and went to work with a top-notch firm. He married. He is generally satisfied. The years of childhood abuse did not defeat him. And he has learned to affirm his worth: "I am at greater peace and share more happiness than I ever thought possible for me."

One of the nice things about asserting your own worth is that it is likely to benefit others. Everybody wins. This is rather dramatically illustrated in the story told by Nan. White-haired and serene-looking, Nan is a housewife who lives at the edge of a metropolitan area. She had a watershed when a well-dressed man appeared at her door nearly two decades ago.

I recognized him immediately, but for a moment or two I couldn't speak. Then I invited him in and told him to tell me what had happened to him. You see, I had first met him about a year before. That time he had also come to my house and knocked on the door. But that time, he looked like a tramp. He asked if I had any work for him. I said I was sorry but I didn't. He looked so weary and so harmless that I invited him in for a sandwich and a cup of tea. We talked for a while, and I learned that he had been in prison for arson. His family deserted him when he went in. When he got out, he couldn't get a job.

But the second time he came, he obviously had work and was doing well. He told me that when he got out of prison and tried to find work, a lot of people treated him badly. They were either afraid or contemptuous of him. When he visited me that first day, he had felt completely defeated. But it seems that I said one thing that made a difference. I called him "sir." No one had said "sir" to him in years. He said it had restored his sense of his dignity. He left the house with a new spirit and a new determination to do something with his life.

Nan closed her eyes as she reflected on the incident.

I guess the first time he came was a watershed for him. The second time was a watershed for me. I almost feel like I've had another child. I gave a man life, and I didn't even know what I was doing. Ever since then, I get a special pleasure out of helping someone else. I think to myself, "I could be changing this person's whole life." Isn't that remarkable?

Self-worth is not like a pie, with a limited number of shares for the world. Affirming your own does not mean detracting from someone else's. Self-worth is boundless. To assert it is not only to enrich yourself but to benefit others as well.

7

Relationships That End
Divorce

Jim and Sandra, a young couple we knew a few years ago, were "made for each other." They came from common backgrounds, shared common goals, and felt immensely attracted to each other. Four years into their marriage, Sandra presented Jim with an unanticipated request: she wanted a divorce. It was the only thing that would satisfy her, she insisted. The marriage was over. She no longer loved Jim. She had been miserable for a number of months as she struggled with her decision, but now knew that a divorce would make her happy.

"I want a divorce." The words were jarring to Jim. But he was unable to stop the process. He was convinced that the divorce would mean extended grief for them both. She was convinced that it would open the doors to renewed happiness. Each of them was in part right and in part wrong. Neither realized the range of potential consequences of divorce.

THE PAIN OF DISRUPTION

The disruption of intimate relationships seriously threatens our well-being. Typically, divorce is a painful process for people. Yet, well over two million Americans go through the process each year. A divorce is relatively easy to obtain today. There is no stigma on the divorcée. Women are not economically bound to their husbands as they were in the past. The legal grounds for divorce have been broadened considerably; many states now even have no-fault divorce laws. And in a generation where the emphasis is on personal gratification—what some observers call the ''me generation''—it is easy to justify breaking a relationship that has problems.

The ease of getting a divorce, however, contrasts sharply with the pain of going through it. Couples who divorce report experiences like those that take place when people grieve for someone who has died. Grief after a marriage breaks down usually occurs even for those like thirty-seven-year-old Steven, a regional-theater director, who initiated his divorce. Although he was the one who started the proceedings, the process was so painful that Steven rebounded into a second marriage and a second divorce before he was able to get his life under control.

With an ever-present cigarette twitching nervously in his fingers, Steven began the story with his first marriage.

I was twenty-three years old when this watershed occurred. I had returned home from school one afternoon when my wife greeted me by asking where I had been. I wondered why she didn't ask how I was, or how was my day. I suddenly realized that she had greeted me this way every time I came home during the past year. For some reason, this time I got very angry and confronted her about why she always greeted me with this suspicious comment in a skeptical tone of voice.

She very coolly told me that she had always distrusted me and that she always knew that someday I would fall in love and run off with someone more attractive. I got furious with her for never revealing this fantasy to me. I had never been unfaithful to her, never even considered it. I was committed to our marriage and that was that.

Steven seethed over the incident for the next few days. As he reflected on it, he began to realize the emptiness of his marriage.

I realized how much her jealousy had separated us, and now our relationship seemed meaningless. I didn't respect or trust her anymore. In fact, I didn't even like her anymore. We separated several times, but things didn't improve. After a while, divorce seemed the only realistic choice.

Deciding to go through with the divorce was not easy for Steven. His parents' marriage had not always been a happy one, but they had worked through their problems and stayed together. Steven thought that if people just waited long enough, they would resolve their difficulties and everything would be all right. In his case, it didn't work out that way. "Two things happened at this watershed," he recalled. "I learned that love doesn't automatically coexist with trust and honesty. And I realized that marriage isn't always forever."

Yet the divorce was not an easy process. He was depressed during the period of separation and felt confused about his relationships with females. He was troubled as he thought about his parents' enduring marriage. Why couldn't the couples of his generation have the same stability as those of his parents' generation? He kept remembering a line from the play *Green Pastures*—that everything that had been nailed down was coming loose. "That's my generation," he said. "We can't seem to keep a family together like my parents could."

During and after the divorce, things got worse.

I felt in turmoil. I had a hard time working. A few months after the divorce, I rebounded into another marriage that was even more devastating to both my self-esteem and my hopes for ever attaining a successful marriage. This marriage lasted only one painful year. The depression that survived the second divorce lasted ten years.

Finally Steven attended a self-help seminar and realized that he would have to take responsibility for his life.

Every time I would blame the past, or my ex-wives, or my parents, or anything else, somebody would challenge me. I remember one woman in the group who very forcefully told me one night that it didn't matter who was to blame for my situation or my feelings. What mattered was what I did *now.* So I had to choose between continuing to sulk in self-pity and setting my life in a new direction.

Steven chose a new direction. He was weary of feeling sorry for himself. He wanted to get on with the good things in life. He is now married a third time—this time happily—and believes he is finally on track for a fulfilling life: "I know that now I can create a healthy environment in which to raise my children—a home with two adults acting, most of the time, like adults."

Steven struggled for a long time to come to terms with his divorces, particularly the first one. Unlike the second marriage, he had thought the first one was good until his wife disclosed her suspicions and distrust. Interestingly, when a marriage is bad, the breakup can still be painful. One woman told us she was married for twelve years, eleven of which were bad for her. But when she divorced her husband, "it really hurt. I cried all the time when I realized it was really over."

Not only is the divorce itself painful, but there frequently may be a residue of pain for some years. Beth has been divorced for some seven years now, but she is still struggling. There are circles beneath her large, brown eyes and a slight trembling of her lips as she talks about it. Her marriage began like a fairy tale, ended like a nightmare, and continues to haunt her.

I met my husband at a party at the university. He was dapper, charming, and witty. We both loved reading, movies, theater, people, parties, laughing, and pizza. We spent our Saturday nights watching "Perry Mason" and talking about our future. He wanted to be an attorney. I wanted to be a college professor. And it wasn't long before I also wanted to be his wife. We were married in our senior year in a classic, formal ceremony with two hundred friends and relatives wishing us to live happily ever after.

We were happy for ten years. I taught school and my husband practiced law. But then the stress of being a lawyer got to my husband. He began drinking more and more. And I began crying myself to sleep. We struggled with it for seven years before I decided that a divorce was the best option for myself and our children.

It was incredibly difficult for me to give up my white picket fence, my ideal family dreams. But at thirty-seven, I turned my life upside down and became a single mother. I thought there was a chance that my leaving would be such a shock that he would change and give up drinking. He didn't change. He still has a drinking problem.

Beth's problems didn't end with the divorce of her husband. In fact, a whole set of new problems confronted her.

I was used to the good life. But I couldn't afford to stay in our home on a teacher's salary. We had to move. My children were angry. They were mad at their father for drinking and at me for failing to keep their home for them. In an attempt to earn more money, I started my own business. I did make more money than in teaching, but I worked fifty to sixty hours a week. It was hard to work so much and be a good mom too. The children resented having to do more around the house. They had been spoiled. Now they had to think twice about new clothes and money for movies.

Beth's financial problems were compounded by the fact that Beth's ex-husband knew how to use the courts to avoid paying her alimony and child support for over two years. The divorce caused bitterness not only between her and her husband, but with former friends, who tended to take sides.

Most of them decided to make my husband the bad guy. This made things worse, because my husband blamed me for their feelings. The estrangement became more difficult. I had hoped that divorce would be an opportunity for us to make our lives easier, not more complicated. I didn't realize how much bitterness there would be over the financial settlement and the question of custody and visitation rights.

Where is Beth headed? She isn't sure.

I have dated other men since my divorce, but part of me is still in love with my former husband. It may be that I'm still in love with the illusion of what might have been. I grew up with the myth that you could marry and live happily ever after. Now here I am starting all over again. But neither I nor my ex-husband seem to be able to get started with a new life. Neither of us can resolve the loss of being a family. We have terrible arguments over the holidays. The times we have shared holidays with the children have been very strained and unhappy, and yet when the children are with one parent, then the other seems to suffer.

Overall, the divorce has affected every area of Beth's life, and continues to affect it some seven years later.

Emotionally, I feel a loss of family stability and centeredness. Economically, I always feel strained. Physically, I've watched myself eat and gain weight to avoid the empty feeling in the pit of my stomach. I am exhausted trying to be Superwoman. Socially, I find myself the fifth wheel much of the time, as many of my friends are married. I have made friends with single women, but I get depressed listening to their complaints and stories of difficulties. So I spend more time alone than I have in the past.

Beth's story is not a unique one. It is not unusual for someone to struggle for many years after a divorce. An extreme example of the inability to adjust to a divorce was reported by a sixty-five-year-old woman who now lives with four other women. She and her companions are a kind of ache-and-pain version of ''The Golden Girls'' television show. The woman was divorced by her husband thirty years ago after she found out he had been having an affair. She recalls that they had a very good marriage for a number of years. They had two children. After the children were both in school, however, she noticed a change in him. He became cold and antagonistic. He finally admitted to the affair and asked for the divorce. She agreed, on condition that she would have sole custody of the children.

The divorce wrecked her self-confidence. She started drinking heavily. She was placed in a mental hospital for six months. She finally recovered and was able to care for her two children.

But she never trusted men again, never remarried, and never really got over the divorce. She has spent thirty years feeling lonely and perplexed about what went wrong with her marriage. She is an extreme example of the bitterness of the rejected spouse, of the anger felt toward the spouse who wants out of the marriage.

But the stories are not all grim, not even when the individual is the one who was rejected. In fact, many of them sound like tales of discovery and freedom. Some people learn to use divorce to carve out new and more fulfilling lives for themselves. One woman married a man "who believed that the husband is God almighty and the wife will do as he says in everything." She now sees herself and her children as far better off than they were ten years ago. "I'm me again. I may not have as much money, but my kids and I are much happier. I think they have a better relationship with their father now than if he were living with us, because we don't live with his constant criticism." And a man we interviewed looked back on his marriage and recalled the regular arguments that he and his ex-wife had and the heavy drinking in which he engaged to escape the tensions. "The divorce has made wonderful changes in my life," he said. "I've stopped drinking. I am peaceful and calm and a far better father to my children."

Incidentally, a number of people named the divorce of parents rather than their own divorce as the watershed in their lives. The divorce of one's parents can have long-term, negative consequences. Young children may blame themselves for their parents' divorce and struggle for years with guilt. A study of the children of divorce in California reported that 37 percent were still depressed five years after the marriage broke up.

But again, there are those for whom the divorce of parents is, in the long run, a positive factor in the growth. Molly is a graduate student who said her watershed was her parents' divorce when she was sixteen. When Molly speaks, her enthusiasm for life bursts through everything she says. She is getting her degree in molecular biology and anticipates with relish a career in research. Oddly enough—it seemed odd at first, anyway—her joie de vivre seems to intensify when she talks about her parents' divorce.

To be exact, it was their separation, which ultimately led to divorce, that initiated the change that occurred in me. For the first sixteen years of my live, I grew up in a home filled with tension, anxiety, competitiveness, anger, and sadness.

Molly attributes her turbulent childhood to the fact that her parents should never have married in the first place.

I cannot remember a time in which they showed any affection toward each other. As I grew older, my mother told me that she would have divorced my dad within the first year of the marriage had she not become pregnant with my oldest brother. She also told me after they were divorced that they had stayed together for twenty-one years because of the children. They wanted to raise their family in a normal environment!

Let's discuss this normal environment. Let me tell you some of my most vivid childhood memories. First, I remember walking into the house in a relatively carefree mood and instantly feeling tension. It formed knots in my stomach. I hated this feeling. I used to run into my room and try to withdraw.

Second, I remember at age ten lying in bed at night, crying, wondering when the divorce would actually occur. There was never any doubt in my mind that they would get divorced. It was just a matter of when. This was scary to me, because I didn't know who I would live with or if anyone would want to take care of me.

Third, I remember making up excuses so that my friends would not come over and play. I was embarrassed. I could not anticipate the situation at home, but I knew it would be somewhere between silent tension, overt arguments, or maudlin tears.

The divorce was finally announced shortly before Molly's sixteenth birthday. Molly had mixed emotions. She was sad and fearful. But she was also "excited at a gut level. I had known for years this was going to happen. I thought to myself, no more fighting, no more tears, and no more awkward silences.'' Molly stayed with her mother. It was a turning point for her. She could come home and feel relaxed for the first time in her life. Her last two years in high school were radically different than her previous school experiences.

> I became much more social, enjoyed being around people, laughed constantly, and best of all, after a long day at school I could actually look forward to going home. There was a peaceful quality to home life and it was wonderful.

Of course, Molly's life did not change instantly. She sees herself as still changing, as still emerging out of the shadows of the tense existence she endured when her parents lived together.

> Since the divorce I have gradually become more secure with myself, and my self-esteem and confidence have greatly increased. I am just beginning to truly like and respect myself, and that is one terrific feeling. I know that a divorce can be very difficult and troublesome for children, but it was a very positive experience for me. I learned one very important message while growing up in a family with two very unhappy parents: Do not stay in a bad marriage solely because you do not want to hurt your children with the process of divorce. Children are very sensitive and intuitive. They know when things are not right. It is much more difficult for them to grow up in an environment in which the parents are strained, unnatural, and constantly arguing than to adjust to the changes of divorce. Change is natural. Resistance, defensiveness, and distrust are not.

FROM DISRUPTION TO WHOLENESS

Clearly, divorce can have quite different outcomes for different people. It can shackle children with guilt or free them to develop. It can leave the ex-spouses mired in self-pity or mark the beginning of fulfilling changes. In the short term, pain is probably inevitable. In the long run, the outcome depends in large part on how you deal with the disruption. Let us look at how, according to those who reported growth experiences, you can turn the trauma of divorce into a positive force.

1. Define the divorce as an important step in your growth. Some specialists in human behavior argue that an individual's growth proceeds from dependence to independence to interdependence. That is, we are necessarily dependent when we are children. We need to assert our independence in order to continue to grow as individuals. But once we have established our capacity for autonomy, we only continue to grow through relationships, through interdependence with others.

A fulfilling marriage is a state of interdependence in which the partners lose neither their identities nor their sense of autonomy. This is achieved through what we call ''zones of freedom within a shared relationship.'' The spouses communicate freely about anything, but they retain the freedom *not* to communicate about some things. They share many or most activities, but they give each other the freedom to pursue individual interests as well.

In some marriages, however, there is a re-creation of the childhood state of dependence. Candy, a professional musician and singing teacher, fell into this kind of marriage when she was twenty. She was very much in love, eager to get married. The marriage would not deter her career, because her husband-to-be was a drummer in a band and understood her musical aspirations. But after the wedding, Candy found herself with a husband who was virtually like a stranger to her, a man who confronted her with demands that she had not heard prior to the marriage.

I had to go by what he thought. He always had the upper hand. I was weak-willed. He made me feel below him. And for a long time, I felt like I deserved it. Then I finally came to the realization that I didn't need to be treated like a child. I deserved much more than that. When I divorced him, I decided that I was not going to be told what to do anymore, that I had some respect for myself, a lot more than I had before. I was an individual and I could make my own decisions.

Candy regained a sense of her self-worth and her ability to function as an independent individual. But Candy also recognizes her need for interdependence: ''Although I had a bad experience with marriage, I still believe in the sanctity of marriage. But a husband must be secure, well established, and allow me to develop my interests. I really want to remarry and have a satisfying companionship.'' For Candy, smothered by her husband, divorce was not merely important; it seems to have been necessary in order for her to develop.

If a marriage is to survive, the spouses must give each other autonomy, space in which to grow. An acquaintance told us about a Maine couple in a rural community who were noted for their constant fighting. The man finally resolved the problem by building a cabin on his land and moving into it. A visitor who came into his cabin noticed that it was immaculate and that there was a fresh pie on the table. The man explained that his wife came in and cleaned and brought him food from time to time. ''No man,'' he said, ''can live with that woman. But she makes an awfully good neighbor.''

One way or another, people will strive to gain their autonomy. For Heather, like Candy, the way to achieve her need was divorce. Heather divorced her husband nine years ago when she was thirty-two. She now runs an art gallery, and appears quite comfortable with herself and her life. She stresses the point that she could not have remained in her marriage and continued to grow as an individual.

I guess it all began with our move to California twelve years ago. We were transferred from the East by my husband's employer. At the time, I was twenty-nine. Our children were seven, six, and four months. I recall on our flight out that my husband told me he would be traveling a great deal in his new position and that I would need to become more independent and develop my own interests. Later he denied that he ever said that, but that really motivated me. I had never been urged in that direction in the past, either by my parents or my husband.

In the beginning, I couched my new adventures as being for the children. But really I began to reach for an independence that eventually led to breaking the bonds of marriage and loosening the bonds with my parents. Slowly there emerged a different me. I met a group of friends who were radically different from those of my past. We were all married and all had three children. Our husbands had created their work and recreational worlds while we were home having babies and raising kids. Now it was our time to expand our worlds. We joined a parenting group, which soon evolved into more than that.

In the group, the women began to explore their feelings about themselves, their marriages, and their futures. Heather felt that her marriage had, for some time, been "less than satisfying," but she never questioned the situation. She accepted the status quo and her own dependency on her husband. As a result of the group experience, however, Heather increasingly believed that her marriage was limiting her personal growth.

I resented my husband questioning where I was going or why I hadn't cooked dinner. As his travel time increased to two or three weeks a month, I grew increasingly resentful of the time he spent at home. I began taking undergraduate classes at the university and focusing my time and attention on schoolwork. I had always loved art, so I thought about an art major, though I didn't know what I would do with it. That didn't matter. This was *my* world. I was discovering life, and in the process I was discovering myself.

In essence, I became committed to school and friends and not to my marriage. My husband became a symbol of the past, of dependency, almost like a ball and chain that I needed to be rid of in order to continue moving. The pressure mounted. The distance grew between us. We could no longer talk without anger. Accusations flew. Trust evaporated. Then we separated.

The separation did not bring the relief that Heather had anticipated. In fact, the separation brought her face to face with new agonies.

It's easy with the safety net of marriage beneath you. But now my dependency needs taunted me. I was frightened at the responsibility. I was hurt by being immediately replaced when my husband moved in with a stewardess he had met. What a jolt that was! I sort of reveled in the fact that I wanted him out of my life. But it never occurred to me that he might also want me out of his. I had a hard time with that. I wanted him to suffer and grieve for me. So I got angry, angry at everything and everyone. Nothing was fair. I felt victimized and full of self-pity. I had gotten what I asked for, and instead of satisfaction I resented and regretted everything.

Heather's bitterness over her husband's behavior carried over into her relationships with her friends. One day one of her friends told her that she cared for her but couldn't stand her attitude anymore. The friend told Heather to call when she stopped pitying herself. In time, Heather did stop feeling sorry for herself. But it took some months. She had to come to terms with her sense of being betrayed by everyone, including her parents and some friends who would not support her. She had to recognize exactly what had happened, and she had to stop playing the victim role. Gradually, she achieved all this. Could she have grown without the separation and eventual divorce? She thinks not.

I had not become independent in my teen years. I was still tied to my parents. Then I switched from parental control to marital control. At the age of thirty, I began to gain autonomy. At thirty-two, I rebelled. At forty, I finally became a person. I mean I finally became me, Heather, an independent human being.

Now I feel whole and self-sufficient. It seems that I had to yank that safety net of marriage in order to realize I can survive without it. I have spent these years working hard and raising three children. I have attained my primary educational and career goals. I am successful.

For a long time, I put my needs for a relationship with a man in last place. But recently I began dating someone who changed all of that. In many ways, I am astounded at my growth, my success, and my increased awareness. I know myself. I like myself. And I accept myself as I never had before. I have paid a price for this—financial reverses, loss of parental support, and, for many years, the loss of a father for my children. But overall, even with the value of hindsight, I would make the same essential choices.

It is obvious, then, that one of the most important ways for a divorce to be a step in your growth is for you to establish or reaffirm your autonomy and independence. Reaffirming your autonomy is also a way of reaffirming your self-worth. For some people, however, *reaffirming* is the wrong word. A number of women told us that they had never had a chance to establish their independence. They went from dependence on parents to dependence on husband. Divorce forced them for the first time in their lives to test their capacity for self-sustained living.

The discovery of your capacity for independence is an exhilarating experience. As the pain of disruption yields to the excitement of self-discovery, the divorced individual tends to cast the divorce into a positive light. Tina works in personnel with a federal agency. Her husband divorced her six years ago. Tina was stunned. "Look at me," she says, laughing and blushing at the same time. "I'm a sexy woman. Everyone tells me that. I couldn't believe it when he said he no longer felt any sexual attraction for me." At first, the pain was so great that Tina could see no hope for herself; like most people, she was jarred by her spouse's sudden and unexpected decision to break up the relationship.

We were married for twelve years. There was nothing that led up to it as far as I could see. In fact, it was a great shock. I thought everything was fine. We were not fighting. My husband just told me one day that he had fallen out of love with me. He said there wasn't another woman. He just didn't want to be married any longer. He moved out immediately.

The next two months were awful. I was shocked and afraid. I had trouble sleeping. I just existed. I didn't see any future for myself. In fact, I felt like this was the end of my life. I went to a therapist, who helped me get through it. Slowly I realized that I was on my own and responsible for myself. Slowly I began to see that I was now independent. A really big change for me was when I started to make decisions on my own.

Tina went to work. She learned the satisfaction of being able to support herself. She feels that what she has gained from the experience is worth more than the pain of the divorce. She now views the divorce as having had a positive impact on her life. She knows she can make it on her own. She knows she does not have to have a man in her life. But she also knows that independence is not necessarily the end point of her growth.

I am now involved with a very special guy. And I hope that it will become permanent. But I know that if it doesn't work out I will survive. I'm satisfied and happy with my life and with myself as a person.

Not everyone needs a divorce to grow in the same sense that Tina, Candy, and Heather needed it. Still, once the divorce has occurred, you can determine that it will be a growth experience for you. Whether or not the divorce is a necessity (and we would underscore the fact that for some people it is), it can be an opportunity. It is not the kind of opportunity that most people welcome. But the alternative to defining it as an opportunity is to endure an extended period of pain and bitterness.

2. *Work through your feelings.* There are at least two mistakes that people can make with their feelings. They may try to suppress or ignore them, or they may get rooted in some emotion that then dominates their lives. We have seen, for instance, that some people may have their lives dominated by depression and self-pity for many years after a divorce. Obviously, this is a no-win, self-destructive situation. It is just as detrimental to try to ignore such feelings, however, to pretend that all is well when you are feeling depressed or angry or hurt. The task that confronts us is neither to ignore our feelings nor get chained to them. Rather, we must confront and work through them.

Working through feelings can be a painful process, and for some people it may require radical action. For example, Chris was divorced in his thirties, two months after he graduated from college and began his work as a pharmacist. Chris had worked full-time while trying to get his degree, so it had taken him far longer than usual. He was unaware that his marriage was crumbling under the weight of all the obligations and responsibilities that he had assumed.

When his wife left him Chris said,

> It shook me to the very foundation of my being. I should have been settling down and enjoying the results of my efforts. I finally had my degree. I had a good position and an excellent salary. I owned my own home and now had time to pursue personal interests.

But all of his achievements seemed to pall into nothing when his wife left. Chris had to face a radically different life than he had anticipated. And he had to somehow work through his own jumbled feelings.

> My initial response to the separation was that of panic as I sought frantically for some solution to my emotional dilemma. I considered seeking support from my parents by moving to the city where they lived, but I didn't want to become dependent on them again. I considered a number of other options, but turned them all down except one.

The one that Chris decided on sounded a bit crazy to his friends. But he decided to follow his intuition to move out to the high desert of California and rent a ranch. For some reason, he had decided that he would deal with his sense of helplessness and loneliness by deliberately exposing himself to more of the same feelings, by forcing himself to survive in an environment that would produce and intensify those feelings. It worked. In fact, he dealt with some other unresolved issues in his life as well as his emotional turmoil over the divorce.

> As a child, I had been bullied on a couple of occasions by

a couple of my classmates. I made up for those failures by getting into two magnificent fights. They were healing experiences. And the general fear that I had from not getting back on a horse that had thrown me as a child was erased by buying and breaking an Arab quarter horse. I overcame my fear of heights—to some extent at least—by going to work for a tree service company and forcing myself to climb the huge trees that grew locally.

Chris stayed in the desert for nine months, a period he now views as appropriately symbolic of his own rebirth. He had earned the respect of the rough-hewn people who lived in the area, and their respect was healing to him.

I had come to their world feeling like something that had slid from under a rock, and I left with a sense of having solidly overcome the worst of my neuroses. They served as my mentors. In their own elemental ways, they taught me by example how to become my own man. I seriously doubt that I could have received a comparable experience in the office of the best therapist anywhere.

Chris returned to the city where he had lived. He was a free man—free of the pain of divorce and free of the heavy baggage of fears and neuroses that had weighed him down for most of his life. He is still single, and is successful and optimistic. He runs his pharmacy and pursues a variety of side interests. He believes that ''a human being can endure and triumph in any testing in his life if he is able to marshal his resources, however scanty they may be, behind a committed determination.''

Chris's solution, of course, will not work for everyone. The point is that people must confront and work through their feelings. For some, radical action akin to Chris's may be necessary. They may be able to work through their feelings by doing things that they always wanted to do but didn't while married. One man we know bought a motorcycle—a vehicle his ex-wife detested—and took a number of trips. For others, support from friends and family may be sufficient. In any case, the feelings must not be denied and suppressed. Only confrontation leads to health and growth.

3. *Balance self-concern with other-concern.*   There is a danger in establishing your autonomy and in confronting your feelings. You may become so immersed in your autonomy that you are oblivious to relationships. You may become so absorbed in working through your own feelings that you lose sight of the value of concern for others. A certain amount of self-concern is necessary and healthy. An excess of self-concern becomes destructive of both your relationships and your personal well-being. A premedical student said that one of his relationships ended while he was romancing a young woman. She discovered that in the course of their passion he had been keeping his fingertips on her pulse, testing her emotional reactions. She decided that he was too scientific for her and broke off the relationship.

The point is to find a healthy balance between the unhealthy extremes of total absorption in the self and total neglect of the self. For those involved in divorce, the maintenance of other-concern may be facilitated or even required because of children. As Karen discovered, it is possible to care for yourself, working through your feelings, while still caring for someone else—in her case, a child who needed her. Karen is a nurse who was divorced sixteen years ago. The divorce occurred when it became clear to her that her dream of a loving family and meaningful career would not be realized.

I married what I thought was a wonderful fellow. We purchased a nice car. And we became the parents of a daughter. Then the problems came. I thought they were simply adjustments at first. But they were serious. My husband was a child. He made demands on me that were unreasonable. Even though I worked as many hours as he did, even after our daughter was born, I was expected to be an immaculate housekeeper, a gourmet cook, a flawless mother, his personal servant, and a sexual turn-on. As our daughter grew, he treated her like me—another servant to do his bidding. I could have forgiven him for what he did to me, but not the way he treated her. I could see that she was growing increasingly troubled because he used her more than he loved her.

In spite of the difficulties, Karen did not find it easy to go through with the divorce. She desperately tried to make the marriage work.

I tried to do everything that I thought would make him happy. I went to marriage counseling sessions. I moved out of the house and returned three times before the final separation. But I finally concluded that the only way out was a divorce.

Karen moved to another city after the divorce. She was still in emotional turmoil. And she was suffering from a condition that typically afflicts those who divorce: low self-esteem. She felt like a failure. She lost a good deal of her self-respect. She began to act out some of her feelings: "I went a bit wild. I went to bars and picked up men for one-night stands. But my daughter's needs quickly tamed me. I settled down and determined to secure a good life for my daughter and myself."

Balancing her concern about her own hurt with concern for the well-being of her daughter, Karen worked through her feelings and carved out a meaningful life for herself. "I will soon witness the high-school graduation of my very bright and beautiful daughter," she said proudly. "And I have reached a point in my career where I am successfully functioning as both a nurse and a consultant." Shortly after the divorce, Karen dabbled in activities that could have taken her on a much different path in her life. It was concern for her daughter that brought her back to a direction that was healthy for both women.

4. *Make use of the opportunity to change yourself.* The aftermath of divorce can be an opportunity for restructuring the self. In a real sense, Chris was reborn after his nine-month sojourn in the desert. He emerged a different person. And he liked the person who emerged much better than the person who began the journey.

Other divorced individuals told us similar stories. They grew because they used the time after the divorce as an opportunity for changing themselves in some positive way. One woman told us that she determined to take control of her life. She got a job and started attending school part-time. She now feels more competent, assertive, and self-confident. And a man who was stunned by his wife's request for a divorce says that he has learned to pay attention to how people feel and not just to what they say. He has remarried, but he no longer takes his spouse for granted. He works at his relationships now. He has transformed himself into a more sensitive individual.

So both men and women may change after a divorce. Ken and Amanda had been married for five years when they divorced. But neither was prepared for the way they both changed after the divorce. The final outcome surprised them even more.

Amanda, a genial young woman in her thirties, is a legal secretary in a large, urban firm that specializes in criminal law. She is attending law school while working in the firm, and already has the promise of a position in it when she finishes. For her, the divorce was a door to a new, assertive self. But she had to fight against everything she was to break up her marriage.

I was almost twenty-four when I married Ken. My parents had taught me to take the marriage vows literally; when I got married, it was till death us do part. My father was dismayed by the rising divorce rate and often predicted that it was the beginning of the end of American society. I accepted those values.

Ken seemed to be all of the things I wanted in a husband. He was good-looking and had a good sense of humor. And, like me, he believed that marriage was permanent. We married a year after my graduation from college.

Ken was an air traffic controller. He had to take regular turns on each shift. Amanda had majored in history, but also had developed secretarial skills in high school. Unable to use her history degree to find work, she enrolled in a two-year course at a college to train as a legal secretary. Ken's working hours increasingly put a strain on the marriage.

For a while after the honeymoon, I accepted it and felt I could adjust to it. But Ken started pressing me to drop out of school and take care of his needs. He hated coming home to an empty house after the night shift. Maybe that's why he started complaining about women working generally. He tried to make me feel like I was destined to be a home-maker and a mother. He ridiculed the idea of a career for me. He pointed out that he made enough money for us to live on; it wasn't necessary for me to work.

Finally, Amanda yielded. She dropped out of school for six months. Ken was happy. She was there when he needed her. But she was miserable.

We didn't want to have children yet, so I had nothing to do but keep house for Ken. I watched soap operas, but they only made me feel worse. They reminded me of all the things other women were doing. You never see a soap opera that exalts the housewife, you know.

In her frustration, Amanda had returned to the college. She didn't tell Ken until after she had paid the tuition.

I thought he might accept it when he knew it was too late to do anything about it. Maybe he would understand how much I needed to do something more than take care of the house. But he didn't. We had a terrible argument. Or I should say, I listened to a terrible harangue. He made me feel like I had betrayed him. Like I was a thief for spending the money without even telling him.

Amanda returned to classes, but without the vigor she had be-fore.

I was in a real double-bind situation. I felt badly every time I went to class, because I could hear Ken saying I had betrayed him. And I knew that if I didn't go to class, I would feel even more useless and miserable.

As she drove to school one day, the thought occurred to her that there was a logical conclusion to her dilemma: the only way to escape the misery was to leave Ken. That, of course, directly contradicted her values and beliefs. She dismissed the idea and told herself that if she only concentrated on loving him more, they could work the problem out. She tried being especially solicitous, but it didn't work. She was nearing the end of her training period. Ken complained that if she was gone so much taking classes, it would be even worse when she started working. Amanda began to feel the desperation that leads people to take drastic measures. Fighting her own values, she left Ken on the day she began her first job.

In a sense, Amanda was assertive. She did go back to the college program. She left Ken and, seven months later, filed for divorce. But in other ways, she was not assertive. She listened meekly when he was angry. She never really tried to convince him that her needs were legitimate.

Ken found the separation and divorce painful. It was hard for him to believe that Amanda would actually go through with it. He moped around the house for months afterward. Then one morning he took a close look at himself in the mirror.

My hair was disheveled. My eyes were droopy. I was getting a potbelly. I looked like shit! I put my razor down, put on my running shorts, and went out for a jog. I felt better afterward than I had for years. I ran every day after that. And as I began to feel and look better, I started to think about Amanda and the divorce in a more rational way.

I wanted to understand why a career was so important to her. I read some books about women. Some were silly. But a couple really helped me to understand. I realized that I had made a big mistake with Amanda. I vowed I would not do that with a woman again.

Meanwhile, Amanda took an assertiveness training course with another secretary. They had decided they needed it to deal with the lawyers for whom they worked. "It was a revelation to me," Amanda recalled.

I discovered that being assertive is not the same as being aggressive or obnoxious. I could be assertive and still be a woman. I wished I had known that when I was married to Ken. Things might have turned out differently.

About a year after the divorce, Amanda put the house up for sale in order to finalize the settlement. She called Ken one evening to tell him she had an offer. He was quiet for a few moments, then asked her if she would wait on the sale until they had a meeting and talked about it. She agreed. They met two days later for dinner. He told her he was sorry about the way he had treated her. He now understood why she needed her career.

I told him I was happy he understood at last. Perhaps he wouldn't make another woman as miserable as he had made me. I surprised him by my assertive reply. But he surprised me by his different attitude. Anyway, the upshot is that we kept talking and talking until the restaurant closed. We met again the next night, and three weeks later we were remarried.

Ken and Amanda have a good marriage now. The divorce was necessary for them to create that kind of marriage, for it spurred each of them to make necessary changes. Those who use the aftermath of a divorce constructively—to understand what went wrong in their marriage and what kind of changes are necessary to avoid problems in future relationships—will grow through divorce. As Amanda put it:

While the watershed itself was very negative, the impact it has had on my life is positive. It's like going to the dentist. You hate those hours in the chair, but you sure love the smile you come out with.

8

Relationships That End
Death

When Ken Bianchi was a boy, he had a troubled relationship with his mother. He would not express his negative emotions to her. Instead, he tried to deny them and to find solace in a closeness with his father as he entered his teenage years. One day Ken and his father took off on a fishing trip. Later, Ken recalled the trip as a marvelous experience in which he was finally getting in touch with both his father and himself. But a few days after they returned home, Ken's father was found dead at work. Ken screamed with anguish. For days afterward, he went alone into his attic and cried and talked with his dead father.

Some two decades later, Ken Bianchi was arrested on suspicion of murder. After extensive investigation, the police concluded that he not only murdered the two women for whom he was arrested, but more than a dozen others. The police identified Ken Bianchi as the infamous Hillside Strangler of Los Angeles.

On the opposite side of the country, another mass murderer, David Berkowitz, the "Son of Sam," also suffered the death of a parent, his mother, in his teen years. David too retreated into himself, spending hours alone in his room or walking aimlessly around his neighborhood.

Of course, the death of a parent was not the only factor in the development of Ken Bianchi and David Berkowitz. But it is possible that their lives would have taken a different course if the parents had lived. Death is the most painful of all disruptions of intimate relationships. For some people, the death of a loved one is a permanent scar on life. But for others, the experience, at least in the long run, can be growth-enhancing.

THE ULTIMATE DISRUPTION

In separation and even in divorce, there is frequently a lingering hope that somehow the relationship can be repaired and intimacy restored. Death shatters all such hopes. There is a finality to death that is qualitatively different from every other threat to our intimate relationships. The death of a loved one, therefore, is the kind of event that we are least prepared for in most cases, and it is the hardest kind of disruption to deal with and overcome.

Typically, there is a grief process that involves a number of phases. Initially, there may be a kind of numbness, almost an inability to realize and feel what has happened. There is a struggle between reality and fantasy, between the compulsion to deny the death and the relentless fact of loss. As a person begins to accept the reality, there is an opening of the floodgates of emotion. Now there is a preoccupation with the one who has died, a craving to experience the relationship once again. Most people also have to deal with depression, anger, guilt, and the inability to function well during this period. Gradually, if the grief process is a typical one, there will be an acceptance of the loss and a rebuilding of one's life through new relationships and new patterns of existence. The disruption is healed, not by no longer caring for the person who has died, but by filling the void with new relationships.

A young dentist, Melinda, illustrated the nature of the healing process as she told of her watershed.

Seven years ago, my two-month-old daughter died in her sleep. Sudden infant death. I was twenty-six years old and loving motherhood. That night I had gone to bed exhausted, like most mothers, dreading the prospect of having to wake up and nurse her in the middle of the night. But she never woke me, and the next morning I woke up with swollen, painful breasts. I knew instantly that something was wrong. My life changed at that moment. I had no idea how fragile life is. How easy it is to die.

Melinda dealt with her grief in part by returning to her practice and keeping busy. In part, her healing involved getting pregnant again two years later. She hasn't stopped thinking about her daughter: "Sometimes her death is vague, like a bad dream. But the impact is within me all of the time." But she has filled the void with her second child, who is now a healthy, four-year-old boy. "I'm not angry anymore. I'm delighted with my son. And I appreciate the gift of life more than ever before."

Obviously, grieving is a painful process. An individual may experience a variety of symptoms, including weakness, tightness in the throat, emptiness in the stomach, problems with sleeping and eating, and weight gain or loss. Some people drink and smoke more heavily than usual.

Interestingly, the better the relationship during life, the more likely the individual is to make a healthy adjustment to the loss. For example, those with happy marriages tend to adjust better to the death of a spouse than those with unhappy unions. Those with mixed feelings about someone may have a harder time adjusting to death than those who have positive attitudes and feelings.

One man in his thirties talked about his father with some ambivalence. His father had died thirteen years previously. The father was strict, an authoritarian who ruled the family and who expected his children to achieve. When the father unexpectedly died from a heart attack, the young man reacted with intense anger: "I was furious. I was totally enraged. How could my father die before I proved myself to him? I hadn't even finished college yet." The man was still so emotionally torn by his father's death that he appeared exhausted after discussing this watershed experience. His ambivalence about his dictatorial father before death carried over into an unresolved grief process that had lasted thirteen years.

Whatever the quality of the relationship with the deceased, we are likely to have to deal with a certain amount of anger and guilt. It is helpful to keep in mind that it is normal to feel guilty and that it is virtually impossible to escape the feeling. There is a story about two New Yorkers who had to come to terms with guilt after their aged mothers died. The one man felt guilty because he had planned on moving his mother to Florida, where life would be easier for her. Before he got around to it, she died. "If only I had taken her to Florida," he moaned, "she might still be alive." The other man felt guilty because he had recently moved his mother to Florida. "If only I hadn't put her under the stress of a move," he complained, "she might still be alive."

Once people work through the inevitable grief, anger, and guilt, they can use the experience to restructure their lives. And therein lies the ray of light in death: in the long run, even the ultimate disruption in human relationships can be used to give us the breath of new life.

FROM DEATH TO LIFE

Among those who named someone's death as a watershed, slightly over half identified the death of a parent. Whether the loss is a parent or someone else, however, there are three common outcomes that turn the loss into a positive watershed experience. First, the survivor may determine to achieve the positive values represented and expressed by the deceased. Another way to turn loss into a positive watershed is for the survivor to decide to avoid the negative values and behavior that led to the death. And the third possibility is for the survivor to take on a renewed appreciation for life, an appreciation rooted in an awareness of both the finiteness and the beauty of life.

Alex, for example, is a corporate lawyer and a senior partner in his firm. He is also a patron of the arts. That isn't an unusual combination, of course. But it is for Alex. He grew up in a closeknit family where the males were taught to be tough and competitive. Alex's father was a businessman. Alex doesn't recall ever seeing his father read a book. The only pieces of art in the house were the inexpensive reproductions his mother had purchased at a department store. There was music, but nothing that would be played by a symphony orchestra. By the time he was an adult, Alex's interests were mainly law, politics, sports, and women.

He married while in law school. He had met Fay, his wife, at a fraternity party. She was a fine-arts major. For ten years after graduation, Alex's career spiraled. Fay worked at developing a name for herself as a painter. She also introduced Alex to a new world.

> We went to symphony concerts, to the ballet, to the theater, and to museums on weekends. At first, I learned to turn it all off and think about my law practice or fantasize about a racketball game during a performance. Fay kept telling me how much richer life is with all those cultural things. I didn't believe her. Or at least I told myself I didn't. Actually, I think I began to enjoy them from the first. But I wouldn't say that to anyone at the time, not even to Fay.
>   And I really never fully admitted it to myself until after her death. Fay was only thirty-five. She was killed when a driver lost control and hit her as she stood on the curb. And suddenly the most beautiful thing that ever happened to me was taken away.

Alex still does not like to talk about Fay's death. He touched on it briefly, then went on.

> I am very involved today in the activities that Fay loved. Currently I serve on the symphony board of directors and also financially support a local repertory theater. I really love the arts now. I can admit that to myself. I guess you could say that I'm expressing my gratitude to Fay for introducing me to her world of beauty.

By achieving the positive values of Fay, Alex was able to turn his loss into a positive watershed. Good consequences of death also can occur even when a relationship was problematic. Nicole, who hosts a radio talk show in a midwestern city, experienced the death of her father when she was eleven. She told us that she had a response that was the opposite of what she would have expected.

> My father was a weak man. He just couldn't seem to cope with the world the way it was. I thought I despised him

because he let other people take advantage of him and because he couldn't seem to handle problems. But when he died, I was very hurt and upset, and wanted him back.

Later, I realized that some people can handle rough times better than others. And some people, like my father, can't figure out a constructive way of solving either complex or simple problems. As a result, I've learned to think of my father every time I have a problem. I force myself to carry on. I'm not a quitter.

Nicole learned an invaluable lesson through her father's inability to cope with the world. She learned not to cave in to problems, to seek healthy solutions to any difficulty she faced. She determined to avoid the negative values and behavior that had characterized her father's life.

The beneficial long-term consequences may involve two or all three of the outcomes mentioned above. For Leah, a speech pathologist in her early fifties, all three outcomes were involved in her watershed. It was not a death, however, but several deaths that transformed her. She talks about her watershed with the authority of a woman who knows who she is and where she is going.

World War Two had a profound effect on me. I was only a child at the time, but my personal life was changed forever by events far away. Although we lived in Ohio, both of my parents were European-born and still had family in Europe. My father's family lived in Germany. We had little contact with them. My mother's family was in Hungary, and we corresponded with them on a regular basis.

By the time I was five years old, I knew all about my cousins, who were my same age, and I looked forward to letters and pictures from their families. I remember an uncle who was in the Hungarian merchant marines coming to visit us in 1941. My mother begged him to stay, but he said he had to go back and try to get his family out. That was the last contact we ever had with anyone in Europe.

Leah and her parents tried to keep in touch with the family. They bought a shortwave radio and listened to news broadcasts from Germany. Leah remembers hearing Hitler in the middle of the night and shuddering at what her father told her Hitler had said. She learned of the camps where Jewish people were herded. Her parents expressed both fury and frustration that the world seemed to ignore them. When the war was over, they hoped to be able to resume connections with their relatives. But that was not to be.

My grandmother lived with us. I was especially close to her. We shared a bedroom and I could see how she changed through those terrible years. After all, she was the only one who really knew those people, who had had face-to-face contact with them.

After the war, we contacted the various agencies and tried to locate any of our relatives who might still be living. But after months of effort, it was clear that no one—*no one*—had survived.

The effect was devastating. It was much worse than *a* death in the family. The family had died. Suddenly all the stories we had heard and the articles in the newspapers and the films we had seen about the terrible things that had happened to those people took on new meaning.

The thoughts of what had happened clung to Leah like an evil parasite. Still a child, she had taken on an adult's sense of responsibility and concern.

I was obligated not only to myself and my family, but to those cousins my age who would never grow up and experience life. I knew that nothing in this world could make me give up being Jewish. They had died for that. It didn't matter if it was willingly or not. It had happened.

More than that, I felt a responsibility to live for them. I wanted to live for them and for myself. They had become a part of me. Although I had never thought about it before, I wanted to have a large family to replace the children that my cousins would never have.

Finally, I knew that I could never turn my back on anyone, any group or individual, who was being oppressed or persecuted. I had to do whatever I could, no matter how little, because I could not stand myself if I did nothing. I don't believe that these were altogether conscious decisions. I didn't sit down and list them to myself. Up to now, I haven't shared them with anyone.

Even though she didn't consciously make up her list, Leah has followed through with the decisions that flowed from her loss. She is determined to implement the values of those who died. She is resolved to avoid the values and behavior of those who killed her relatives. The experience of loss is no longer a source of profound grief, but it is as real and significant to her as it was more than forty years ago.

Even today the death camps are with me as if I was there myself. But from that moment to this, I have fought for my identity as a Jew and that of my children in the public schools of this country. I married a Jewish man and had five children. I tried to teach them to be caring and just people.

For many years I have been an active volunteer for Amnesty International, working for prisoners of conscience and the abolition of torture worldwide. Of all the things I do, I consider this to be one of the most important. As my mother used to say, it is like trying to empty the ocean with a teaspoon, but if you work at it long enough you will succeed.

FROM COPING TO TRIUMPHING

Most people eventually cope with the death of a loved one. Some seem to adjust rather quickly. There is a gravestone in an English churchyard with the following inscription:

Sacred to the Memory of Jared Bates
Who died August the 6th, 1800
His widow, aged 24, lives at 7, Elm Street
Has every qualification for a good wife
And yearns to be comforted

Apparently Jared's widow had recovered from her grief quickly enough to advertise for another husband on the gravestone.

The question here, however, is not merely how to cope but how to triumph. How do you turn the experience of loss into a positive watershed experience? How do you go from a wrenching disruption in your life to a meaningful growth experience? It is not possible, of course, to avoid the emotional pain of loss. But the longterm consequences may be very different, depending upon how you react. Those for whom loss through death became a positive watershed experienced many different kinds of loss—loss of parents, spouse, relatives, friends, and even children. Their experiences suggest a number of ways to produce ultimately beneficial consequences.

1. Work out unresolved issues with the dying person.   Some of us, of course, will never get the opportunity to do this. The death may be sudden. It may occur far away from us. The dying person may be in too much pain or may not be lucid. Unfortunately, some people do have the opportunity but do not use it. They may not want to acknowledge the fact of impending death.

Researchers who have studied the interaction between dying patients and their relatives note that there are four different kinds of "awareness contexts." An "open context" is one in which everyone knows of the coming death and each knows that the others know. A "closed context" is one in which the patient, the relatives, or both do not know about the impending death. A "suspicion awareness context" exists when the patient, the relatives, or both suspect that death is near even though the physician has reassured them that there is hope. Finally, there is the "pretense awareness context," where all the people know but all pretend not to know that death is near.

Some people get the mistaken notion that the pretense awareness context is best for the dying person. But that deprives everyone of an opportunity to express some thoughts and feelings that may be lost forever. And when there are unresolved issues, it deprives everyone of a final chance to work them through.

Hannah, a free-lance photographer with an itch for travel, was able to establish an open awareness context with her father on his deathbed. His death thereby became a watershed experience for her and allowed her to work out some problems in their past relationship. Hannah left home at an early age to pursue her desire for an adventurous career. Although she had had good relationships with her parents in her early years, her father was very hurt by her decision to leave. They had a bitter argument, and she left in anger. The issue was never resolved. After some years, Hannah married and settled in a city on the East Coast.

> There was always a strain with my father when I returned home for a visit. But we never discussed the matter. I still resented the fact that he tried to hold me back, that he didn't send me off with hope and pride. And I guess he still resented the fact that I refused to listen to him, and that I felt the need to leave home.

Hannah's trips home grew more infrequent over the years. Then one day she got word that her father was dying. She returned home immediately. How would she relate to this man for whom a childhood love had given way to years of resentment? She couldn't just go back and act the loving, concerned daughter, pretending that the years of bitterness never existed.

Hannah decided that she would have to be open with her father about her feelings. He made it easy for her, because he was a different man. As he got older, her father had become more accepting and forgiving. He was not the angry, wronged parent now, but the loving father she had remembered as a child. It would have been easy to have forsaken her decision to talk openly with her father, to pretend that all was well, and to offer him some fragile hope for life.

But Hannah pursued her initial intention. And she found her father receptive to talking about it. In his last days, they cleaned up the painful parts of their relationship. Because they worked through some of those issues, Hannah reports now: "I have a new sense of freedom since his death. I no longer feel angry and guilty like I did before. I feel that I am a whole and independent person."

2. *Stay engaged with life.* Wounded by loss, it is tempting for us to retreat from life, to retire within ourselves, to disengage

from relationships and activities. In part, this is because grief requires great expenditures of energy and often there is little left for other relationships. But this tendency also stems from the fact that disruption hurts so much. If we don't have the attachments in the first place, then we cannot be hurt by death.

Marcus, a product manager for a manufacturer of hydraulic equipment, illustrates this tendency to retreat. He was only a small boy when his watershed occurred: his mother committed suicide. He is articulate but virtually without emotion as he relates his story. There is no sharing of whatever feelings he has. It is as though there is a barrier that disallows us entrance into his real world.

Neither Marcus, nor his father, nor his brothers suspected that anything like a suicide could happen. They were all stunned by her act. Marcus realizes that from that time on, he began to distrust people. He was reluctant to get involved with friends. He became suspicious of others and their motives, feeling that few people were genuine and reliable. Now, some twenty years later, he still maintains a certain separateness. He is successful in his career, but he recognizes and acknowledges that his interpersonal relationships—including even those with his own family—are shallow. Deeply wounded by his mother's suicide, Marcus chose to disengage himself from people to prevent a recurrence of that hurt. His watershed left a scar on his life.

In contrast, Ann, a retiree in her sixties, suffered one of the most painful of all losses when she was thirty-seven. But she kept her engagement with life, and she now talks about the positive impact of her watershed.

We moved west when I was twenty-four. It took a great deal of courage on my part. It changed my life-style. I became more Americanized, and lost the Italian and New England family traditions of my early years.

Over the next few years, I gave birth to four sons. That may sound like a busy, full life. But I was feeling a little bored with my life. I was home most of the time and had virtually no distractions. Only my four lively children. Then one day my second son wasn't so lively anymore. After a time we took him to the doctor. He was diagnosed as having leukemia. At that time, there was nothing we could do but watch him die.

After his death, I used to long for that "boring" life I had before. I kept wishing I could go back, and I thought how happy I really was then and didn't even know it.

Ann was tempted, as we all are when faced by such a loss, to retreat. But she could not. She had the responsibility of her husband and three other sons. She kept engaged with life, including relationships. "I learned to appreciate whatever I had at the moment," she says. "And I wouldn't put anything off to the future. I learned to be content with my life as it is."

3. *Increase your "what" understanding.* We are cognitive creatures. We want to understand our world and the things that happen in it. But there are different kinds of understanding. We can distinguish between "why" understanding and "what" understanding. To understand *why* something happens is always difficult and sometimes impossible. For example, it never will appear fair or reasonable or just that a child should die. The "why" understanding will always elude you. But even in that situation, you can gain a "what" understanding—an understanding of what happens to the dying person, what happens to the survivors, and what the survivors can do to deal effectively with the situation. The latter kind of understanding can be achieved because loss through death is one of the common experiences of humans. And we gain the "what" understanding by tapping into those common experiences.

There are various ways to gain this kind of understanding: talking to people who have had a similar experience, reading books that explain the process of loss, or working through the death with a counselor. Nathan, the publisher for a house that specializes in cookbooks, endured a great deal of distress before gaining this understanding. Once he had it, he was able to use it to help others. At the time of his watershed, Nathan was thirty-two. He cupped his cheek in his hand as if to support himself while he discussed the event.

It began to unfold fifteen years ago when my best friend, Vince, was working on his gas water heater. It blew up, and Vince was badly injured and burned. Vince and I grew up together. We went to the same school, and now we worked for the same company. We were the proverbial two peas in a pod. Or two balls in a jockstrap, as we liked to say.

I was at the hospital with his wife when they brought him in. I'll never forget the doctor's words to us. He thought Vince's chances for recovery were poor, but that there was always a chance. We clung to the "always a chance." We wouldn't let ourselves believe anything except that sooner or later Vince would recover and return home.

At the time, I was married and my wife had recently given birth to our daughter. Vince and his wife already had two kids. Instead of the expected recovery, we watched over the next couple of weeks as life slowly ebbed away from a great and loving friend.

It was a devastating experience, with the doctors doing everything they could and Vince's wife trying her best to cope with the situation. We couldn't accept what was happening before our eyes. We wouldn't let ourselves admit that a death was taking place. I was obsessed with helping his family cope and keeping their hopes up. I kept looking for the answer that would make this nightmare go away. But it never came.

Finally, I not only realized that we were helpless but that the doctors were in the same position. I went to the hospital daily. I started to resent Vince's wife because I felt she was abandoning him. Actually, she was torn between her responsibility to him and to her kids. Each day the doctors would say that the end was near. I didn't like the way some of the nurses were treating him. I was mad at the entire world.

Nathan's hand dropped to his lap and he smiled briefly as he remembered his outrage. "The world wasn't moved by my anger," he noted. "I guess it helped me. But it didn't help Vince."

Nathan went through a prolonged period of depression following Vince's death. He had periodic bouts of crying. He dealt with his feelings first of all by increasing his work load. Intuitively, he sensed the need to stay engaged with life. He did not cut himself off from people or activities. He talked with a physician, who helped him understand the nature of Vince's injuries and the fact that everything possible had been done for his friend. He read a number of books about death, and increased his "what" understanding. He learned the stages that a person goes through when dying. He learned about the grief process. And he then realized that he, Vince, and the two families had been through one of the common experiences of humankind. He saw in the experiences of others his own journey of pain. And he recognized that he could emerge from that as others had, a stronger and healthier individual.

Vince's death was a watershed for Nathan because through it he achieved a new level of maturity. Some years later, an older friend of Nathan's died suddenly from a heart attack. Because of his experience with Vince and the understanding he had gained, Nathan was able to help the family deal with their grief. He says his own family has benefited as well.

> The experience with Vince has given my family a stronger emotional bond. I felt a little guilty about it, but the summer after Vince died, we had the best family vacation we had ever had. I think we all had decided to appreciate and enjoy each other as much as we can whenever we can.

4. Reach out to others.   The second guideline emphasized the importance of maintaining activities and relationships. This one stresses the notion of taking advantage of the support offered by people. You can "put on a happy face" or "keep a stiff upper lip" and refuse to share your grief with others even while continuing to interact with them. Or you can tap into the resources represented by other people who care about you.

Frequently, it will be a family member who cares and who helps. But it may also be someone other than a relative. You can usually distinguish the person who says "Let me know if I can do anything to help" as a form of politeness rather than real concern, from the person who says it—verbally or nonverbally—because of a genuine desire to be available. Chelsea is president of a New York marketing and trend-analysis firm. She had a struggle with death when she was a teenager. She was able to survive, in both a physical and emotional sense, because she realized that a teacher cared enough about her to give her some desperately needed guidance.

I was fifteen. I was very depressed and suicidal. I don't even know why. I only know that I had been unhappy for a long time. I don't know if I would have actually committed suicide, but I know that I really considered it. I just didn't have any incentive to live. My feelings were intensified by the tragic death of my sister, who died in a swimming accident. That was a breaking point for me. I know my parents cared about me, but they were so caught up in their own grief that they couldn't help me.

I was really at the end of my rope when I went to a teacher I had had the year before. I felt that she really cared about all of her students. She gave me an anchor to sanity. She became my friend. I talked with her about my feelings and my situation. She met with me every time I needed her. Eventually I began to feel better about my sister's death, about myself, and about life. She saved my life. I think I would have exploded—emotionally—if I couldn't have found someone to help me.

There are sensitive, caring, supportive people everywhere who are willing to listen and to help. The point is to call upon them. Do not fear that you are presuming upon their time and energies. Drawing upon their strength, you can grow to the point where you, in turn, will have the resources to help others. Thus, you do not deplete the sum total of caring and support available in the world; you increase and distribute it more widely.

5. *Review what is important, and what you want to be, and reorganize your life accordingly.*   In the early 1960s, Attorney General Robert Kennedy was vacationing in Colorado. He and two of his children were in a store when a man overheard the girl tell her younger brother, whom she thought was not behaving properly, to remember his "age, manners, and Boston accent." The boy, however, continued to misbehave. She looked

sharply at her brother and said: ''Do be quiet. You are losing votes like this.''

At an early age, Kennedy's children were learning one of the things that was important in that family. Their family's life was organized around the crucial matter of political achievement. Some people never have their lives so organized. They have never taken the time to think about what is really important to them, about what is sufficiently meaningful to serve as the central organizing principle of their lives. But we need to be centered in order to grow. We need to have our lives revolve around something significant, something that gives meaning to our existence.

For many people, the loss of someone through death is a means of learning, or relearning, what is really important. Again and again, people who had gone through a traumatic loss indicated to us that they learned to gain a new perspective on life, to put a new emphasis on people rather than material things, to appreciate life each day, and to refuse to be frustrated by trivia. It is that kind of rethinking and restructuring of life that turns a loss into a positive watershed.

Unfortunately, many people live by inertia. They keep going in the direction in which they started independently of whether that direction is the most fulfilling. Loss through death will jar some of them out of that inertia. They will change directions. And the loss, in that sense, will become a positive watershed experience. This is what happened to Robert, who spent twenty years in a business that he despised. Robert no longer looks like a businessman. His curly hair is long, and he dresses casually. He still talks with the aggressiveness of a successful businessman. But he punctuates his account of his watershed with moments of deep emotion.

My job was managerial, supervising fifteen people in a computer-oriented paper flow. I was well paid, respected, and sought after for other positions. I had the ultimate American dream, the beautiful house in the country, pool, cars, trips, the whole pie. But . . . I was miserable.

I hated what I was doing. I got no satisfaction from doing it. And I also felt guilty because I thought I should have been thankful for being so lucky and having so much. But so many mornings I would get out of the car, look at the building, and just stand there. All I wanted was to somehow just get through to five o-clock.

Robert was forty-one years old when he was jarred from his inertia in this life of unhappy ease.

I got a call one day that my kid brother was in the hospital. Some kind of heart problem. We had no idea he had a bad heart. He was only thirty-eight. He didn't smoke, and didn't drink very much. I always thought he was something of a health nut. And there he was. And the doctor told us he was sorry, but we had to face the fact that my brother was dying.

Denial was my main resource at the time. I had a firm belief that this could not really be happening to us. This guy was my best friend. He was my baby brother, who could make me laugh like no one else could. I couldn't handle all the emotions.

I spent as much time as I could with him in those few days he was in the hospital. But he died alone. Early in the morning. I spent most of the days that followed his death moving but with no real purpose. I was numb. I can still recall most images, but I can't conjure up any of the feelings. Numbness must be a human defense to survive and to handle a situation like that.

But then it hit me. I broke down and cried off and on for three days. I wasn't only grieving, though. I was mad at him for dying and mad at myself for being angry with him. And when I wasn't crying or mad, I was depressed. I kept thinking about the way he looked just before he went into the hospital. He was such a happy guy. So full of life.

I guess you can only grieve like that for so long. I finally started feeling like I was getting my feelings under control. My life, my family, and my work had been overshadowed by his situation. Now I had to face myself and my situation again. And I didn't like what I faced.

The situation at work got worse. I went back and looked

and listened in a way that I had never done before. I saw my work and my life in a different light. I knew now that I had to be honest with myself. I couldn't pretend anymore that everything was good or even tolerable.

My life had become a farce. I had become a business machine. All those youthful dreams and ideals were lost somewhere in my past. I kept thinking, Is that all there is? The lies were over and now it was time to put up or shut up. I knew how dramatic this crossroad was, but I also knew that a choice was at hand and that I had better do something about it.

Robert spent time talking with his wife about where they were in their life together and where they wanted to go. With the approval and encouragement of his wife, he quit his job. They had four daughters to support. His wife went to work and Robert returned to an early love: art. He works as a free-lance artist and maintains a small studio where he sells his work. He doesn't make much money yet, but he is optimistic about the future.

Truthfully, it is very exciting. But very scary, too. Change has no guarantees. But it does start things to happen once an individual takes the first step. I wish I could convey to you the intense love between two brothers, one who died and one who lived more fully because of that death. His guts gave me guts. As he faced his death, he taught me to face my life. I hope that in sharing this the pain is not the only aspect you see. There was unbelievable growth too. . . . I just wish that he could be here to see all that has happened. I wish that he could share in my joy.

Like others we have met, Robert struggled with his loss and emerged with a new life. It wasn't that he merely coped with the loss and regained his ability to enjoy life. Rather, through self-examination and reorganization he mastered the loss. He determined to seize the future and shape it to achieve the abundance of life that his brother had. The loss became a gain.

9

Transitions
Moving into
New Social Worlds

We all have the Alice problem. Recall that when Alice went "through the looking-glass," she encountered the Red Queen, who suddenly started running rapidly hand-in-hand with Alice. When at last they stopped, Alice discovered that they were still in the same place. The Queen informed her that in this country "it takes all the running you can do, to keep in the same place."

We live in an age of rapid change, where it seems that we must run as fast as we can just to keep up. Electronics textbooks are outdated almost as soon as they are printed. The appliances we buy will be superseded by better models before we have paid for them. And new fashions appear in everything from clothing to music before we have become fully accustomed to the old fashions.

As if all that were not enough, most of us experience some kind of transition into a new social world at some point in our lives. The sudden shift into a different social world is the most radical and rapid kind of change. This can happen through an actual physical move, such as traveling or relocating to a home in a new community or being inducted into military service. It can happen by becoming part of a new group—the kind of thing that happens in religious conversion—or by getting involved in politics, social movements, or a transforming cultural event of one kind or another.

161

We face so many changes that at times, like Alice, we may feel breathless. We may feel like one of James Fenimore Cooper's fictional characters, who said that the entire nation was in "a constant state of mutation." And we may wonder whether it is healthy to live under such rapidly changing circumstances. Was Alvin Toffler right when he argued that we are suffering from "future shock"?

Actually, humans have a remarkable capacity to change. Like other experiences we have discussed, social transitions yield different consequences for different people. They may be traumatic, life-enhancing, or even boring or inconsequential. It depends in part on how people define them.

Some people will view a particular experience as painful but useful in the long run, while others will view the same experience as only painful. Some will view a particular experience as a moment of joy, while others will view the same experience with a yawn. For example, one of our acquaintances visited the Grand Canyon. On his return, he summed up the experience with a shrug of the shoulders and eight words: "It's just a big hole in the ground." Others have stood at the rim of the Grand Canyon and felt a sense of awe and wonder. For some people, then, a transition into a new social world is nothing out of the ordinary. For others, the transition can be a watershed.

TRAVEL

One of the paradoxes of life, wrote the philosopher Alfred North Whitehead, is that the world "craves for novelty and yet is haunted by terror at the loss of the past, with its familiarities and its loved ones." A favorite way of dealing with the dilemma, of satisfying our craving for novelty while holding on to the familiarities of our past, is to travel. For travel is a venture into novelty that ultimately returns us to the comforts of the familiar. That is why John Steinbeck found people looking at him with envy and longing when he set out on his travels across America with his dog Charley. Nearly everyone he met expressed a desire to do the same thing, to spend time wandering from state to state. None wanted to do it permanently. They all liked the places where they lived. They wanted both the new and the familiar, and they saw travel as the answer.

Travel has the inherent potential, therefore, for a watershed experience. But not everyone has a watershed experience during travel. Some people return grimly, like the woman who went camping for a week, only to endure rain every day of the trip. Others come back with a few interesting tales, like the woman who visited the Leaning Tower of Pisa some years ago. She noted a man handing a slip of paper to the tourists who parked their cars nearby. He asked, and received, a sum of money from each driver. The tourists thought they were paying for parking. But the woman, who spoke Italian, looked at one of the pieces of paper and saw that the man was insuring the parked cars against damage in case the tower fell over.

What happens to those who return not merely with interesting stories but with a changed life? Among those for whom a travel experience is a positive watershed, there is a sense of personal growth, of a new independence, and of a heightened awareness and openness.

Personal growth, for instance, was the payoff for Jason, a graying optometrist, who looks like a textbook example of conventionality. But Jason hasn't always behaved in conventional style. When he was eighteen, he took off for the mountains, isolation, and discovery. Jason thinks that his watershed experience had its roots in discontent that began to gnaw at him when he was only nine.

I was in the fourth grade of a Catholic school. I was for the first time beginning to closely examine and question the teachings which I had previously accepted wholesale. There is one phrase that echoed in my mind repeatedly. The phrase was ''everlasting life after death.'' I was really caught up with all the teachings about life and death and eternity. I was only nine, but I wanted to know more. In response to my queries, however, they just told me to have what they called faith. The echoes continued. Faith was not going to be enough.

I didn't stop thinking about the issues. You can't hardly go to Catholic school and ignore them. By the time I was eighteen the conflict between needing to know and being incapable of comprehending these concepts built to an unbearable level. I had to seek some sort of resolution. Or at least some balance.

I was drawn to the Rockies of Colorado. Why the Rockies, I have no idea. I don't even recall choosing. It was simply where I had to go. I packed my bags and took leave from my summer job. Once in the mountains I drove straight to a state park and parked my van in a deserted area of the campground.

For the next two weeks, with the exception of supply runs back to town, I spent my days hiking and thinking and my nights trying to keep my campfire burning so I didn't freeze to death. During those two weeks I watched various animals as they lived their day-to-day lives and occasionally died. I watched shooting stars and sunsets and birds that court and mate in midair. And I thought of my death, what will occur after, and what it means to me both now and in the future.

There was no one event, but rather a gradual awakening. So that by the end of the second week I knew that I had my answers, and that it was time to return to the world that I had fled. The main impact that these two weeks of introspection had on my life was to remove a conflict which had impeded my ongoing development as a person. Those two weeks yielded a much calmer person. Gone was the wired sense of urgency. I was at peace with myself.

For Jason, the days of isolation in nature meant a new perspective on life and death. He began to see himself as part of a monumental drama of life process, a drama in which he could comfortably participate without having answers to questions raised by his parochial education. He made his peace with the process of life, and that opened the way to further growth.

Allison, a Los Angeles banker in her late twenties, had a very different experience as a result of travel. But she, too, found it to be a watershed. Her experience occurred some six years ago when she was graduated from college. She decided to celebrate in style, since she was the first member of her family to even go to college. She chose to join a friend in Colombia, South America.

> I was ready for the adventure, even though I didn't speak a word of Spanish. When I arrived at the Bogotá airport, I saw my friend in the distance and started to walk toward him. A policeman stopped me and spoke harshly in Spanish. I became petrified that I would die instantly in this strange land. I couldn't talk to him to explain what I was doing. After much confusion and commotion, I understood that I had to go through customs.

Allison began her journey with romantic notions of escape to an exotic land. She anticipated being welcomed by people who would admire and appreciate her as an American. She imagined participating with them in their festivals, smiling at them as she strolled through their markets, and savoring their cuisine as she dined with them. Her romantic notions were blunted by her encounter with the policeman at the airport. Her fantasies completely evaporated, however, when she arrived at her living quarters.

> I found myself in an apartment which was below my own notions of poverty. Yet some of the locals hated me because I had running water. I was living in luxury in their eyes. The disorientation with new ways, the frustration with my inability to communicate, and the pain of being an outsider continued for a while. And being a tall, blond woman made me stand out conspicuously wherever I went. To top it all off, I had health problems. There were bacteria in the food and water which most people adjusted to quickly. I was ill for the entire five months of my stay.

Allison's response to all the strangeness was one of shock. She initially thought about returning immediately to her home. But she decided to stay with her decision to meet the people and learn about their culture. She enrolled in an intensive language course, got a job teaching English, and began slowly to meet the people and understand their ways. Her persistence paid off.

But it was not until she returned to the United States that she realized how much the experience had changed her.

> I walked into the Los Angeles airport and was again shocked. The airport looked positively antiseptic. The trip had irrevocably changed my view of the world. I can no longer say, "I'm an American," for there is a North and a South America. I now say that I'm a United States citizen. I am very sensitive now to different cultural ways. And my political views are much more oriented toward global peace.
>
> Reflecting back on that trip's impact on my life, I am surprised even today as to how powerful an event it was. It still influences me. For instance, I soak up with pleasure any place that has an international flavor. I am honestly a better citizen of the world and of my own country because of it. I am sensitive to the power of cultural differences on individual behavior. And I tend to think that what was good for me would be good for all. Everybody should live in a foreign country for a while.

Tracy, a young architect from the Midwest, spent three months in France with only minimal knowledge of the native language. She experienced some of the same culture shock that Allison did—and enjoyed some of the same benefits.

> I managed to get by with a combination of English, French, and sign language. I definitely became more creative through it. I could beg for help, get directions, and tell somebody off without knowing half the right words. I usually traveled on my own. And I gradually grew more self-reliant and confident of my abilities to deal comfortably with a broad range of people and situations. I am now willing to have more adventures and challenges, to risk more. I chose to become an architect rather than a draftsman directly because of that experience.

Thus, travel can be a means of growth, of self-discovery, and of the discovery of the rich diversity of humankind. At times, people report an experience that is akin to a recapturing of aspects of childhood. As one man put it: "I was like a little boy again, discovering once more something of the fascination and wonder of the world in which we live."

CHANGE OF RESIDENCE

Travel is a relatively brief exploration of a new social world. Changing one's residence is likely to be a more long-term commitment to a new social world. Like travel, change of residence is tied up with romantic notions of escape to a new and better life. Mona Simpson captured the idea well in her novel *Anywhere But Here*, which is the story of a mother and daughter who leave their small midwestern town to find fame and happiness in California. They envision a meteoric rise to stardom in Hollywood. As usual, the reality turns out to be quite different from the fantasy.

Even if our fantasies are not fulfilled, we may experience enough of them for the move to be a positive watershed. But change of residence is a more radical step than travel. It may not be as easy to return to the comforts of the familiar. Some people, therefore, initially have a sense of insecurity, anxiety, or even anger and depression. Even a move in the same general area may be stressful. Carolyn, who owns a small gift shop, recalls a move from one town to another when she was seventeen as her watershed experience. It sounds like a relatively inconsequential event, but the move made her realize how important it is to her to live in a place where she is surrounded by caring people. And that realization has affected her subsequent life.

My home, the house in which I live, has always been very important to me. Even as a very young child, I can recall the sights, sounds, and smells of my home and the homes of others who are dear to me. We had to move because my stepfather was promoted. My parents were happy because it meant greater financial stability. But they were also sad, as I was, because we were leaving a community of very caring and supportive friends. To this day, the memories and visual pictures of that house appear in my mind. For many years, my dreams involved that particular house, especially in stressful times like when I moved west, got a divorce, and started a new career.

My parents had built that house in the suburbs in the early 1950s. Then my father unexpectedly died of a heart attack. Our house was filled with grief and sorrow. But a new beginning occurred with my mother and stepfather's wedding. Babies were born and brought home. The attic was completed to accommodate a growing family. There were lots of holidays to share with aunts, uncles, cousins, grandmas, and grandpas.

The house was significant because it was associated with my childhood and adolescent years. What made it most meaningful, though, were the exceptionally caring neighbors. After my father's death, there were a few families that kept a special eye open for my sister and me. Whenever my family needed help, the neighbors found a way to give and still allow my family to maintain its dignity. I got a sense of community from this special neighborhood that has remained with me all of my life.

The experience of growing up in that neighborhood and then moving into a different one has structured Carolyn's relationships with others. Wherever she has lived, she has attempted to form "a mutual sense of sharing and trust" with neighbors. She feels a need to be a part of a community wherever she is.

The community I grew up in has imprinted itself on my psyche. I still find it important for myself to get close to people who live nearby. That gives me a sense of inner security. And it's not just a matter of receiving. I believe that growing up around caring people has made me a more caring person wherever I live.

Virtually no one we asked viewed a change of residence as a long-term negative watershed. Once the initial period of negative emotion has passed (if there is such a period), there is an overwhelming sense of the move being very positive. There is likely to be the perception of personal growth, of freedom and independence, of broadened perspectives and new opportunities. Indeed, in some cases the change may be essential to an individual's well-being. In the case of Danny, a city manager in the Northwest, the decision to move may have saved at least one life. And it certainly altered for the better the lives of an entire family. Danny is a short man in his middle thirties. He has a booming voice, which has lost none of its New York accent. He grins frequently as he speaks, giving the impression that he is less affected by events than is actually true.

I grew up in New York City in one of the toughest neighborhoods around. My dad died when I was seven. My mom had to work all the time to support us six kids. We had little, and if we wanted more we had to steal it. I joined the gang my brothers were in shortly after my dad died and it soon became the most important thing in my life. My brothers had already been in and out of trouble with the police, and my oldest brother had done time. But it made him a big man in the gang.

When I was thirteen, our gang had a war with a rival gang. My brother Dom was killed. We were really close. I was really angry. I wanted to kill all of them. My oldest brother was even more enraged. He was crazy. He got a gun. I tried to stop him, to get him to realize that he needed help, but he wouldn't listen.

Somewhere along there my anger changed to the fear of losing another brother and I realized how stupid and futile the whole thing was. Well, my brother did kill one of the members of the other gang, and the police shot him.

The deaths of his brothers had a tremendous impact on Danny. His perspective changed. He no longer wanted to be a part of a gang. The gang seemed to be taking more from him than it was giving to him. He determined to see that the rest of the family would stay free of the gang warfare. He got a job and went back to school. But he soon discovered that he could not make such a decision with impunity.

The first few months after my brothers died were really rough because of the gang giving me and my family a hassle. I was supposed to be in the gang for life and I was supposed to avenge my brothers. So we moved out of that neighborhood. It was really hard for my mother. She had to leave all her friends. But my younger brother was already in a gang. . . . My sister had gotten pregnant when she was fourteen. It seemed that no matter what my mom or I said or did, they were being captured by the culture of the city.

Moneywise, we were doing better than ever before. I had a good job and my mom was working. But I knew that we had to go. We had to get away from this kind of life, from the influence of the city and the gangs. I wanted to get far enough away that people would have to ask where we were from when they heard us talk.

So really, without much notice to anyone, my mom and I quit our jobs, sold everything except a little furniture, and moved. We ended up in a medium-sized town in the state of Washington. I was just eighteen. My mom got a job on the third day. My brothers and I got jobs within a week. We had some problems with the younger kids, but it was as if we all sensed that this was right. My mom married again. All of us kids have gone to college, have good jobs, and families.

Few people had as dramatic a story to tell as Danny. But again and again, they spoke of the positive effects of moving to a new locale:

- ''I became more sophisticated and aware of different cultures.''
- ''It gave me more of a sense of freedom to do what I wanted, work where I choose, and make my own decisions.''
- ''Even though it is hard at times, I wouldn't trade what I've gotten—a far better job and a new and interesting group of friends.''
- ''It did everything for my ego; it was a challenge, a new environment, and it has taught me not to be afraid of a

struggle. I feel as though I proved to myself and others that I can be independent in my career and my personal life.''

CONVERSION

All of us have a need to become involved in something that is greater than we are, to become a part of something that transcends our personal pleasure and pain. One way that happens is through conversion, which can occur in both religious and non-religious contexts. Religious conversion, wrote the pioneer American psychologist William James, is the process ''by which a self hitherto divided, and consciously wrong, inferior and unhappy, becomes unified and consciously right, superior and happy.'' A consequence of conversion, James noted, is a sense of newness that pervades the individual's world. He quoted Jonathan Edwards: ''The appearance of everything was altered; there seemed to be, as it were, a calm, sweet cast, or appearance of divine glory, in almost everything.''

Similarly, two contemporary social scientists, Peter Berger and Thomas Luckmann, assert that religious conversion is the prototype of an alteration of an individual's outlook on life. They point out that such a change can also take place in political indoctrination or psychotherapy. Thus, particularly in the case of adults, conversion is likely to be an even stronger break with the past; it is an affirmation of, perhaps an eager plunging into, newness.

The experience of Charles Colson, once labeled the ''hatchet man'' for President Richard Nixon, exemplifies this kind of transition. His conversion was a religious one. As the Watergate scandal unraveled, Colson struggled with his own world view and his own identity. He met an old business acquaintance who had been converted and who startled Colson by his changed manner. Partly through the influence of that businessman and partly through his own reading and introspection, Colson had a conversion experience. In writing about it, he pointed out that he gained a new perspective both on himself and the world. He felt the negative emotions he had been experiencing flow out of his life. He felt the presence of God, filling up the void that had been in him for so long and bringing with it a new awareness of all things.

Colson subsequently spent time in prison for his involvement in the Watergate affair. Some thought his conversion was a ploy by a clever and devious man to avoid prison. But Colson's commitment never wavered. In prison he carried on a Christian ministry. After his release, he worked to develop a prison ministry, donating speaking fees and some of his book royalties to the cause.

Colson's conversion was prodded on by his inner discontent and perplexity. Frequently, it is emptiness, a lack of purpose, or personal problems of some kind that precede a conversion experience. In some cases, however, the individual reports that the conversion took place because he or she suddenly confronted something that resonated with an inner desire. As one man put it: "I came into contact with the faith when I was nineteen. And when I heard about it, I knew that this was something that I wanted. It wasn't a matter of feeling guilty or inadequate. Instead, I made a discovery that drew me forward by its irresistible appeal."

Once converted, people report newness in many ways: love, acceptance of others, personal growth, purpose in life, and peace of mind. There is also a change in behavior—such as that reported by Kevin, who was in a downward spiral when he had his conversion experience. Kevin looks like a professional football player, but he is an urban planner in an eastern city. He spoke of his experience eagerly.

Without question, the greatest event or experience of my life was the spiritual journey I began several years ago. I was twenty-one years old, in college, majoring in sociology and urban studies. I was also majoring, in my personal life, in a course of self-destruction which encompassed the entire spectrum of illicit drugs, sexual encounters, and certain criminal activities. All of this was a result of trying to run from intense feelings of insecurity, confusion, and lack of purpose in my life.

I was angry and rebellious. I got involved in student activist groups and other organizations that let me lash out at all the phoniness of my parents' world, which, from my perspective, had brought so much pain to my life. I resented a society in which my father was viewed as successful because he had a Ph.D. and was a respected professor and then he dumped my mother and the children for another woman who better fit his respected life-style. My second father and my third father only increased my anger and desire to fight the system.

Looking back on that troubled period of my life, I realize that I was ripe for something. Maybe anything that would offer a way out of my destructive behavior and bring a little stability into my life. Yet, somehow, even without the trauma and pain, I believe I still would have felt the need for a purpose and meaning beyond myself and my personal goals.

My spiritual pilgrimage was precipitated by the accidental reading of a book entitled *The Cross and The Switchblade* by David Wilkerson. I came across it when I was doing some research on street gangs and delinquency. But I found more than the data for a class project. The book contained the testimony of one man's personal relationship with God. If those experiences were actually true, I told myself, then this man had an authentic and meaningful relationship with God, and I wanted one, too.

Shortly after Kevin read the book, David Wilkerson spoke at the university Kevin attended. It was during the speech that Kevin had his conversion experience. It was a memorable moment for him.

The only way I can express the magnitude of that moment is in terms of the feeling that swept over me. I felt an immediate rush of peace and tranquility, coupled with an awareness of a love so total and complete that I burst into tears at the realization of its beauty. At that moment I knew that my life would never be the same again.

POLITICAL ACTIVISM

The conversion experience, the sense of being rescued from a more or less unsatisfying past and thrust into a vibrant new life, can, as mentioned, also occur in a nonreligious context. The secret is to discover your own "magnificent obsession," that which thrills your inner being and transforms your life. For some people, politics or political activism is the answer.

People often don't associate politics with growth and fulfillment. A lot of us feel like the woman in a southern city who said she was planning to vote for a local candidate who had the reputation of being, at best, dishonest. "If a man isn't ruined when he goes into office," she explained, "he's ruined when he comes out. And there's no use to ruin a good man."

In spite of such views, some people find that the political world offers a transcendent experience that adds rich meaning to their lives. And some have a conversion experience through participation. Emily's conversion occurred in a social and political movement. Now in her early fifties, Emily works as a reporter. Her watershed occurred in a large eastern city when she was thirty-nine, divorced, and the mother of two teen-aged daughters.

Probably at no other time of my life had I experienced such terror, such lack of certainty, and so much anticipation about my life. While in this state, I decided to attend a meeting of the National Organization for Women. I had been very interested in the women's movement, although I was more than a little wary of these women promoting the wonderful but radical concept of women's liberation.

One hot summer evening, I climbed the steps to the NOW office with a sense of excitement. There were posters announcing events for women in music, theater, and art; political notices and notification of literature for women by women; newspapers and periodicals containing stories, essays, poems, and want ads all directed to the concerns and interests of women. The thrill came, I think, from the knowledge that I had at last come into my own. At last, I felt whole, accepted, and real. To a woman like me, who had so suppressed her own needs to be there for others, this event signaled a kind of rebirth. From that point on, I had a family again—a family of women. I was welcomed, connected, and supported by a community of women.

She participated in various activities, such as a freedom train that was organized to support the Equal Rights Amendment and to honor the memory of the early suffragettes. For a time, she served as the president of the local chapter. Her involvement clearly changed her perspective on herself and her world, an alteration that has remained with her. She recalls that as she left the national conference one year, driving through the rain to catch a train home, she had intense thoughts and feelings.

I felt such gratitude that I am living at a moment in time that permits the experience of women's consciousness. I resolved then to work toward a better and more conscious world, believing then, as I do now, that feminism is the cutting edge of humanism.

Emily is still a member of NOW, but she is no longer an active participant. However, she continues to live by the principles she gained: "I think my feminist commitment is played out day by day in the various segments of my life." Like the lives of those who experience a religious conversion, Emily's life, including her lifestyle, her perspectives, and her behavior, changed dramatically as a result of her conversion to feminism.

People need not get involved in a particular cause like feminism to be affected by political ideas. Andrea is an active Democrat. Now in her forties, she became a political animal in 1969, just after she passed the bar exam. Andrea was a serious student throughout her college days. She avoided any involvement in the campus protests that raged throughout the nation. But the head of the law firm where she got her first job was active in local politics. He invited her to a meeting of his Democratic club.

I went expecting to be bored. I really only agreed to do it because I wanted to please him. But I heard some heated discussions about the Vietnam War, about domestic problems like poverty, and about the need to mobilize people—people like me, who were so immersed in their own lives that they barely realized there were problems in the world.

I suddenly came alive with feelings that I had never experienced before. It was a combination of guilt and enthusiasm—guilt because I had spent most of my life until then contemplating my navel; enthusiasm because I suddenly came alive to my world. I was determined from that moment never again to get so wrapped up in my own career and life that I would be oblivious of my world and all of its problems.

Andrea has remained active in politics for nearly twenty years. She has run for office and been a delegate to the Democratic National Convention. As she puts it: "I'm hooked. Politics is my addiction."

WAR

The experience of war is like that of travel in that it is a temporary journey into a new social world. But it is far more likely than other kinds of transitions to be psychologically disruptive and dehumanizing. Soldiers in combat may have serious psychological problems, particularly when they have engaged in acts of massive and indiscriminate destruction against the enemy. Vietnam veterans seemed to have special problems in coping with the stresses of war, in part because of the nature of the war and in part because of the lack of support when they returned home. Some reported having nightmares for years after coming back.

Most people would expect the experience of war to be, if anything, a negative watershed. Yet a number of men who served in Vietnam told us that the experience was a positive watershed for them. Consider, for example, the story of Greg, a financial planner who is married and the father of two children. When he was twenty-four, he volunteered for duty in Vietnam. He was an Air Force pilot at the time, flying C130s. He regarded a tour in Vietnam as part of his professional responsibility.

One of the greatest impacts Vietnam had for me was the dedication to teamwork that I experienced. We were interdependent and we had to trust each other if we were going to stay alive. But being there also led to a strong disillusionment with government for getting us into the war. I made the decision then that I would not make a career out of the Air Force after all. I was convinced that our presence in Vietnam was an effort to impose changes on people who really didn't want them.

More than anything, being there gave me a greater appreciation of being alive and a determination to live life to the hilt. The small, petty frustrations we all have seem so insignificant. And what I was doing was so unfulfilling. Of course, I was successful from society's point of view. I was an officer in the Air Force and a good pilot. But I was not successful at a personal level.

I decided that I needed to be in control of my life, to control the decisions that had to be made. I no longer wanted the government to control my life. Once I started making my own decisions, I liked it so much that I now own my own company. I'm in control.

Greg discovered his need for autonomy while in Vietnam. Jamie, another Vietnam veteran, was also in the Air Force. He reported more trauma than Greg, but none of the disillusionment with government.

My assignment to serve a year away from my family in Vietnam was a significant watershed in my life. My engineering job brought me into close contact with many returning pilots and I flew with them and listened to their war stories on a daily basis. The assignment was to be my first real test in a combat situation and I was very apprehensive about leaving my wife and two children. I didn't know how I would react to the danger. The survival training that preceded the assignment did little to prepare me for the job at hand in Vietnam. Standard survival lectures and ditching training—how to escape from a crash landing in the water—

took up the first five days. The compound phase and the survival trek were scheduled for the next week.

The compound phase included some time spent out-doors—in a barbed wire enclosure, in winter weather, with a watery fish-and-rice soup to eat—and then a standard course on Chinese interrogation techniques. This whole experience was new and very different for me. I felt better after getting through the day stripped naked in a cell with loud Oriental music, shouting guards, and high tempera-tures, but was still worried about an extended stay in that atmosphere.

Next came box time, where you were placed in a very small box and the noise started again with sticks hitting the box. The box was so small that your head hit one end and your bottom hit the other with your legs tucked under you. Being above average in size, it was a very tight fit for me. With two people shoving on the door to get it closed and locked, I resisted as much as possible to get extra room. My small act of resistance made me feel better, and I passed this short test without a problem. Before I was finished, I had also completed jungle survival school and small-arms training.

When my days at survival school were over, an airplane dropped us off at Da Nang Air Base. I was a major and assigned to a forward operating location in the central high-lands. They were short of experienced people there and considered rank a stabilizing influence on junior pilots. Combat finally was a reality when I saw fires and explo-sions on the ground as we flew into the base. The reality became even greater when we landed and I could choose between living quarters rebuilt after the Tet attack of the previous year or those that had not been hit yet.

Our mission was to slow the transportation of supplies to South Vietnam via the Ho Chi Minh Trail by directing air strikes and artillery fire from border fire bases. Being shot at in the air became the norm. Combat presents unique challenges to each individual, and each faces these chal-lenges in a different way.

Many of my new friends began to change life-styles,

some slightly and some drastically. In the air, some would fly higher or in areas that were considered safer with little regard to mission performance, while others were always coming back with bullet holes. On the ground, a pilot who had been a very religious person turned to erotic art and drinking for the first time in his life before being shipped back to a Da Nang desk job. We all drank more than normal, and a few became alcoholics. The year passed with but two short weeks in Hawaii as the only respite.

In spite of the trauma, Jamie sees some positive outcomes from the experience.

Vietnam intensified my involvement with life. I literally could taste and feel the danger. And it changed me. It's hard for me to express, but my engagement with life is more vivid. I see and hear more; I'm just generally more aware. Also the knowledge that I survived—that I didn't panic, that I maintained my wits, values, and even my sense of humor—has allowed me to face new challenges in my life with greater confidence and a belief in myself.

THE WORLD OF CULTURE

War is humankind in its most destructive mode. Culture—the worlds of art, music, dance, and literature—is humankind in its most creative mode. People have watershed experiences in both modes. Pat, a husky football coach in a small college, had a watershed experience through a rock-and-roll record. He was an outstanding football player in high school and college, but too small for the professional ranks. Pat has found fulfillment in being a coach, however—though only with the help of Bruce Springsteen.

When I was a sophomore in high school, I was already a good athlete. I didn't have any special ability in anything else, so I knew that I had to do something with sports. But that wasn't going to be easy. My father wanted me to be a doctor or a lawyer. We didn't get along too well in those years. In fact, we argued a lot, because he didn't like how much time football took and he insisted I could become something more than an athlete.

My watershed happened after a family vacation. My father and I had a heated argument in the car on the way home. I stormed into the house and picked up my mail. In it there were some records from the club I belonged to. One of those records was by an artist I didn't know—a guy by the name of Bruce Springsteen. When I listened to it, I knew the music and the lyrics were for me. Right from the first song. Everything I heard seemed to apply to me and to my life. I listened to it for the next month. It was my life's story. And it helped me get through the next year in many ways, especially in terms of the problem with my father. It gave me hope and energy.

One of Springsteen's songs that was particularly helpful to Pat was "Growin' Up." The words reflected his situation and what he wanted to do in it—namely, he, too, stood alone in the midst of anger but determined that he would not be subdued or conquered by it.

You can imagine my excitement when Bruce gave a concert in our city during my senior year. When I went to it, the ideas were suddenly no longer abstract. Seeing him in concert, living his philosophy, made me realize that whatever you do in life, you can work hard at it and know that someday the benefits will appear.

The very next day, Pat got an acceptance letter from a college. He felt it was a sign. He could play football at the college and major in physical education. His life would be a good one after all.

It took some time, but my father finally accepted me for what I am. It was hard for him to give up the dream of having a son who is a doctor and accept the fact that my heart and my future were in football. But he finally gave in. In fact, I would say he's real proud of me today. Maybe

I would have made it to this point in any case. But every time I hear his name or his music, I still pause and say, "Thanks, Bruce."

Cultural experiences help some people master a difficult situation. They help others to establish new direction in their lives. Theresa, a small, vivacious woman, is a lawyer and the wife of a neurosurgeon. Ten years ago she watched tearfully as her youngest son left home to go to college. At a relatively early age, Theresa faced the "empty-nest" problem. Of course, she had a busy social life and she had done some volunteer work for the hospital. But there was an unease in her.

I felt a little empty. At times, I felt something close to panic, as though my life had no particular purpose or direction. I enjoyed doing things with the women at the club. But I felt that my life had to have something more, that I had to do more and be more than a woman of leisure.

Theresa had no direction until she read a once-forbidden book. She was a voracious reader as a teenager, and decided to enjoy once again the pleasures of fiction.

I went to the bookstore one afternoon and started browsing. I had about five books in my hand already when I noticed one that had been labeled pornography when I was growing up: *Lady Chatterley's Lover* by D. H. Lawrence. My curiosity was piqued. I wondered why the book had been condemned. And I wondered if it would still be considered obscene in the days of X-rated movies. I started to move on, but then, impulsively, I picked it up and added it to my stack.

I was excited that night about spending an hour or two delving into my stack of books. The first one I picked up was *Lady Chatterley's Lover*. I never put it down until I had finished it. I remember telling my husband the next night how excited I was about the book. "This isn't pornography," I told him. "It's a book about women and their needs."

Theresa pondered the message of the book in the days following. She discussed it with some of her friends.

> I told them that Lawrence really understood women, that he realized that society had put women into a stifling mold, and that women had the full range of needs that men have. I realized that my husband would never think about giving up his profession at this stage in his life. But isn't that what I had done when I sent my son off to school?

Stimulated by these ideas, Theresa decided to pursue a life-long dream of becoming a lawyer. One part of her said it was crazy to go back to school—three years of study seemed almost wasteful at her age; yet another part—the part that Lawrence had reached—said why not? And the latter won out. She entered law school, made law review, and, when her studies were completed, was recruited by a well-known local law firm.

> I have, in many respects, a new life, and I love it. Don't misunderstand me. I loved having and raising my children—in many ways, this was the most creative thing I ever did. But I was ready for new and demanding challenges, and the law gave me those. And, in some ways, I owe it all to D. H. Lawrence.

An excursion into the world of literature led Theresa into a new life. She had hesitated when she first saw the Lawrence novel. She had always thought of it as forbidden territory. Even if not forbidden, however, a new social world may threaten us. To enter it is to step into the unknown. But the risk can yield a hearty payoff. For many, the venture becomes adventure. The new social world turns out to be a transition to a new direction in life.

10

Turning Transitions into Watersheds

A year in Italy became a turning point in the career and family life of novelist John Cheever. The adventure began with little or no planning. Other families might have had some doubts about such a move, his daughter Susan Cheever said, but they did not. And it was an important experience for all of them. For John Cheever, the trip began a lifelong love affair with Italy. His immersion in Italian culture and history greatly enriched his future life and work. For many years, Cheever had a drinking problem and struggled with anxiety. But Italy gave him a measure of joy. Even when he was feeling fearful or miserable, he could find solace and pleasure in reflecting on his experiences in Italy.

The time in Italy also had a major impact upon his relationship with his daughter. During these months they began a practice, which would last for the remainder of Cheever's life, of intense dialogues over various intellectual issues. The unique father-daughter relationship that they had was forged in the context of travel in a new culture.

Not every transition makes a positive contribution to a person's growth. Sometimes travel is merely a break in one's routine; it leaves no lasting impression. Some people never adjust to a new location, or they find that the new location makes little change in them. Or war leaves scars rather than a positive watershed in its wake. And some people are bored rather than enchanted by the world of culture.

What makes the difference? There are some specific techniques, but underlying them all is an important principle: you can turn the ordinary into the extraordinary. The principle is illustrated by the experience of a traveler who was taking a rural vacation. As he drove through the New England countryside, he passed a barn with a number of targets drawn on it. In the center of each target was an arrow. The man, intrigued by the sight, stopped and inquired of the farmer about the "incredible marksman" who lived there. "No one around here is good with a bow and arrow," the farmer said. Pointing to the barn, he told the traveler that the arrows were all shot by a neighbor's young son. "He shoots arrows into the barn, then goes and paints targets around them."

The ordinary always has the potential for becoming the extraordinary. The following techniques, which draw upon that underlying philosophy, are useful for turning transitions into positive watersheds.

LOOK AT CHANGE AS A CHALLENGE

Some observers have accused Americans of being neophiliacs, of having an insatiable hunger for the new. Actually, people are ambivalent about change. They have a need both for new experiences and for anchors to the past. There is an old story about a man who got a new boomerang and then killed himself trying to throw the old boomerang away. Something about the story rings true. You can't blithely toss away the past. There is security in the known, even if it isn't particularly satisfying. Few of us easily give up our security.

In addition, there are risks in change. There are unknowns. There is the possibility that the new will not even be as satisfying as the old. Even people who willingly plunge into the new tend to go with some apprehension. A number of those who decided to move to a new location talked not only about the excitement but the anxiety. There is always a threat in a transition. For that reason, it takes courage to venture into new experiences. Those who have the courage and accept the risks, who look upon change as a challenge and not as an undesirable intruder, are likely to find the transition to be a positive experience.

We should note that new experiences do not always turn out well, even when the individual desires the change. Not everyone will step boldly into the new and emerge with a sense of exhilaration and gratitude for the experience. But perhaps your willingness to try the new will be enhanced if you keep in mind the risks of avoiding change. Those who resist change are fighting the essence of the universe, for change is the nature of life.

We all get to some point in our lives when we would like to freeze existence, to maintain things just the way they are. When our daughter was seven, we went into her bedroom one night to tell her good night. We found her weeping and asked what was wrong. "Nothing," she said. "I was just thinking how happy we all are, and I hate to see it change." We tried to help her realize that change is necessary, that we would continue to be happy even though we would all be different, and that not changing was more of a threat to our happiness than changing.

In other words, the present is elusive. You cannot freeze it. You cannot keep things they way they are. Progress or decay are the only two options we have. Those who are unwilling to accept the new will find themselves continually frustrated and depressed.

On the other hand, those who view change as a challenge are more likely to emerge with something positive. Danielle is that kind of person. Danielle was twenty-five when she completed her master's degree in dance therapy. She had a desire to travel, but she also wanted to start her career. She decided to move to London in hopes of fulfilling both desires. Danielle did not realize at the time that dance therapy was virtually nonexistent in London. But after a month, she secured a job at a private school for autistic children.

I had mixed emotions when I began the job. I felt jubilant, but also lonely, scared, and incompetent, wondering what I was doing in England. Why hadn't I stayed at home where I had friends, support, and where a safe and easy job awaited me? Walking to work in the rain day after day gave me plenty of time to think about it and come up with some answers.

I realized that I needed to move to England in order to

objectively evaluate and direct the course my life was going to take. I needed the distance from school and my family in order to make a sound judgment about my future. Because of the work laws in England, dance therapy was one of the few jobs available to me. So I either made it in my profession there or I would have to go back to the States.

During the next year, Danielle made it in England. She developed a number of programs in schools and hospitals in various parts of London. She was a success. More important, she learned some important things about herself.

My experience taught me the positive value of commitment and change. It taught me that commitment overrides fear because it enables one to confront fear and deal with it. It also clarified my goals. I realized that I needed to go on and get my Ph.D., because dance therapy could only work for me as an adjunct kind of therapy.

Danielle is back in the United States now, in Boston, studying for her Ph.D., expecting to move to California to establish her practice. She continues to view change as a challenge. Change has become her ally, not her enemy.

PERSIST

There is an ancient saying: "The falling drops wear the stone at last." Persistence, in other words, is the necessary ingredient of any achievement. Nothing worthwhile ever happens easily and quickly. Nor is it merely a matter of luck. The famed football coach Vince Lombardi scoffed at the idea of luck as a form of chance. "Luck," he insisted, "is when opportunity meets preparation." In our study of couples who had long-term, satisfying marriages, we found that persistence through difficult times was essential. None of the marriages was trouble-free. And none of the spouses believed that they had merely been lucky. Instead, all stressed the importance of effort and persistence in spite of problems. As one woman put it: "Our marriage is firm and filled with love and respect, but it took time and work. . . . Our marriage took twenty years and we are still learning.'' She noted that she and her husband worked through some problems that seem to break apart marriages today. And she is grateful that they did not allow those problems to separate them.

Persistence, then, implies vigor as well as perseverance. Pete Rose set a number of records, including most lifetime hits, as a major-league baseball player. Rose is not a large man, and he never had much power as a hitter. But he got the nickname Charlie Hustle because he gave his best every game. While other batters strolled down to first base after being walked, Rose always ran. A friend of ours who lunched with him told us, "One thing that really impressed me about him is his belief that if you just do more than the other guy, and keep on doing it, you are going to be a winner."

So persistence means determined and continued effort. Persistence also means confronting problems and refusing to back down in the face of difficulties. Christine, an interior designer in her thirties, told us that her watershed occurred some four years ago when she began running. Running, she says, changed her into the trim, energetic person she is today. Her husband had started running and urged her to run as well. Her initial reluctance quickly turned to dismay.

I had never exercised. I was in terrible shape. It was painful and I wanted to quit. It was like torture. Every breath hurt. It was only because of his encouragement that I continued. Then, after a few weeks, I noticed that it wasn't as difficult anymore. I began to increase my distance. Eventually, I settled into a routine of running three miles a day several times a week. Occasionally I run six miles.

It was a turning point for me. I was really tempted to stop. I could easily have gone back to being a slouch. But I kept on. I began to feel good physically and mentally. It boosted my confidence in myself. I lost weight. I had always been somewhat disappointed in my appearance and physical abilities, but now I was proud of them for the first time. And my husband and I became closer because of the new shared activity.

Transitions are frequently painful in their initial stages. In some cases, such as war, persistence is required rather than voluntary. In other cases, however, the individual has the option to back away, to return to a former state. Persistence through the initial pain may bring about a positive watershed, as it did for Christine. A similar experience was reported by Jodi, a woman whose watershed involved the world of fencing. Twenty years ago, when she was a teenager, she began an intensive, three-year formal training program in fencing. It was one of the most demanding experiences of her life.

> Even when I was ill, had a high temperature, or was exhausted, I had to practice, sometimes all day. When school was out, I and the rest of the trainees had to go away from home to train. We didn't get a vacation like everyone else. But at the end of the three years, my team won first place in a national competition and I took second place individually.

What motivates someone to commit to such intensive training? In Jodi's case, it was not an unyielding drive to master the sport.

> I thought of quitting the training program several times. But I think the embarrassment of giving up would have been too great to bear. And I'm glad now that I didn't quit. I'm proud of the way I stuck with it. I learned that anything of value is worth working hard for. And I also learned that discipline works. It brings rewards.

A foolish persistence is the hobgoblin of little minds, to extrapolate from Emerson. But the lack of persistence because of some initial pain or difficulties may rob you of a positive watershed experience.

GET INVOLVED WITH NEW PEOPLE

A study of emotional experiences in eight different countries concluded that relationships were the most important factor in generating various emotions. In particular, when people were asked the kinds of things that brought them joy or happiness, relationships with friends were mentioned most frequently. Relationships with family members and making new friends were also among the most frequent sources of joy and happiness.

Unfortunately, transitions may separate us from our friends, thereby removing one of the major sources of gratification in our lives. It is important, therefore, to make new friends, to form new relationships. These new relationships need not be permanent. In the case of travel, for instance, getting to know local people rather than mere sightseeing may turn the experience into a positive watershed. One young man said that a trip to the Samoan Islands was a watershed for him because he found the people so "giving and warm. I'd walk down the street and they would invite me in for dinner and the next thing I knew I had a place to stay." He was deeply moved by the fact that the Samoans "genuinely cared about their fellow human beings." Although he has not been able to return, the people are still with him. "The impact it had was profound," he noted. "I will never forget the way the people treated strangers. I still feel that I have some of Samoa in me. I don't foresee ever losing it. I vowed that after I got home, if anyone needed a place to stay or a meal and I could help, I would."

Moving to a new location may also mean a permanent rupture in a relationship. Elizabeth, a California talent agent, speaks with some emotion about her move from Oklahoma over twenty years ago. It enabled her to change a situation that was distressing her. One of the values of transitions is that they may allow us—indeed, they may be the only way—to deal with troubled aspects of our lives. In Elizabeth's case, the move was forced on her. It led to her declaration of independence and her subsequent acquisition of a surrogate family. Elizabeth still wrestles with twinges of guilt, but she knows that she made the only choice that would allow her to grow.

I was eighteen and just out of high school. I had been brought up in a very strict family. My father ruled the home like a dictator. He controlled what I wore, my language, my efforts in school, and even my choice of friends. And my mother went along with whatever he did. She wasn't as stern as he was, but she wasn't any help to me in dealing with his endless rules and regulations.

Elizabeth's father was particularly concerned about the possibility of sexual activity on her part. He would not allow her to have any contact with boys at school without his permission, which would only be given after he had considerable information about a particular boy. Her social life was very restricted.

I could date boys as long as my father approved. But there were very few that he ever approved. He could always find something wrong. He didn't trust one boy because his sideburns were too long.

I didn't believe in open rebellion, but in my senior year I secretly began seeing a boy at school. My father had never met him. And I knew he wouldn't approve of him because he smoked and drank beer. Near the end of the year, my father found out. He was really angry, and he was afraid that the relationship would grow during the summer break even though the boy was going to college in the fall. So he decided to send me on an extended trip to California to visit my sister.

The move to California was the beginning of Elizabeth's watershed experience. It was not a move that she wanted. In fact, she felt torn between her feelings for her boyfriend and her father's insistence. Reluctantly but obediently, she boarded the bus for the trip. She was eighteen years old, but she still felt she should do whatever her father ordered. Once she arrived on the West Coast, however, she experienced a taste of freedom that she had never known. The contrast to the stifling atmosphere of a dictatorial father and a say-nothing mother was nothing less than startling to her.

I was like a filly at the races. When the gate opened, I took off. And I never went back. The move became permanent. If I had gone back, I know I would have never led my own life.

In spite of her father's authoritarianism, Elizabeth felt a certain closeness in her family life. She believes that her father cared about her. He apparently believed that the rules he imposed on her would protect her. She could not grow in that atmosphere, but she felt an emptiness when she broke with her parents.

In the years since, however, she has found a surrogate family. As she puts it: "I have become close to several people, both men and women, who have become my adopted mothers and fathers. They are there when I need them, but they don't force me to do things their way." Getting involved with other people in California filled the void that was created by the move. Elizabeth's transition brought her freedom, but she knows that the outcome could have been quite different if she had not gotten involved with new people. She needs the closeness of a family. Unable to maintain that closeness with her own parents, she found a surrogate family in a new location.

LEARN THE ART OF POSITIVE REFLECTION

Like the harried man who said he coped with multiple demands by putting his mind in neutral and going wherever he was pushed, some people wander through life without giving much thought to their experiences. Others think about their experiences, but they focus on the troubling aspects. For example, they may reflect on a trip, but think about the costs or about the unexpected bad weather or a problem at a hotel. They may reflect on a move, but grimly hang on to thoughts of what they have left behind.

Positive reflection is an alternative to the negative thoughts that run through your mind during the day. *Reflection* means that you think about your experiences and the implications of those experiences. *Positive* means that you learn to sift out and value what you have gained from the experiences. Transitions frequently involve painful experiences. But there can always be a gain as well, even if it is nothing more than learning not to repeat a mistake.

Brooke, a lovely model who is now in her late twenties, learned the value of positive reflection when she was only eight. It led to a lifelong attachment to water. Brooke recalls a sickly childhood, including trips to the hospital in her father's arms to get relief from asthma. Brooke had to learn to live within severe limitations.

> I remained puny and sensitive for years, and it seemed that every wayward grass and pollen brought on a miserable attack of itchy nose, tearing eyes, and sneezes. I couldn't play outside very much. I often spent an afternoon on my grandparents' farm watching other children playing, wishing that I could join them, but realizing that that enticing long grass was my mortal enemy.

When she was eight, the family moved from the Midwest to a military base in the Philippine Islands. They had access to a private beach that was set aside for officers and their families. Brooke's sister spent time playing on the beach with the other kids, but Brooke fell in love with the ocean.

> All I wanted to do was to be in the water. I was a stringy-haired and scrawny little kid, but staying afloat in the water was easy for me. I began to love the ocean because I could be outside in the sun and there weren't any obnoxious grasses and pollens to drive me and my nose crazy. But my dad wouldn't let me go in the water without an adult, and my mother didn't swim at all. I nagged him constantly. He would hold my hand while I jumped waves, and sometimes he'd support me and we'd swim around out beyond the waves. Unfortunately, my dad ran out of enthusiasm long before I did. We would have to come back in so he could chat with his friends.

Finally, he hit upon a plan that I remember as vividly as if it were two days ago. He stood me on the beach and wrapped me up in a big orange life jacket, the kind that fits like a coat, buckles tightly, and is inflated behind the neck and down both sides of the chest. Then he carried me to the water and towed me out to sea. He parked me near a buoy and swam back to the shore, leaving me bobbing free like a baby buoy. At first I tried to swim as I was used to—on my stomach. But I couldn't roll over, so I learned to lie on my back and let the vest hold me up.

Brooke found floating an exhilarating experience. She watched the waves come in and felt herself lifted up by them. She counted birds in the sky. She watched her toes wiggle. She thought about the life jacket and what made it work. And just as she wondered about how long the life jacket would hold her up, her father appeared. He had been watching her all the time. When she got to a certain point, he swam out and towed her back to the buoy and let her drift again.

Initially, she reacted instinctively to the experience. She had discovered something that made her feel like a different person, something that brought zest and excitement into her restricted life. As she grew older, Brooke thought a good deal about the experience and what it meant to her. She realized that being in water brings her a peace that she finds nowhere else. And it was the positive reflection that made the experience a permanent turning point for her.

Since I first realized what a difference it makes in me, I've been hooked on being surrounded by water. I've gone swimming in snow-lined mountain lakes and have stood under thirty-two-degree waterfalls. I'm even at peace when I'm in a Jacuzzi, or in the same room with an aquarium. It may seem to be an undramatic event, just a little girl enjoying a summer evening at the beach. But the impact on my personality was profound.

The experience in the ocean was the first time I learned to relax mentally. In the ocean, I learned that I could rest, just float around and let the water hold me up. And from there I progressed to a little more activity and adventure, gaining confidence and physical endurance. Soon I was spending every afternoon at the pool, screaming and chasing and making new friends. If I hadn't had this early experience at the beach, I may have continued to be treated like a semi-invalid by my parents and have had very few friends. But I had the chance to learn to float, insulate myself from stresses and aggravations, and from that position to exercise and gain the strength I need to enjoy my life.

We are frequently too harried to spend time in positive reflection. Too often we feel like we are on a ten-day trip around the world, with every moment filled and little or no time to reflect upon what we are doing. It's a mistake to get that busy. Louis, a New York advertising copy chief who looks more like a shy college professor, had a watershed experience in Africa. It was a turning point in his life because he spent the evenings reflecting upon what he had done during the day. He had finished his business twelve days early in Nairobi and wondered what he would do. He wanted an unusually "nontouristy" experience, so he contacted a knowledgeable friend, who put him in touch with a society of missionaries. Louis offered his services and the society asked him to visit six missions in Kenya and write stories for their magazine. There were both positive and negative aspects to his experience, but he chose to focus on the positive ones.

While with the missionaries, I witnessed a completely different life-style. In the bush country of Kenya, the people live in poverty, but they always manage to smile. They welcome visitors with open arms and are willing to share what little they have with visitors.

My initial reaction to their situation was pity, but it gradually changed to admiration. I lay awake at nights attempting to analyze what was happening inside of me. I wondered what I was really learning. By observing the blending of African and Western cultures, I knew that I would somehow be affected.

Louis could have spent his nights in various ways. He chose to think about his experiences. And the fact that it was positive reflection helped make it a positive watershed.

Since this memorable experience, my outlook on life has gradually changed. Prior to this, I was a fiery personality. I had arguments over all kinds of things. I would do anything to prove a point, whether I was right or wrong.

Upon my return to the United States, I noticed a change in my attitude about life's petty annoyances. I remembered the Africans who toted water for many miles to their austere dwellings. I now saw my leaky faucet as a petty annoyance which I was able to live with. My bad ankle was now part of life, and life continues rather well with it. Instead of bar hopping, I now spend my spare time visiting hospitals and doing outdoor activities with my family.

Louis feels that he has a much keener awareness of what is really important than he had before his watersheds. He believes that he has a greater respect for his fellow humans, and that he tries to treat them "as people and not as commodities or inanimate objects." He thinks that he is better able to relate to others, and he likes the person he is much more than the person he was.

LEARN THE ART OF ACTIVE SEEING

Psychologists point out the importance of active listening. By active listening, they mean doing whatever is necessary in order really to understand what someone else is saying. We may appear to be listening to someone but not really hear what the person is saying; our mind is wandering or we are not listening carefully enough to absorb the information. Or we may hear the words, but attribute a meaning to them that the other person doesn't intend. Active listening involves such things as attention to nonverbal cues as well as to the spoken words, allowing the other person to speak without interruption, and rephrasing what he or she has said to see if we have really understood the full meaning. Active listening, therefore, requires effort and energy.

Active seeing is similar. You can look at something without really seeing it—that is, without taking it in and having it become a part of your consciousness. Or you can see a part of it, but miss something that could be very significant. An industrial scientist reported an interesting incident that illustrates the point. It occurred in the years before the First World War when Sir William Ramsay, who discovered the gases argon, xenon, neon, and krypton, was lecturing on his work. The scientist had helped to set up the experimental demonstration equipment and listened with interest to the lecture.

Sir William told the audience how he had discovered the gases and the meaning of the names he had given them: new (neon), lazy (argon), hidden (krypton), and strange (xenon). In his last lecture, he noted that each of the gases would emit its own special light when an electrical charge passed through it. As he subjected each tube of gas to the electrical charge, the audience saw a different color glow. The scientist noted that it was a striking display. The five hundred people in the audience applauded politely and went home—not one of them realizing that they had seen the first neon light. Only some years later did another scientist watch the demonstration and recognize the commercial importance of it. That scientist engaged in active seeing.

People who have watershed experiences in transitions have learned the art of active seeing. When they travel, they look at their surroundings and try to assimilate as much as possible. They are engaged with both the people and the things in their environment. Listen to Kelly, a department store executive in her thirties, describe her watershed experience, which occurred when she was nineteen:

I had a summer job working in a hotel restaurant in Switzerland. It was my first time out of the United States. I was the only foreign employee and knew no French, the common language in the area. The work hours were very long, but on my break I would wander in the beautiful countryside. On my days off, I would take trips to nearby towns.

I was constantly bewildered and confused by the cultural differences, from the way they scrubbed floors to the way they sold milk. I had to ask my boss to explain to me why things were done in such different ways. I went there thinking of myself as the sophisticated American. I began to feel more like a country bumpkin in the city, a dummy who barely knew the world.

Kelly engaged in active seeing, because she didn't just observe something different but saw details, thought about them, and inquired about their meaning. She was troubled by the differences until she had a flash of insight one evening.

I was watching the sunset in a field and thinking about the differences. I realized that, yes, it is different. We are not all the same. And places are not all the same. There is so much to see and explore and discover, so many new worlds. And that is wonderful! It isn't necessary for other people to be like me. Or for me to be like them. Our differences are what make life fascinating.

Active seeing, then, requires effort and reflection. It means absorbing your surroundings rather than casually encountering them. Leonard, a business consultant who specializes in conflict management techniques, practiced the art of active seeing when he was a teenager; as a result, an experience that could have been a rash fling became a positive watershed for him.

Leonard has always been sensitive to his environment. He tunes in quickly to the feelings of others. He notices his physical surroundings. Those qualities make him effective as a consultant. They also paved the way for his watershed experience. He was only fourteen at the time, living in a town in the Northwest and doing well in school, both socially and academically. But Leonard decided to strike out on his own.

I was the youngest in a family of nine children, and from what I could see, we were all going nowhere. We had been sharecroppers, ranch hands, lumber-camp cooks, and service workers in a hotel. We were off and on welfare.

My brothers and sisters accepted our life-style. But I had had a taste of the good life through visits to my friends' homes, through jobs for wealthy folks in my town, and through fantasy trips from my readings. When *The Grapes of Wrath* was assigned as a reading project, I remember

thinking that this was the story of my life put to paper, and
I decided to leave and to find and make my own fate.

It was a difficult decision. Leonard really didn't want to leave
before the end of the school year because of the friends he had
made. More important, he didn't want to leave his girlfriend
and her parents, who had been like a second family to him. But
he felt that his home life was intolerable. He had to leave. He
departed for the farmlands of northern California in the spring,
before he graduated from the ninth grade. He would be in time
for spring planting and for the harvest of the winter wheat. He
figured he would be able to get work easily before the flood of
summer workers came.

But it was 1952, one of the worst winters for the logging
camps. Many loggers had come into the area looking for work.
And there were the hobos who had also come. Leonard joined
them all in a camp while they waited for the crops to be ready
for harvest. He hadn't brought much money, but he made some
friends among the loggers and hobos.

I didn't have blankets. The nights were very cool. We were
sleeping in a hollow near a stream and the moisture seemed
to hang in the air. I was cold. One of the hobos took me
under his wing and told me to go to the butcher shop the
next day and get a big roll of paper and wrap myself in it
for a sleeping blanket. It worked. Unfortunately, all my
tossing around at night and the crackling of the paper sleeping bag kept some of the others awake. When I went into
town looking for work, they burned my sleeping bag in the
campfire. They all elected to share a part of their wraps
with me, so that night I had different shirts and pants to
roll up in.

I was rapidly running out of money, so my meals were
cut back to a cup of coffee and a quarter-pound candy bar
for breakfast, lunch, and supper. By the end of the second
week without work, it was a cup of coffee for breakfast and
supper and a candy bar for lunch. By the end of the third
week, I just had lunch.

Everyone wanted work. Everyone would do almost anything for money. But none of the townspeople really needed anything more done, and they couldn't afford to pay wages, either. All the wood had been cut, all the houses repaired, painted, and cleaned. The barns were clean and the weeds cut and the machinery repaired. And some fifteen thousand of us scoured the town for work.

Leonard watched the men shoot craps during the day, sometimes gambling with wages that they were yet to earn. He saw them wager clothing and services on a throw of the dice. He learned of a murder, which occurred when a big logger was caught cheating at dice. The logger was challenged by a small crop-worker with a fast knife. Leonard had watched as the logger's hand got pinned to the floor and the third die rolled out. He never saw the cheater again.

Those who broke the rules faced severe sanctions. In addition to punishing offenders within, outsiders who were not workers or friends of workers often were beaten and thrown out of the camp. But insiders who followed the rules found the camp to be a refuge. Although food was scarce, people shared what they had with others. And Leonard was safe; he was an insider.

Maybe because I was the only kid in camp, or maybe because I didn't beg, or maybe because I reminded them of themselves when they were younger, I was included. I learned to make stump coffee, hobo stew, dandelion tea, and grass soup. And I learned to trap my own game.

Finally the crops ripened and work was available. Life became easier and more relaxed in the camp. Soon, however, the father of Leonard's girlfriend tracked him down and insisted that he return to school. Leonard did extra work and was graduated with the rest of his classmates. He believes that the concern of his girlfriend's father and interest of his teachers in "salvaging a runaway" helped him complete that year of school.

Looking back on his experiences, Leonard saw more in the camp than a group of desperate men. He saw more than the gambling and the violence. He saw the sharing and the care, even as men hung near the edge of desperation. He absorbed his surroundings, reflected on them, and grew.

> My hobo days are always with me. I learned about the rules that one society makes inside of another society. Without this watershed experience, I would not have tolerance for the needy people of the world today. I would not be involved in organizations to end world hunger. I would never have tried to understand peoples of other countries—and even other corporate cultures.
>
> I have had the opportunity to live in different strata of society during my lifetime. As an American migrant worker, as part of the poor working class, and later as an upper-middle-class businessman, I have seen the world through different eyes. My intolerance of my family's social status really colored my views of the world. I might have been a thief or a robber, using force, stealth, and strength to get my ways had I not seen that individuals in hunger and poverty still have honor.

Active seeing turned a potentially negative experience into a positive watershed for Leonard. It can also turn a potentially trivial experience into a positive watershed. Derek is the president of an airline, an executive who speaks and smiles with self-assurance. He thought a few moments about watersheds in his life, then said: ''The one that is uppermost in my mind is giving up cigarettes. I smoked from the time I was eleven until I was thirty-five. Quitting affected more than my health. I am literally a changed person.''

A seemingly trivial incident in which Derek practiced active seeing provided the stimulus for his decision to quit. Derek and his wife had just moved into a new home. They were invited to the neighbors' for a get-acquainted drink. The neighbor was a chain smoker who talked rapidly and nervously; his conversation was punctuated by deep coughs. But he was a highly successful businessman, an interesting person, and a living storehouse of jokes. Derek and his wife returned home in high spirits.

But I kept re-creating the scene—partly to enjoy the laughs again, but also to watch him in my imagination as he puffed and fidgeted and coughed. I couldn't get that picture out of my mind. Over the next week, I would see him every time I lit up. He became the mirror of my future—that was me in a few years.

Ten days after the visit, Derek threw away his remaining cigarettes. He has not smoked since. He feels that his life is much different because of it.

For a long time, I would quit and then start up again. I was able to see my personality change back and forth. As a nonsmoker, I am much more relaxed, calmer, much more in touch with my emotions, and an all-around healthier person.

After I quit, I even became a better tennis player, winning more than I lost—a real change in my performance. I could concentrate on my game instead of my need for a cigarette. Smoking had affected almost every part of my life, just as quitting has affected almost every part. Literally, I am a new person.

Derek took a relatively insignificant event—a drink with new neighbors in a new environment—and used active seeing to turn it into a positive watershed. His experience underscores the power of active seeing, which can transform the trivial as well as the dramatic into a time of growth.

11

Growing by Choosing

According to the Greek historian Herodotus, the Persians had a definite procedure for making important decisions. They would discuss the matter while they were drunk. The next day they would reconsider their decision after they were sober. They also used the reverse process, and made the initial decision while sober and the reconsideration while drunk. In either case, they had to agree with the decision under both conditions before finalizing it.

Although Herodotus is not known for his infallible accuracy in recording history, the story underscores the sense we all have that important decisions should be made with caution. That is, how they are arrived at is of critical importance. Many watersheds discussed in this book involve decisions of one kind or another. However, the watersheds that we are concerned with here are those in which people said that the decision-making process itself was the significant experience.

TO GROW IS TO CHOOSE

We do not grow by default. Nor do we grow by playing it safe and hoping that all will turn out well. We grow (or fail to grow) because of the decisions we make. Those decisions may come in response to some external event or experience. Or they may be a result of some internal process, such as trying to reach a new plateau in one's life or following one's own inclinations.

David Hartman, until recently the host of ABC-TV's *Good Morning America*, prepared himself in college for the corporate world. After graduation, he served a tour a duty in the Air Force. He was in charge of a Strategic Air Command computer system. One of the things he discovered was his dislike of putting on a tie and going to a desk to work every day. He also disliked working in an organization in which he had to follow the orders of others. In other words, if his military experience was any indication, he had trained to work in a world that he would not find fulfilling, the world of business. Nevertheless, a few months before his discharge, he accepted a job with a large corporation. That, after all, was what he was prepared to do.

His life took a different direction when his roommate suggested that since they both loved show business, they should go into that instead. Hartman was struck by the idea. He had the inclination and he had the aptitude. He played six different musical instruments. He had been involved in choral music in his school days. In his third year at the university, he worked part-time as a radio and TV announcer. And, most important, he had enjoyed it all immensely.

Hartman reflected on his parents' admonition to him to find work that he would enjoy. He realized that it was the security rather than the enjoyment that attracted him to the corporate job. He decided to forego the security and start over on a different and uncertain career. It was a decision that was necessary for him to grow, to become his own person.

Usually such a decision is a response to both internal and external factors. For example, Carl is a self-made millionaire, an entrepreneur who has succeeded in a variety of business ventures. He has been successful at most things he has attempted in his life, but his watershed occurred because he was dissatisfied with one of his careers. "I've always loved business," he said in his rapid-fire manner of speaking,

> and I've always loved teaching. So I combined the two in my first real career. I got my D.B.A. and began teaching at a state university. I taught well, did my research, published fairly much, and rose in the ranks. I became an associate professor in the matter of a few years. And then a combination of things changed my life.
>
> First, I became increasingly disenchanted with academic

life. The students were fine. But the faculty in my department was basically a group of isolates. In faculty meetings, there was no camaraderie, no sense that we were a group of like-minded people pursuing similar interests. And no one seemed to care much what the others were doing. Each faculty member was greatly interested in what he or she was researching and greatly uninterested in what anyone else was doing. I considered trying to move to a different school. But something else was gnawing at me.

I was researching successful innovators and writing about them. And I kept thinking to myself that I could do what they were doing. The financial payoff would be tremendous. I would miss teaching, of course, but I surely wouldn't miss my detached colleagues. I decided to hold off on trying to move elsewhere until I knew what I really wanted to do with my life.

Carl's dissatisfaction with the atmosphere of his department and his unfulfilled aspirations for achievement in the business world itself were the internal factors at work. Then an external factor appeared that led to his decision. A franchise fair was held in his city. He attended it, not to consider buying one of the franchises but to see the extent to which innovative ideas were presented. Carl stopped to chat with a salesman who was representing a company franchising wallpaper outlets. Then he began criticizing the operation, pointing out certain areas in which the company needed to improve its approach. The salesman listened politely until a few people gathered around and listened to Carl's critique.

I loved it. I had an impromptu class. So I started to give them a lecture. But the salesman got agitated when he saw the others listening carefully to what I was saying. He interrupted me and asked one question: "How many successful companies have you owned?"

"I'm a university professor," I shot back at him. "I teach this stuff."

He just snickered and said, with obvious sarcasm in his voice, "I believe you." I noticed some smiles on the faces of the others and they dispersed before I could get my lecture going again.

Carl was humiliated and angered. But more than that, the incident spurred him to a decision.

> I stalked out of there determined to show them that I knew what I was talking about. It was five miles, but I walked all the way back to my apartment, thinking about what I would do now. By the time I reached the apartment, I had my plans formulated. I would have to resign my university position at the end of the year. Meanwhile, I would start my business, make it successful, and franchise it out. That's the way to make money. Get your own ideas and sell them. Don't buy into someone else's idea.

Carl opened a combination bookstore and coffee shop. It was an innovative idea. The enterprise succeeded, and he successfully franchised it to others. The following year he branched out into other ventures, always striving to be innovative. Franchising has paid off for Carl. But the decision to leave the university and plunge into the world of business was not easy. He still misses teaching. It took courage to resign a tenured position and take on the risks of a new business. Watershed decisions are not necessarily easy to make. But on the other side of that decision-making process there is the promise of a new life.

Is "new life" too strong a metaphor? Can a crucial decision make that significant a change in us? Not always, of course. But those who grow by choosing, those who have experienced watershed decisions, tell us that the outcome is frequently a dramatic change. Moreover, the change is not just a result of the kind of decision made, but of the very fact of making a crucial decision. In our early years, we necessarily lean on others to make decisions for us. If we are to continue growing, we must learn to make decisions on our own. The consequence can be a whole new perspective on life.

Pam, a young investment banker, found herself in a crucial decision-making situation when she was twenty. She was a junior in college, majoring in biology. She hoped to go to veterinary school, her goal since she was a child. Pam's love of animals continues; in fact, her dog and cat competed for her attention as she told us of her personal turning point.

> I never even thought about doing anything with my life other than treating sick animals. But in my junior year I faced a crisis. I went into biology knowing that the next step of getting into veterinary school would be extremely difficult. I just assumed that everything would work out the way I wanted it to. Some of the science and math courses weren't too bad. Others were so beyond me that I don't know how I made it through.
>
> At first, I tried to ignore the growing anxieties about my ability to complete the increasingly difficult coursework. I refused to think seriously about the situation for fear that I might find out something I didn't want to know. One characteristic of my personality at that time was that once I made a choice, I did not change my mind. I equated changing my mind with a show of weakness.

But then she had to enroll in a physics course. Pam had no trouble with courses in English, literature, sociology, and psychology. She had done well in her other science courses, even when she had to struggle. But physics was her Waterloo. She could not grasp it. She could no longer avoid dealing with the issue, either, for she was failing the course. Her feelings at the time, she recalled, could only be labeled as "terror."

> I had left myself only one option, and it was slipping away from me. I started having nightmares—death, cadavers, and someone squeezing my ribs until I couldn't breathe. Finally, I tried to analyze the situation as though I were somebody else. I realized then how dumb and stubborn I had been. I was like a cat insisting on being a dog. It would never happen.
>
> So I started to think about the possibility of changing my major to business. I talked to my friends. I began to like the idea of a change for myself. I started to experience both feelings of excitement and peace inside. And to my sur-

prise, the final obstacle of telling my parents was met with their support and concern.

Pam sees the situation now as one in which she had more alternatives than she believed at the time. She realizes that she could have been tutored in physics and passed the course. But, she said,

> I believe I was at a turning point in my life where I needed to make a change. There is the possibility that I would have made it on the path I had chosen. But suddenly new possibilities were opening up to me. Something inside was pushing me to make a change. For so long my head had been telling me which way to go. This decision resulted in my learning to listen to my heart.

Pam occasionally wonders what her life would be like if she had continued on in her determination to be a veterinarian. But she is content with the decision she made. She realized later that the experience was a true watershed for her, because she was no longer terrified about making choices.

> I began to meet choices and changes with the attitude that just about anything was open to me. It led me to greater introspection. It helped me to start being an adult instead of my parents' little girl. I began to shift from living up to what I perceived to be their expectations for me to living up to my own expectations. By taking control over what I wanted for myself, my expectations began to be more realistic. My thinking became more flexible. I no longer felt the need to hold so tightly to a decision. I could laugh at myself.

For Pam, the decision to shift her career aspirations meant a great deal more than a change in the kind of work she would do. It gave her a new perspective on herself. "I began to believe that we can find value in any choice we make," she explained. "I discovered what it means to be free." Independent of the content of the choice we make about something, the very act of making an autonomous decision can be a watershed experience.

Of course, the content is not unimportant. Not every decision-making experience has the potential for being a watershed. The decision must involve something that the individual regards as significant in his or her life. The most common kind of decision-making occurrence reported as a watershed was one dealing with work or career. People talked about a variety of other decision-making experiences, ranging from becoming a vegetarian to stopping smoking to bringing suit against the board of directors of a condominium complex. But most commonly, the occasions of decision-making that people reported as watersheds involved work and career.

There is good reason why people regard work and career decisions as significant. A good part of life is spent at work of one kind or another. Work therefore is a crucial element in our well-being. People who lose their jobs frequently experience stress. For more than a hundred years in this country, the rates of admission to mental hospitals have gone up during times of economic depression and subsided during times of prosperity. When unemployment goes up, suicide rates and death from certain ailments such as cardiovascular disease and cirrhosis of the liver also go up. People who are unemployed are more prone to depression, anxiety, aggression, insomnia, and marital problems.

Unfortunately, working in undesirable conditions or an unfulfilling job can also be stressful. Heart disease, migraine headaches, peptic ulcers, and hypertension are all associated with stressful working conditions.

Ted is a good example of someone whose watershed experience involved a decision about a career that was stressful. His enthusiasm as he talks about his life now is in striking contrast to the frown that clouds his face as he discusses his first career. In his thirties Ted was the manager of a West Coast company dealing in medical technology. He had risen to his position in a matter of four years. But there was a price to pay.

I had sacrificed everything for success, or for what I thought was success at the time. I had no outside interests. My wife was contemplating divorce. I had traveled forty-five weeks during the previous year. My children did not like for me to come home. I was entirely detached from the world and lived and died by the technology. I could not understand why my family was so unimpressed with the way that I was so wonderfully successful. I knew that it was only a matter of a few months until all my work would bring me great financial rewards. It was at that point that I learned that the company was being sold to a British firm that had no desire to conduct business in the U.S.

The sale of the company jolted Ted from his blind rush to financial success. His whole perspective on life was shaken. Like many Americans, he had thought of himself in terms of his work. His identity and his worth as a person had been tied to his success in business. Fortunately, he had the inner resources necessary to rethink his views. As he did, he saw things in a new light.

I had spent a long time denying everybody that was close to me and alienating myself from all aspects of a normal life. I had deferred all living to after we reaped the rewards from my hard work. Now, without warning, there would be no rewards—which, as it turned out, might not matter, because the way I was going, there wouldn't be any family either. What good is a fat paycheck when you bring it home to an empty house? The realization hit me—helped by my wife's assessment of our life—that I had made a terrible mistake. Not only had I lost my career, but I was on the verge of losing my family.

Ted realized that he had to attend to one matter immediately: his career. Whatever the outcome of his marriage and family, he had to have a job. His options were to accept a position in London, find a similar job with another firm, or take a job as a salesman with a new and different kind of company. For the first time in years, he used considerations other than income to make his decision.

My main concern was to salvage my marriage and family. In discussing the opportunity in London, it became apparent that if I accepted the position I would go alone. That choice was out. If I were to accept a similar position here, I would once again travel extensively. That was out. I saw at the time only one option, which was to accept a position as a local salesman.

Unfortunately, Ted found it was more difficult to find such a job than he thought. Every interview led to an offer to do something similar to what he had left. After three months of unemployment, he was in serious financial trouble. It was time for drastic action. Ted decided to go back to college in the fall. He found summer work as a lifeguard in Los Angeles to help support his family. And a camper in the parking lot on the beach became their temporary home.

In spite of the uncertainties and financial problems, the summer on the beach was "the most enjoyable summer of our lives," according to Ted. But school was starting, and they had to find a place to live. Ted and his wife found an apartment, put their three sons in one bedroom, took one for themselves, and also used it for an office. Finally, he contracted to do market research for a local company. By the time he finished the project, he had decided to become an independent market researcher and to attend school part-time. "One morning in September," he recalls, "my business was started on a card table in the bedroom of our apartment."

After some difficult times, Ted has once again become a successful businessman. But he did not gain success at the expense of his family this time. His home life is going well. And he has a new element in his philosophy of life: "Never allow a company or anything else to dictate the quality of your life." Deciding for himself was a major turning point in Ted's experience.

THE POWER OF CHOOSING

When we make our own choices (rather than allowing parents or a spouse or our friends to choose for us), we are using a powerful tool that will further our own growth. There is power in choosing, because crucial decisions open up unexpected doors. But, as the case of Pam demonstrates, the process itself often produces results that we do not anticipate. Pam thought she was merely changing career lines when she gave up her plan to become a veterinarian. She did not realize that her willingness to make the decision would also open the door to greater freedom for her—that the very act of making a decision would accelerate her growth.

Freedom is one of the positive consequences of choosing. We use freedom here in a twofold sense, both as increased autonomy and as liberation from a burden. For many people, the freedom that comes from choosing is similar to that experienced by Pam—a new sense of autonomy, a sense of being in control and of being able to fend for oneself in the world. The discovery of such personal power is exhilarating.

Consider the experience of Sarah, who was graduated from college in the mid-1970s. Sarah is a cheerful, red-haired woman who admittedly "frets too much about everything." On graduation day, which occurred just one year after her wedding, she took her diploma and then confronted an unsettling fact: she was "in that condition which so personifies the traditional woman—pregnant." Sarah agonized over what she should do.

At once I was thrust into the eternal debate of working mother versus loving homebound mother. And while I rode a continual emotional elevator in a futile attempt to resolve the issue, there was no doubt, at least as far as my conscience was concerned, as to which side in the debate would prevail.

Sarah felt that she had no choice but to stay at home and care for her baby. But she also feels that society doesn't reward such a choice.

Motherhood seems to be an anomaly of life. For example, whenever you are introduced to someone, invariably one of the first questions you are asked is, What do you do? Motherhood doesn't qualify as doing. Just about the only justifiable doing is hauling the kids to Little League and accompanying your husband to company functions. As more evidence of motherhood's flirtation with oblivion, I was quite often referred to only as Karl's mother or Bert's wife.

Sarah spent ten years fluctuating between frustration and anger, depression and blaming her husband and children for her feelings. Then she made the difficult decision to give in to her thirst for autonomy and enter the job market. Eventually she found a job in public relations handling the account of a real-estate developer. "My only regret," she says, "is that I didn't do it sooner." She finds that "nothing makes a person feel as significant and powerful" as earning one's own income. Moreover, feeling more powerful and autonomous has enhanced her relationships with her family. Frustration no longer prods her into lashing out at them. Becoming more autonomous has not separated Sarah from others; rather, it has given her the sense of personal power that she needs in order to fulfill her responsibilities to her family more cheerfully.

In other words, becoming more autonomous doesn't mean becoming more isolated or aloof from the struggles and strivings of other people. Watershed experiences frequently do just the opposite. They give us the inner strength we need in order to "be there" in a meaningful way for others. They give us the inner resources we need in order to be sensitive to people's needs. This is what happened to Andy, a promoter of rock and jazz concerts. When Andy sat in a Boston chapel in 1978 questioning the meaning of life, he didn't realize that he was in the anguish of a transition that would ultimately make him both more self-reliant and more sensitive to others.

A balding, whiskered man in his late thirties, Andy has been through a number of careers. He was born and raised on an eastern farm. Like many other rural young men, he opted for work in the city. He became a manager of real estate. He also married, and for a time both his marriage and career were doing well. But Andy grew restless with his work. About the same time, marital problems developed. In 1974, his marriage ended. He made a clean break with his past by also leaving the property-management field. It was as if he had to get away from everything in that phase of his life.

In order to reconstruct his life, Andy decided to get into the promising discotheque industry. He began by opening a number of nightclubs. He worked with record companies and magazines to promote disco music. In less than a year, he was highly successful. But the president of the company that controlled the nightclubs made some decisions that led to financial disaster and to Andy's loss of a job. After eight months of unemployment, he convinced the owner of another discotheque that he could operate it successfully. He got the job. For a time, he was spectacularly successful. But increasing competition and decreasing demand led the owners eventually to close the disco. Andy had immersed himself in the job. Losing it was like the death of one's beloved.

As Andy sat in the Boston chapel, he realized that he was

a broken man with a broken spirit. I was suffering from battle fatigue and executive burnout, and there were no doctors to help me. I was in such a bad condition that my dad came to the city and took me home. He felt I needed time and the quiet of the farm to mend myself. I hated to leave the city. I was afraid that I would never see it again. But my father was right. The time on the farm was just what I needed.

Eventually, Andy found his way into the work of promoting concerts. The more he reflected on what had happened, the more he was convinced that there was some purpose to it. His road back began in that chapel experience. It was there that he raised questions about the meaning of his life. As he continued his reflections during the days on the farm, he decided to change his life. He became convinced that whatever he did in the way of work, he would always have to do something that would enrich the lives of others.

Andy regards himself as a kind of "wounded healer," one who has been through the fires of bitter disappointment and who thereby is equipped to help others who have similar experiences. Currently, he is back in the city promoting concerts. But there is a difference in his approach to work: "I don't work just for money anymore. Don't misunderstand," he added quickly. "I have nothing against money. But I won't put on a concert just to make a bundle. I only work with musicians that I believe make people feel better." Andy says that he can do this only because he himself learned to become self-reliant, to "find strength and courage within, to dare to dust off" after falling down, and continue.

Autonomy, a new sense of self-reliance that results in greater sensitivity to others rather than more isolation, is one aspect of the freedom that many people have experienced in their decision-making watersheds. The other aspect of freedom that comes from choosing involves the sense of a burden being removed from our lives. Peter, for instance, is a digital-network engineer in his thirties. Four years ago, Peter "came out": he openly admitted that he is a homosexual. When Peter was in high school and college, he dated women but he "longed to be intimate with other males." However, he felt guilty a good part of the time. He tried to suppress his feelings. He talked with a college counselor, but that left him feeling "only more confused and guilty." He entered adulthood still struggling with his feelings.

It was not until after he had established his own home that he came to terms with the issue. It happened one day in February, he recalls, when a heavy snow made traveling to work impossible. He sat in his apartment and reflected on his life. As he looked out the window, he saw his married neighbors in their front yard, laughing and playing in the snow. He envied their happiness. But his envy turned into grateful insight as he continued to watch them.

At first I thought to myself that I wished I was in his shoes. Then I said, You're just kidding yourself. You wouldn't want to be married to her. You're gay.

It was the first time I ever frankly admitted, even to myself, that I not only have homosexual feelings, but that I am gay and I want to be gay and I want to have relationships with men. I decided right there to accept that.

More than that, I decided to let other people, including my family and friends, know about it. I was tired of pretending it wasn't true. I wanted to have fun with someone I love just like my neighbors were enjoying themselves together.

Peter experienced an intense sense of relief. Even so, it was not easy for him actually to tell his family and friends. But once he did, he had a feeling that he describes as "liberation." He realizes that he could not have continued to grow without accepting and openly acknowledging his orientation. "Now," he says, "I feel joyful and free."

Less dramatic but equally liberating was the experience of Sam, a radiologist, who decided in his late twenties to lose weight. Sam remembers the exact date that he made the decision: March 24, 1983. He doesn't know why he made his choice on that date, only that he had been building up to it for some time. "Basically, I felt like hell. I felt that it was time for a change." He decided not only to lose weight, but to improve his appearance generally. He joined Weight Watchers, went to a clothing consultant, and started exercising. He feels "like a new man. And it's a funny thing, but I remember feeling better the moment I made the decision. I didn't have to wait until I actually started losing weight."

In addition to enhancing our sense of freedom, making important decisions typically builds our self-esteem. To make a choice and to act upon it is to assert control over our life. It is an expression of confidence in our ability to be discerning, rational, and active. As such, it naturally builds self-esteem.

The new level of self-esteem may not come easily. Once the decision has been made, the individual may be assaulted by self-doubts, by second-guessing friends, and by disapproving family. The doors opened by decision making rarely present us with a downhill path. If making the decision is difficult in the first place, following through with it may require considerable determination and courage.

Martin, a chemist in the research lab of a large corporation, came face to face with the consequences of decision making when he decided to go to graduate school. At the time, he had an excellent sales job with a nationwide pharmaceutical company. He had high income, great fringe benefits, security, and the promise of advancement. But he quickly tired of waiting for doctors to fit him and his wares into their tight schedules. He resented the demeaning way in which some of them talked to him. He was annoyed by the long hours he spent in his automobile. He wanted a new challenge.

Martin decided to resolve his problems and deal with his aspirations by going back to school, earning his Ph.D., and becoming a chemist. That's when he encountered his first problem. Martin's father thought his plan was totally irresponsible. He couldn't believe that Martin would throw away the financial security he had for a new career that might or might not work out. It wasn't easy to convince his father, but Martin was persuasive. Eventually his father agreed, reluctantly, with Martin's plan.

Martin returned to school with enthusiasm. He was in love with chemistry. And he soon fell in love with an undergraduate student. She finished her B.A. at the same time that Martin completed his qualifying exams. They decided to celebrate by getting married. Martin's father reminded him of the financial obligations of marriage and urged him to try to get his old job back. His urgings made no impact until Martin's wife unexpectedly got pregnant. Then the thought of a secure job with a high income beckoned Martin to leave his dream and take care of his responsibility as a husband and father.

But I couldn't do it. Selling drugs to doctors was just too limiting to me. There was something in me that prodded me on to complete my degree. I knew that I would never be satisfied if I quit school and gave up on my dream.

Martin's wife initially supported the decision to stay in school. But neither of them anticipated the financial problems they would encounter. Martin's stipend from the university was their sole source of income. It was barely sufficient. Martin was too proud to ask his parents, who could well afford it, for help. He wanted to demonstrate to his father that he could make it on his own. A crucial time came when his wife, weary of the endless chores of a new mother, suggested that they find a baby-sitter and go out to dinner.

I told her we couldn't afford it. She said we could afford a lot of things if I weren't so stubborn and would ask my dad for help. I told her that was out of the question. I couldn't ask my father to subsidize something he didn't even want me to do.

We argued for quite a while. I know now that it was a terrible time to have a fight. We were both tired. She was tired from mothering a cranky baby all day and I was tired from the demands of graduate school.

Unfortunately, they didn't resolve the matter. They kept sniping at each other. The thought of ending all the problems by quitting school and going back to the firm prodded Martin repeatedly. The fact that the thought came to him alternately seduced him and made him angry. When he got angry, the arguments with his wife intensified. After a few months of conflict, Martin's wife left him. Martin persisted in his quest.

I loved this woman and our child, but I also felt compelled to complete the journey that I began. In my mind, this was the final test of who I was and what I wanted to do with my life. During the next two years, I continued going to school, I started working part-time and summers, and I saw my son regularly. And, oddly, my wife and I seemed to grow gradually closer together even while we were separated. We seemed to be better able to recognize qualities in each other that we valued. We ended up getting back together just before I graduated.

Getting his Ph.D. was the "end of an arduous struggle" for Martin. He feels that it marked the "beginning of a new stage of development, one founded on increased self-confidence, maturity, and commitment to the future." Martin's decision led him on a path of growth, but the path was filled with obstacles along the way. It cost him much financial anxiety and nearly cost him his marriage, but Martin has no doubt about the appropriateness of his decision.

We have seen how self-esteem results from making an important decision and following through on it. But isn't it true that self-esteem is a necessary foundation for making such decisions rather than a result of making them? Aren't people inhibited from making decisions if they lack self-esteem?

It is true that people with a high level of self-esteem are more willing than others to make crucial decisions. But the relation between self-esteem and decision making works in both directions. For we have found that some people, apparently impelled from within by a yearning for growth, make decisions in spite of relatively low self-esteem. They emerge from the decision-making process with a new perspective on themselves. Their self-esteem is much higher, and that makes subsequent decision making far easier.

Consider the case of Phyllis, a retired naval officer who is now an engineer. In her early twenties, when she was a senior in a Colorado college, she made an unexpected and bold decision to respond to an ad. Doing so changed her life. Phyllis had changed majors in her junior year, from physical education to English. She had also applied and been tentatively accepted in the master's program in English. During the summer after her senior year, she planned to stay with a friend, work part-time, and study for the qualifying examination she would have to take to be fully accepted into the graduate program.

But when she asked her parents for some financial help, they told her they preferred her to return to their home in the East for the summer. Her father would get her a job as an editorial assistant, and she could make more money than she could from the part-time job she hoped to find. Phyllis couldn't do it.

In the first place, I was very unsure of my abilities. And I was terrified of getting a job as a result of my father's influence and failing at it. I had a definite inferiority complex. At this point, not knowing exactly where to turn, and desperately seeking another alternative, I received a brochure in the mail from the navy. I had always been interested in the navy. My cousin was in the naval reserve during World War Two and Korea. I investigated it and decided to apply.

Although she had not yet been accepted, Phyllis faced the difficult task of telling her parents of her decision. As she expected, they opposed it. But she said that she was only postponing her graduate work for two years while she served in the armed forces. They finally gave in and accepted her decision. In October of 1956, Phyllis entered officer's candidate school. Instead of two years, she spent the next twenty-five as a naval officer.

Reflecting back on her decision, she realizes that she chose what she believed at the time to be her only alternative. "I felt trapped in a situation over which I had no control," she says, "and I felt I could not cope with it. The navy offered adventure, excitement, new friends and experiences, and an opportunity to untie, finally, the apron strings of my parents."

There were, of course, other options. One of her professors had suggested that she apply to the Ph.D. program at Yale. But Phyllis had no confidence in her ability to succeed at an Ivy League school. Besides, that was the professor's plan for her, not her own plan. "Looking back," she notes,

> the strongest feeling I can remember is that of being trapped, of having someone else—my parents or my professors—choose the way I was going. I wanted to break out of that pattern. My problem was that I did not feel strong enough to make that break myself. So when the navy brochure arrived, I saw an alternative. I decided to let the navy make the break for me. I substituted the navy for my parents. But at least the navy was *my* choice.

Once in the service, Phyllis liked the work. She became interested in engineering and eventually the navy sent her to school to earn her master's degree in electronics engineering. She has no doubts about the appropriateness of her decision.

> I learned self-confidence. I gradually got rid of my inferiority complex. I was successful. I made a lot of friends, had many different experiences, got to travel, but, most importantly, I gained pride in what I was doing, and in myself, in what I was.

People who have developed higher levels of self-esteem are likely to be more accepting of others than those who have lower levels. An individual with high self-esteem has less need to manipulate others in order to protect himself or herself. Thus, it is not surprising, as the experiences of Sarah and Andy suggest, that another outcome of a watershed decision is better relationships with others. Having developed a greater sense of self-esteem as a result of making and following through with an important decision, a person is able to relate to other people more openly and helpfully.

The "other people" to whom a person can relate better includes family members. Of course, not every relationship is enhanced because of an important decision. As in the case of Martin and his wife, a relationship may suffer. Martin had a good relationship that degenerated to the breaking point, but he was able to rescue and restore it. Some people have the opposite experience. They make a decision that reverses the downward spiral of a deteriorating relationship.

Marcia, a sixty-year-old fashion designer, owns her own business. But only eight years ago, she was a bored housewife with an enduring but somewhat stagnant and unhappy marriage. Knowing that she had to make a change, she decided, at fifty-two, to go into business for herself. She had spent years making clothes for family and friends. Now, she decided, she could make a business out of it.

She began in her home, and with her friends. Success brought articles in the local paper and more clients than she anticipated. She needed a larger place to work. She rented a shop and now has a steady group of customers.

The decision led to a new relationship with her husband. Marcia had a stable but unexciting marriage. For three decades, she played the traditional wife and mother. After the children were all gone, however, she realized that she and her husband had crystallized their marriage around the children. Most of their conversation focused on the children. They had built a family but not a marriage.

When Marcia first announced her decision to her husband, he was taken aback. Why would she want to start a business at her age? What would friends and neighbors think about his ability to support his family? How could she carry on a business and still take care of the house? And above all, he was stunned that she presented him with a decision that had already been made instead of an idea that could be explored.

He was really perturbed, but I can see now that telling him afterward was the wisest thing I could have done. I shocked him right out of his shorts. If I had just discussed the matter with him, I would probably still be sitting at home all day. But when I told him I had already decided what I was going to do, I think he realized how little he knew the woman to whom he had been married for thirty years. I guess I didn't even know myself all that well. I sort of shocked myself by telling him what I was going to do instead of asking him to discuss it with me.

One of the unexpected results of Marcia's decision to start a business, she says, was "new insight into myself and my husband and our marriage. He battled me a long time over the business. But he has really come around. He even cooks some nights. For the first time in thirty years, we are living as friends who care about each other. Isn't that a miracle?" Marcia started her business to find new meaning in her life, to deal with her restlessness and boredom. She not only got new meaning, but also a new phase in her marriage.

As Marcia discovered, decision making is necessary for opening new doors. In his autobiography, Lee Iacocca asserted that decisiveness, the ability to make a decision and act on it, sums up the meaning of a good manager. It also sums up the character of the individual who grows.

12

The Techniques of Choosing

Some people make crucial decisions at a very early age. A. J. Foyt, the famed race-car driver, was only five when he decided to devote his life to the sport. From the time he was three, he had played in and driven a toy race car. He wore the car out in a couple of years, so his father, a mechanic who worked on race cars, built him a midget race car that would go fifty miles per hour. One night his father took him to a track in Houston where he was to drive the midget car around the track as a kind of opening ceremony. Even as a child, he knew that one car did not make a race. So he challenged one of the top drivers at the track. It was only after Foyt insisted, and his father consented, that the disbelieving driver agreed to a three-lap race in midget cars. Foyt won, and from that moment he committed his life to race cars.

A. J. Foyt became one of the nation's finest drivers. But it was a risky decision. What if he had failed? What if he had only been mediocre? What if he had gotten trapped by a childhood career decision that didn't bring him fulfillment as an adult? Decision making, at any age, is a risky business.

THE RISKS OF CHOOSING

There is a word, *abulia*, that means a strong inability or unwillingness to make decisions. Some psychologists think that the problem of abulia is widespread. If it is, perhaps one reason is that we almost instinctively recognize the risks of choosing.

Let's look at a few cases of people whose watershed decisions left them far short of the benefits they had expected.

In some cases, people experience negative outcomes simply because a decision sets off a chain of events that they did not anticipate. In other cases, however, the decision itself may be faulty. Terry, a forty-six-year-old sales manager for a shoe manufacturer, looks back on a crucial decision he made on a whim. It turned out to be a very bad decision. He was seventeen, contentedly living at home and attending high school. He was a good student and a second-string guard on the basketball team. He can recall no serious problems he had at the time. But his best friend told Terry one day that he was quitting school to join the marines. Impulsively, Terry replied that if his friend would join the navy instead, Terry would join with him.

"He agreed," Terry recalls ruefully.

He wanted fun and excitement. And it sounded exciting to me. The whim would have passed if we had waited. But we acted in the heat of the moment. And I have been dealing with it ever since.

I effectively crippled myself. I had planned on being a professional of some kind, maybe an engineer. Instead, after I got out of the navy I went from job to job. I've struggled to better myself, but it was the worst decision of my life. I've paid for it ever since.

Terry is financially successful now. He is an effective motivator and manager. But there is a void in his life, a yearning for what he missed. He is like the Hollywood waitress who is quick to tell customers: "I'm not really a waitress. I'm an actress." Unlike the waitress and the many others who yearn for more in their lives, Terry will probably live out his life with unfulfilled aspirations. Unfortunately, his parents allowed him to follow through on a significant decision that he made impulsively, and his rashness continues to rankle him nearly thirty years later.

If Terry made his decision rashly, Fran made hers blindly, without having adequate information. She is now thirty-seven, and the director of front-office operations for a resort hotel on the West Coast. Fran blushed slightly as she spoke of her watershed.

> I've always thought of myself as a rational woman with strong aspirations. But I did something really stupid when I was in my middle twenties: I fell in love.
>
> Actually, I fell into infatuation. We had a whirlwind romance of three weeks and one night at a party he asked me to marry him. Would you believe that I still didn't even know anything about his background? All I knew was that he was a good-looking guy with a good job and he seemed to be crazy about me.

On impulse, Fran agreed to the proposal and they were married two months later. At her husband's insistence, Fran got pregnant almost immediately. They had a son. And at her husband's insistence, she quit work to stay home and raise the child.

> I can't imagine myself doing all that. But I did. We had never talked about having children before we were married. You can imagine my surprise to discover that he wanted a very traditional wife who would bear him a large family and stay at home to care for them. I wanted children. And I love my son very much. But I didn't want to raise my own baseball team. And I didn't want to stop working.
>
> For the next few years I went on the pill. He didn't know. He wondered why I didn't get pregnant again. When he found out that I was taking the pill, he was furious. Our relationship deteriorated quickly after that and we were divorced.

Fran returned to work. And she feels she learned a valuable lesson: how to retain her rationality in her decision-making process.

> That was the one time I remember letting my feelings run away with me. I didn't bother to learn anything about him before we were married. At least, I didn't bother to learn

the important things, like what he expected in a wife and what he wanted out of marriage.

Overall, she regrets her decision.

I do have my son. But once I settled down and realized what I had gotten into, I was determined not to let my husband have his way anymore. Basically, I feel like I lost nearly five years of my life in that marriage.

Rash decisions. Blind decisions. They can leave an individual with long-lasting regrets. And so can starry-eyed decisions. Some people are idealistic to the point of being unrealistic about the consequences of a decision. That describes Jack, who also made a decision that was later regretted. Jack made his watershed choice in 1968, when the nation was embroiled in the Vietnam War.

At the time, it seemed like a necessary war to me. I had grown up in a home with very conservative and patriotic parents. My political opinions were largely influenced by a conservative attitude which dictated that nothing short of an American victory would satisfy true social justice. I was fully convinced that the only answer to the Vietnam issue was an unconditional victory by the United States. And I believed that until I was twenty-seven years old.
So I thought of my enlistment as a golden opportunity to perform my patriotic duty and fulfill my share of the citizenship bargain. The following summer I found myself going through basic training at Quantico, Virginia. Right after, I was sent to Vietnam.

Now a captain in the army, Jack has thought a good deal about the war and about his decision to enlist. But he still finds it difficult to assess the total impact of his decision.

By most standards, my life has been not only successful but happy as well. However, during the last four or five years—about the same time that I admitted to myself that our involvement in Vietnam was a major blunder—I have been less and less content with the course of my life.

It's difficult for me to conduct a realistic analysis of my discontent, but I suspect that a great part of it lies in envy. I find myself envious of my civilian counterparts, who seem to have far more alternatives in the conduct of their day-to-day lives.

The thought of resigning my commission began to enter my mind approximately three years ago. Since then, I've contacted a number of companies and received some favorable responses to my resumés. However, no one has been willing to start me at any position above the entry level of management.

The upshot of it is that I am faced with a major career dilemma. I can stay in the military, where I have established a solid reputation and I'm moving up in the ranks with no setbacks to date. Or I can start over at the same level as a newly graduated college student. I'm not real happy about either of those choices. But given the alternatives, I have decided to stay in my current position.

Jack now waits for the day when he can retire from the military. He thinks he'll have a better perspective on his watershed decision then. But at present he feels quite certain that he would have been happier and more satisfied with his life if he had remained a civilian and pursued a business career.

Is there any way to avoid making the kind of decisions that leave a residue of regret in their wake? No. We can't guarantee that. There are always risks to decisions. In 1981, David Stockman, the federal budget director under President Ronald Reagan, granted an interview that was published in *The Atlantic*. It was a risky thing to do. He embarrassed the Reagan administration by his forthright and detailed answers to questions. Eventually, Stockman resigned his position. The decision to give the interview may have been the turning point in his career in government.

Others in the world of politics have made decisions that almost seem, from an observer's point of view, to be self-destructive. President Richard Nixon's decisions about the Watergate break-in led inexorably to his resignation from office. It may have been, as his administration called it, a "third-rate burglary," but the decision to try to cover it up brought his presidency to an end. Similarly, Senator Gary Hart decided in 1987 to spend some time with an attractive model, first in Miami and then in Washington, D.C. He claimed innocence of any wrongdoing. Nevertheless, the ensuing publicity forced Hart, the front-runner for the Democratic presidential nomination, to retire from the race for several months.

Still, the answer is not to avoid choosing, for that will stagnate our growth. And even if we avoid rash, blind, and starry-eyed decisions, there is always the possibility that our hopes for fulfillment will be shredded into disappointment by unpredictable consequences. But there are ways to minimize the undesirable. There are ways to maximize the probability that the consequences of a decision will enhance our growth.

CHOOSING FOR GROWTH

Since decision making is so integrally tied up with growth, it is important to know how to make good decisions. Indeed, the multitude of decisions that we make during our lives, whether or not they are watershed experiences, have varied consequences. Some pain us. Some enrich us. The question is, how can we make good decisions, the kind that enhance our well-being?

There are a number of steps that enter into a good decision-making process. These steps will increase the probability of your making an appropriate choice in any situation. In essence, you must treat the decision-making process as a problem-solving exercise. Let us phrase the steps in the form of five questions for you to answer in sequence:

1. What is the problem?   Sometimes people attack a symptom rather than the real problem. If, for example, you are dissatisfied with your career and you try to soothe your discontent by indulging yourself in such things as a new car, a new home, or a new stereo system, you are only treating the symptom rather than the problem. An essential first step in any decision-making process is to decide the nature of the problem, and then to determine whether the problem is such that it really requires you to make a decision.

2. What is it that you want? What do you want to achieve? What are you looking for in a career? In your marriage? In your life generally? What are your standards? What are your priorities in life? With specific reference to the problem you have defined, what would you like to see happen?

3. What are your possible options? What choices do you have? Don't accept your inclination to think that you are trapped, that you have no alternative. There are always options. If the problem involves someone else, explore your various options with that person. If the problem is yours to resolve, ask a friend or relative to brainstorm with you about possible choices you can make.

4. How realistic are the options? Psychologists tell us to "reality-test" our ideas—that is, to think through the implications of each option. Is an action you are considering realistic? Will it help you achieve what you want? Are the possible benefits worth the costs of pursuing it?

Carefully evaluate each option before selecting one of them. It helps to write down a best-case and worst-case scenario for each option. With the best and worst possible outcomes before you, you may want to apply "the minimax principle": choose the option that best minimizes your possibility of loss while best maximizing your possibility of gain.

For instance, suppose you face two alternatives for investing money. One has the potential for a 10-percent gain and the risk of losing up to 20 percent of your investment. The other has the potential for a 30-percent gain and risk of total loss. The minimax principle directs you to take the first option, because the greater potential for loss that goes with the second one outweighs the relatively smaller gain available. Even if you have a great tolerance for risk and don't follow the minimax principle, it is at least wise to ponder the best and worst cases.

5. What will you do if the option you choose doesn't work? Before you make a final decision, always ask what could go wrong with each possible solution. Have a contingency plan in case things do go wrong with the option you choose. Then act upon your decision, but be prepared to pursue the contingency plan.

Important decisions should be made in the context of asking the above kinds of questions. But a decision-making process that enables us to grow involves more. The following thoughts and suggestions are based on the experiences of the people we interviewed about watersheds in their lives.

AFFIRM GROWTH

Base your decisions on the determination to experience personal growth. But don't we all prefer growth over stagnation? Isn't that a given?

Actually, we prefer to grow, but we don't necessarily prefer to face the uncertainty and pain of growing. And sometimes we may come face-to-face with what Freud called the death instinct and find ourselves in a self-destructive process. Paula, a forty-two-year-old divorced mother of two children, had her watershed experience in a confrontation with her own self-destructive tendencies.

Paula is an artist for a mail-order company. Seemingly, she had everything life has to offer. Although she had experienced a stressful marriage that ended in divorce, she had good relations with her parents, her siblings, and her two children. Her watershed began shortly after the divorce, when she became seriously ill.

> I had always thought of myself as indestructible. In my family, with its German heritage, we learned to bear up under our problems without complaining. So I had a tendency to downplay illness.

This time, however, Paula clearly had a problem. The doctor diagnosed it as an infected gall bladder and she was rushed to surgery. That didn't end her medical difficulties, however.

> My recovery was extremely slow and further complications developed. I began to experience a great deal of leg pain, but I only weakly referred to it when visited by the doctors

or nurses. The pain didn't stop when I got home. One day I looked down and saw that one leg was swollen twice the size of the other one and it was purple. It turned out that I had a major thrombosis in my left calf, and a stubborn case of phlebitis.

I returned to the hospital and once again became the good patient. I stoically lay flat, took my medications, and tried to adjust to being strapped down to a warm pack on one leg and having a constant I.V. on the other side. But I didn't get any better.

The change in my condition, my watershed, occurred when the specialist returned on the tenth day of his treatment program. He was alarmed that I wasn't responding and confronted me with my will to live. Or rather, the lack of it.

I realized that he was right: I was flirting with death. I was at a low point in my life. Indestructible Paula, whose marriage was shattered, was flat on her back with one serious illness after another. My self-esteem was devastated by it all. So I was killing myself. And I didn't even realize it until the doctor pointed it out to me. It was right then that I made the decision. I decided to live! In three days, I had recovered enough to go home. In two weeks, I was back at work.

Paula has never been incapacitated since that time. Her decision to affirm life involved a determination to quit being the passive victim she had become after her divorce. The physician had startled her into a realization of the downward spiral into which she had blindly fallen. But she had to make the decision to reverse the process. She had to decide whether to change or allow events to control and suppress her. She chose life and growth.

BE WILLING TO TAKE RISKS

There are always risks in decision making. The minimax principle gives you one way to handle the risks, but it does not eliminate them. Robert Frost portrayed the dilemma of making decisions in his poem "The Road Not Taken." When we come to a fork in our travels, he pointed out, we must decide which way to go. We can't have it both ways. We would like to know what is on both paths, but we must choose one or the other. And our choice will make a significant difference for the rest of our days. So, the risk cannot be eliminated. You cannot know whether the well-traveled or less-traveled road will bring the greatest fulfillment. You only know that you must choose one of them.

Indeed, it wouldn't even be desirable to get rid of risk, for frequently it is risk that pays off large dividends. Entertainer Mary Martin's career took off after a Sunday-night talent show at a New York nightclub. She sang two numbers. One was "Il Bacio." Because the aria was "so grand," she tended to giggle in the middle every time she sang it. To hide that, as well as to have some fun, she had turned the middle part into a jazzed-up rendition. On this night she made the risky decision to do her version—at a time when no one else had even thought about swinging the classics.

She began in the traditional fashion. The room was very quiet as she sang in her best operatic voice. Then she launched into her jazzy version. She finished to a standing ovation and a new career. She took the less-traveled road, and the risk paid off. She could have taken the more-traveled way and sung the aria in a conventional manner. That would have been a risk also; her rise to fame could have been delayed or taken a much different route.

There is another sense in which we need to be willing to take risks. At times, the decision that is needed may involve breaking with the present rather than plunging into the future. That is, there may be no goal in sight, no known door to open, no particular alternative that is beckoning. Rather, there may only be an oppressive present from which we need to be liberated.

Sheila, a registered nurse in her forties, is a stocky blonde who looks as though she could tough out anything. She got a chance to try when she was thirty-six. At the time, she was in a fifteen-year-old marriage that was troubled. Her husband wanted an open marriage, with each spouse free to have sexual relations with others. Sheila had no desire for such a marital arrangement.

In addition to her marital problems, Sheila was facing physical and professional difficulties.

I had surgery, a large tumor removed, which left me with physical limitations and a tendency to tire more easily than previously. I knew I was not able to have the physical stamina to do bedside nursing as I was then doing. I had to face the reality that I needed a job that could support me financially. I had enough personal pride that I did not want to be dependent on my husband.

Sheila found a new position that seemed to be ideal: she would educate hospital staff members in physical rehabilitation. Soon after she took this job, the head nurse retired. A new head nurse had experience in rehabilitation and decided that she could train her own personnel. Sheila's position was eliminated. She was then offered, and took, the position of supervisor of an alcohol rehabilitation in-patient unit at the hospital. Her problems began immediately.

I was particularly concerned with patient safety on the unit. I couldn't get standard safety equipment until a patient convulsed and almost died. I was given a very low nurse-to-patient ratio. I would staff my unit for twenty-four-hour coverage, but since the staff nurses were hospital employees, they could be used elsewhere if needed. The alcohol unit was not perceived as needing much help, because the patients were not really "sick." Two Saturday nights in a row, I received a phone call at nine P.M. telling me that my unit nurse was needed in Intensive Care, where the patients were "sick." This left an unlicensed nurse's aid as the only staff member on duty.

There were patients in the detoxification stage of rehabilitation, and, fearing for their safety, I went in and worked the unit myself. This was on top of the already long hours I was putting in during the day. (I was only compensated for forty hours, by the way.) I made repeated requests to the administration for a safer staffing ratio, but was totally ignored, except for building a reputation of being unreasonable. This went on for five months, until the week that I put in ninety-three hours' work.

It was the ninety-three-hour workweek that finally brought the situation to a head. Sheila could no longer cope with the unrealistic demands and responsibilities of the position. Instead, she submitted her resignation to the director of nursing. She had to be able to support herself, but she had no job lined up. She didn't even have an idea of what she would do. But she knew that she had to extricate herself from the hospital.

For a short time, as she searched in vain for a job, Sheila feared that she had made a terrible mistake. Finally, she found a position managing the medical unit of a retirement home. It was, and still is, very satisfying to her. Even eight years later, she can see the value of her risky decision.

But that isn't to say that it wasn't a scary decision. I didn't know what the future held; I only knew that I had to get out of that job. It was physically and emotionally killing me. . . . Both my personal and professional integrity demanded drastic action. And fortunately, the risk paid off with a position that I love.

TRUST YOUR CAPACITY TO REDEEM A BAD CHOICE

What if you take a risk and the outcome falls short of your expectations? Or what if the decision turns out to be a disaster? Then you have to trust in your capacity to redeem the situation by another choice. To twist the words of Tennyson a bit, 'tis better to have chosen and lost than never to have chosen at all. It is better to find that some of your decisions were not the best than to sink into the stagnation of letting others make decisions for you. Indeed, it is probable that you will make some bad decisions, or some decisions that lead to results other than those for which you had hoped. The point is, you must trust your capacity to deliver yourself from the unwanted consequences of those decisions.

When Bruce finished school with his bachelor's degree in

business administration, he was sure he had an edge on other people. It was 1981, and he wanted to go directly into management. Trained, tanned, and healthy-looking, Bruce was confident that he would succeed at anything he tried. "I thought of myself as God's gift to women and business," he says. He decided to go into the restaurant business.

The philosophy I used was that of the big fish in the small pond. Almost no one in the restaurant field, including high-level managers, has a college degree. Thus, I thought it would be easier to move up quickly into management. I got my first job at a fast-food restaurant and then moved to a national restaurant corporation as a management trainee.

The job was absolutely terrible. I had to work long hours—sixty to seventy hours a week—dealing with employees who were very different socially and who viewed the world differently from me. Most of the employees were shortsighted and did not give much thought to long-range goals.

And to top it all off, my only contact with customers was when they had a complaint. The food was burned, or it took too long to cook, or it was the wrong order. That kind of thing gets you down after a while, especially when you don't have co-workers with whom you can share your annoyances.

In addition to other problems he encountered, Bruce found the high rate of turnover to be unsettling. He constantly had to deal with new employees and different managers. Moreover, the longer he was in the job, the more pressured he felt. As he became more efficient, his work load was increased. And he never liked the constant juggling of multiple tasks such as ordering, cooking, cleaning, and supervising. He preferred to work on one thing at a time and do it thoroughly.

Clearly, Bruce was in the wrong occupation. He stayed with it for a year before he finally changed direction.

I thought long and hard about where I had been and where I was going. I saw myself as either continuing what I was doing, with the constant stress and fatigue, or getting out of this field entirely into something else that would be enjoyable. The decision was easy. Becoming an old man at forty years of age wasn't very appealing. I made the decision to get out.

Almost precisely at the time that Bruce decided to leave, he saw an ad for a marketing manager in an electronics firm. He had majored in marketing, so he applied and got the job. He loves his new work. His brief stint in the restaurant field was a "bad experience," he says, but it led to something good. He is happy now that his earlier work made him so distraught. Had it been even minimally acceptable, he might have stayed with it and missed something much better.

If the restaurant job had worked out, it is conceivable that I might never have gone into marketing. And that is the field that I really love. That's my niche. I don't care about being a big fish or a little fish anymore. I just want to work at something that I find fulfilling. The restaurant job was a watershed that pointed me in the right direction for my life.

DON'T LIMIT YOUR CAPACITY TO CHANGE

There are some folk sayings that suggest limits to how much people can change: "You can't teach an old dog new tricks." "Can a leopard change its spots?" On the other hand, there are numberless therapists and advice columnists who offer the promise of quick and relatively easy change. From the brief counsel of Ann Landers to the promise of a California therapist that you can stop smoking in sixty minutes, we are told again and again that we can change our ways.

In between the pessimistic sayings and the offerings of instant relief, there is the fact that people do change. We break old habits. We acquire new skills and improve old skills. We learn new and better ways to relate to people. We take a class and become more assertive. We enter therapy and learn to overcome neuroses. We get into a small group and develop more self-confidence. We shift directions in our careers.

Sometimes we decide to change ourselves at a remarkably young age. One man told us that as a young boy he was shy, withdrawn, and insecure. But just before he was to enter the eighth grade, the family moved to a different town. At this point, rather than being intimidated by the new situation, he made a conscious decision to be outgoing, friendly, and confident. He decided that because no one knew him at the new school, it would be a good opportunity to break out of his old pattern. As a result, he became one of the more popular boys in his class. And he believes that his present personality is a result of this change.

Another man, Bob, a middle-aged loan officer for a mortgage company, related a similar decision to change his personality.

When I was younger, I was sarcastic and temperamental. When we would play football, I screamed at my teammates when they made a mistake. I was the angry one. Then one day a friend pointed out that I was acting in a very obnoxious manner. He did it kindly, almost as a parent who was hoping that I could be different. His gentle admonition was like a mirror in which I saw myself clearly for the first time. Not only did I see myself, but I didn't like what I saw.

I decided right then that this was not the kind of person I wanted to be. I decided to change. And I did. I learned to control my temper and to choose my words more carefully. I did it by reminding myself every day of the kind of person I wanted to be. Sometimes, I had to practically bite my tongue, but I refused to give in to my impulses.

I am now seldom sarcastic about anything. And my friends regard me as an even-tempered guy. I think we have a lot more control over the kind of people we become than most of us realize.

If we really want to, and if we choose to, we can make changes in our lives, our habits, our attitudes, and our patterns of interaction. It is important not to allow our choices to be constrained by the belief that we are hemmed in by inflexible boundaries that limit the amount we can change.

BE WILLING TO CONSIDER THE UNUSUAL

If one way to stifle personal growth is to put limits on how much we can change, another way is to put limits on what kind of change we will pursue. When considering options, it is well to avoid a knee-jerk rejection, a dismissal out-of-hand of something because we think it is unrealistic, impractical, or too bizarre. To maximize the possibility of your growth, be willing to consider all possibilities. At least give them the benefit of thinking them through.

Is it possible, for example, that the best decision is one that initially seems contrary to common sense and goes against the advice of others? Norman, an articulate and vigorous man in his early thirties, believes that the answer is yes. Against the advice of his parents and his friends, and contrary to his usual pattern of behavior, Norman left a job for which he had trained for eight hard years. He had worked at the job for only a few months when he made the decision to leave.

My parents could hardly believe me when I talked to them about it. My friends told me I just needed a vacation. There I was, a Ph.D. in biology working in a research lab. It was the fulfillment of a lot of years of hard work. And to most of the people I know, it seemed that I was blithely chucking it all away and taking a job that had nothing to do with all those years of training.

Norman left the lab to work as the director of a consumer advocacy group. He got the job through a college friend. Neither his parents nor his friends could understand why he would toss aside his career in research so quickly. Actually, the decision had been building in him for some time. It was the day of what he called "the Big Kill" that helped him make the final break.

I've always loved animals. At first, I didn't mind the animal research because it was all with rats. But believe it or not, I even began to get attached to them. I was the only one in the lab who would pet them before lopping their heads off.

Researchers in the adjacent lab were using dogs for their experiments. During my break, I would sometimes go over and play with them. I was really miserable. And my misery intensified as the day of the Big Kill approached. We had to slaughter a whole batch of rats that day to complete a set of experiments. The more I thought about spending an entire day killing rats and removing some of their brain tissue, the more I felt a sense of revulsion.

I wound up calling in sick that day. I let the lab assistants handle it.

Norman isn't opposed to animal research. He knows it produces a great many benefits for people. "It has to be done," he says. "It's just that I can't do it." Fortunately, Norman had an alternative. As his concerns about his future research had increased over the months, he had shared his feelings with a friend from college who was a national director of the consumer group. His friend had offered him a position with the organization. The day after the Big Kill, Norman called and accepted.

I told my other friends I would be making just as much money as I had at the lab, and would probably earn more in a few years. "But you have a Ph.D.," they said. "You mean you're not going to use your degree anymore?" I told them: "I don't know. Maybe I'll be able to use it some way. If not, it doesn't matter. It isn't as important as my peace of mind."

I don't think I've ever done anything like that before, something that my parents and all my friends thought was stupid and self-defeating. But every time I pass that lab I'm grateful I had the courage to leave. Three years ago, I was a down-hearted researcher. Today I'm a happy consumer advocate.

Norman is sure that it was not only the right but the most beneficial decision he could have made. And that should be the focus of decision making. What matters is not whether we choose something that is "normal," or that most people would choose or prefer. What matters is that we choose options that help us to grow, regardless of how unusual they may be.

PURSUE YOUR OWN DREAM, NOT THAT OF YOUR PARENTS

Unknowingly, many people pursue a dream that is not really theirs. Our parents have dreams for us. And sometimes their dreams persist even if we don't share them. Television news commentator Ted Koppel is Jewish and is married to a Roman Catholic woman. His wife's mother was not happy with the union; it was not in accord with her dream of a husband for her daughter. After twenty years of marriage, Koppel's wife pointed out to her mother that the marriage had worked out better than she had expected. The mother simply replied, "Only time will tell."

We do not like to disappoint our parents. But it is a mistake to make decisions based on a dream created for us by them. Unfortunately, some people do not realize what they are doing until someone jars them into awareness. Adam, a building contractor, told us that his parents planned on his being a lawyer from the time he was a little boy. It was not until he was married, had experienced rejection by a number of top law schools, and had had his wife confront him with the reason for his behavior that he realized what was happening in his life. He was mechanically filling out applications to more law schools when his wife asked him why he had to live someone else's dream. Why couldn't he just be himself? They had a heated argument, but Adam realized that she was right. He decided to pursue his own desires rather than those of his parents.

Similarly, Audrey, a nutritionist in a suburban medical center, recalls how her parents filled out her high-school program for her when she was in eighth grade. It was a secretarial program. When she took it to her homeroom teacher, the teacher looked at her and asked: "Is this what you really want to do?" She recalls the ensuing scene with gratitude.

I don't remember what I mumbled in reply. She considered it again before quietly tearing it up. Then she completed another form indicating a college preparatory program, and told me to take it home for my parents' signature. My life turned around in that moment. From the bottom of my heart, I am grateful to her for having the courage to do that for me.

For Joan, a free-lance writer and novelist, the awareness came like an "aha." Joan is thirty-seven, but looks more like thirty. She is clearly happy with her life, and loves to talk about both her past and her present. It was, she told us, a flash of insight that changed the course of her life. She grew up in a family in which the lives of the three daughters were defined early by their parents. The older sister was labeled brilliant, and she has carved out a promising career as a scientist. The parents labeled the younger sister as a trailblazer and something of a rebel. She is also a successful professional, but only after years of such things as flying hot-air balloons and traveling to Europe with an older man. For Joan, on the other hand, the label was quite different.

My parents said I was the sweet one, the normal one, the home-loving one. And while my older sister got Erector sets and chemistry sets for Christmas and my younger sister got kites, I was given dolls, nail polish, and pretty sweaters. I was destined to become the perfect wife and mother. Since they also wanted economic security for all of us, I was to be a schoolteacher, a job my parents felt was not too intellectually demanding, but one that could draw on my nurturing talents and not interfere with my primary purpose. And so I grew up and married a handsome man and we had two children. We were the storybook couple who had the storybook wedding and the storybook marriage.

But as stories go, there must come climaxes. And that is where my watershed really begins. We were living in Hawaii, and my husband was working hard to establish his law practice. I was home changing diapers and fixing bottles and hooking rugs. . . . Meals were elegant and promptly on the table at the appropriate time. I prided myself on the fact that I never served the same meal twice in a period of a year. All of my husband's shirts were starched and ironed, and our house looked like a picture out of a home magazine.

In the midst of all of this perfection, Joan says, she became increasingly aware that something was wrong. She did not experience the fulfillment that was supposed to come to her. She started having fights with her husband. She grew despondent. She wasn't sure herself what she wanted or why she felt as she did. She only knew that something was nagging at her. She was living out her parents' dream but felt more as if she had slipped into a nightmare. After struggling with the disquiet for more than a year, she received a letter from her mother that led to a crucial insight.

It was my twenty-sixth birthday. My mom sent a sentimental letter along with a card and present. One sentence in the letter grabbed me and hung in my consciousness for days afterward: she said that I was just what she had always hoped I would be. What *she* hoped I would be. She meant it as a compliment, of course. But I realized that she inadvertently had hit upon my problem.

What I hadn't dealt with before was that I was living my parents' hopes, not my own. When was I going to do the things that I wanted to do, to live my dreams and not theirs? The funniest thing about that to me is that when you have spent twenty-six years living a master plan, it is difficult to ferret out what you really want from what you have come to accept as what you should want.

Joan's experience evokes a story told by comedian Woody Allen. He had a dream once, he said, in which he was to be burned at the stake. His life flashed in front of him. He saw such things as his mother knitting and his father chopping wood. And then he thought, here I am about to die, and the wrong life is flashing in front of me.

Joan, too, saw the wrong life flashing in front of her. It was not the life she had chosen. It was a life picked out and conferred upon her by her parents. She and her husband discussed the problem. He encouraged her to pursue a new plan, and agreed that it should be her plan. He was willing to support her in whatever she chose to do.

Joan had majored in English and had loved writing, so she decided to try writing as a career. The two children went to a babysitter for the first time in their lives. Joan stayed at home with her typewriter and wrote all day. Her parents strongly disapproved of these steps. And Joan and her husband had to deal not only with their reproaches but also with the resistance and tears of two children who had rarely been separated from their mother. But they all survived.

In fact, they more than survived. They now share the rewarding family life that had eluded Joan in the earlier years.

Jerry and I have been married for seventeen years, and we're terrific together. I'm not sure where I would be if I had not finally realized what the problem really was— perhaps in the looney bin! I still hear the parent voices. They're not all bad. I still have to deal with guilt I sometimes feel when I am finding fulfillment in being more than mommy and wife. But I'm really happy. I know who ''me'' is and what direction I want to travel.

I have a wall hanging near my typewriter that I absolutely love. It says that the only two lasting things we can give our children are roots and wings. I was certainly given roots, but the wings came with great difficulty.

At least they came. And they came because Joan was willing to make the difficult decision to pursue her own goals rather than those of her parents. Such decisions are not easy. You run the risk of hurting or upsetting others. But if you shy away from them, you run the risk of stunting your own growth. In the long run, neither Joan's parents nor her children would have been happy if she had remained a despondent wife and mother. Making a decision to pursue her own dream eventually benefitted everyone. ''My parents and children are really proud of what I have done,'' says Joan. ''You would think now that they wanted me to do it all along. My dreams have lifted the whole family.''

Joan urges her children to discover their own dreams and pursue them with passion. Their dreams may or may not be the same as hers. That doesn't matter. As she found out, when you make a decision that gives you wings to go with roots, you are likely to increase not only your own well-being but also that of those you love.

III

Commencing

Do not because a thing is hard for you yourself to accomplish, imagine that it is humanly impossible; but if a thing is humanly possible and appropriate, consider it also to be within your own reach.

Marcus Aurelius

13

Learning to Master Life
Ten Principles

"Ten of the happiest women in America" read the headline on the advertisement. And who were they? Ten women who had lost weight by the method offered in the ad. Another advertisement promised happiness to any child who learned to play the piano. And still another suggested that clean breath was the way to bliss. American advertisers know about our quest for happiness. They know we are much like one of Turgenev's characters, who said: "I expect happiness. I demand it." And they offer us their various wares as a way to increase our happiness.

At a more basic level, happiness is not a matter of doing this particular thing or receiving that particular thing. It is a by-product of being involved in the process of growth. It is a recognition of the fact that any experience or situation presents us with an opportunity, and that even the unexpected, the unpredictable, the undesirable and painful times are ultimately opportunities for growth and mastery. But that insight leads to some important questions: How do you use situations and experiences for personal development? How do you keep from succumbing to despair in a traumatic situation? How do you keep from passing by and ignoring an opportunity for personal enrichment? How do you master life?

People have sought answers to these questions throughout human history. Some of the answers are not useful. They are like the ancient Egyptian cure for the common cold, which employed a rite of exorcism. The sufferer would utter an incantation: "Depart, cold, son of a cold, you who breaks bones, destroys the skull, makes ill the seven openings of the head. Go out on the floor, stink, stink, stink." Arguably, the method may be as effective as any in use today, but it is not the answer to the problem.

The answers we advocate and the methods we suggest are based on the experiences of the hundreds of people who shared their watersheds with us. Out of those experiences we have culled certain principles that seem to be broadly applicable. In particular, there are ten principles, each of which can be used in a variety of circumstances in order to generate a positive watershed.

1. TAKE RESPONSIBILITY FOR YOURSELF

Illness, death, the loss of a job, and problematic love relationships are among the painful experiences of life. Some people deal with them by blaming God, fate, or others. To be sure, there is an element of luck or chance in what happens to us. And we may be exploited or wronged by other people. But ultimately we have to take responsibility for our own lives. We cannot retreat into the false comfort of regarding ourselves as victims and continue to grow. Whatever else we do, we do not have to play out the victim game, no matter how much we are mistreated.

Amy, a Mormon woman, feels that she was wronged and forced into a situation that became a watershed experience for her. Nothing in her life had prepared her to deal with the situation. For as a good Mormon, Amy learned early to acquire the skills that would make her a good wife and mother. In contrast to her present assertive and outgoing nature, she was taught to be passive and obedient to men. She recalls learning to embroider in a church youth class and hearing her teacher admonish the class to "do it neatly so that your future husbands will be impressed with your homemaking skills." She remembers growing up knowing that the major goal of her life was marriage, a "happily-ever-after" union. At first it appeared that she had achieved the Mormon goal. She was married in the temple and the union was sealed for eternity.

I did the prescribed wifely things of my era, helping put my husband through college, moving with him around the country as his employment required, giving the perfect dinners and parties, volunteering for the right charities, and generally being a supportive wife. I also loved the man I married.

But to my astonishment and horror, after twenty-four years of marriage I was fired from my job as a wife. My husband divorced me. In a short six-month period I lost not only my identity, which had been to be a good wife, but also my home, my social role, my connections with other couples who had been our friends, my financial standing, and, most painful, my eternal companion.

Amy joined the ranks of mature single women. She found that the rules for women and their roles had changed. She discovered that women were increasingly expected to have careers, to be self-supporting and self-sufficient. This put her at a disadvantage, since she had neither the education to pursue a particular career nor the belief system to support such a move. Amy clearly had been wronged by her husband, who violated Mormon belief and left her stranded. She had been wronged by married friends who abandoned her. At that point, she could have slipped into self-pity and stayed there for years, stagnating and blaming others for her plight. Instead, Amy took responsibility for herself.

My first step was to resolve not to become a woman wrapped up in her past, clinging to it like a life raft. I wanted to be able to move beyond the hurt and pain and make something special out of my life. I began by taking a real-estate course and getting my license. Then I got a job with a developer selling lots for vacation homes. From there, I moved into my own real-estate office. Soon I'll be the largest independent broker in this city.

Because of her religious beliefs, Amy still struggles with the fact of her divorce and her single status. But by taking responsibility for the course of her life, she has turned a painful episode into a positive watershed.

If I were given the choice, I never would have chosen to be divorced. Nor would I wish it for anyone else. But it has truly been beneficial in my life. I have grown in more ways than I can comprehend. I am happier and more peaceful than I ever was when I was married.

Amy knows other Mormon women for whom life after divorce was basically a grim story. Amy didn't allow that to happen to her. By taking responsibility for her own well-being, she used the divorce to create a new life-style for herself.

2. AFFIRM YOUR OWN WORTH

Crises often assault our self-esteem, a tendency that makes it more difficult to deal with those crises. For we must believe in ourselves and have a sense of our personal value in order to maximize the benefits of any situation. People with a high level of self-esteem tend to get more involved with others and to relate to them in a healthier fashion. They also are more likely to strive to cultivate their personal strengths and to excel in whatever they do. To affirm your own worth, then—to increase your level of self-esteem—is to arm yourself with an invaluable weapon in your struggle to grow.

Affirming your own worth is not something that you do only once. Self-esteem is a precarious possession. We all find ourselves needing to affirm our worth over and over again through our lives. And particularly in a time of crisis, you may find yourself doubting your own abilities or capacities or value. It is important to address that issue in order to grow through the crisis. Keith, a dentist, discovered this when a critical situation in his life led him to raise a question: What kind of person am I if I could kill someone else?

Keith doesn't seem to be the kind of person who could kill anyone. He is a slender, gentle man, who enjoys getting to know his patients personally. He talks freely about his work and his family—a wife and three children. But there is a stony edge that creeps into his voice when he talks about his watershed.

The question of whether Keith could kill emerged as a result of his tour of duty in Vietnam in the early 1970s. As a military dentist, it was unlikely that he would have the occasion to kill anyone. But in Vietnam the combat zone was everywhere. Besides, Keith was sent periodically to mobile medical units near the front lines. What would he do if he came face to face with the enemy?

Keith also worried about his safety and his future. He was distraught over leaving his family, over the possibility that he might kill someone, and over the possibility that he might be killed and never see his family again. Although he never killed anyone, nor even saw anyone killed, the crisis did not abate but deepened when he returned home.

I was bitter. I was bitter that my country sent me there and wasted nearly a year of my life. At the same time, I was aware that my values about obeying orders and responding to my country's needs required me to go. So there it was. A dilemma.

I began to resent my country and to resent myself for meekly obeying. I began to examine my beliefs. I had been trained as a healer. My work is to help people, not harm them. But the country sent me to Vietnam to help those who were killing people. I was torn between my abhorrence of war and my duty as a citizen.

As Keith reflected on his experiences and his beliefs, he found himself embroiled in other conflicts. He felt a need for having control over his life, but felt that going to Vietnam represented a lack of such control. He sensed a need for faith in himself, but wondered how much he could have when he felt betrayed and perplexed by his own value system. He began to wonder what he could believe in. He had long agreed with the notion that men should be strong and self-sufficient and thoroughly rational creatures. He now saw himself changing.

The macho idea notwithstanding, it is okay to cry, to feel, and to express feelings. I discovered that I am happier and more at ease with myself as a person who can be tender, show love outwardly, and cry if the emotion calls for it. I realized this one rainy Saturday when I thought about a young man I treated in Vietnam. He was so full of plans for the future. He was going to be married as soon as he returned. I hope he made it.

At any rate, I thought about how great it is for people to be that excited about their dreams for the future. And then I thought about how insane wars are, how they wreck those dreams for so many people. I got tears in my eyes as I thought about it. My wife noticed them. I was embarrassed, but I told her about my thoughts. Then *she* got tears in her eyes, and told me it was great that I was that sensitive.

The impact of all this on my life was that I began to get in touch with myself and to get some answers to the age-old question, Who am I? I became more aware of the fact that I was a decent human being. That means that I might still get caught up in situations like Vietnam. But I now have the confidence that whatever situation I'm in, I'll choose to act in a way that will be in the best interests of both myself and others.

Keith's affirmation of his own worth—his decision that he "was a decent human being" after all—was an important part of working through his bitterness. And he now can see his crisis of values as a "healthy experience" that marked a turning point in his efforts to grow.

3. BALANCE SELF-CONCERN WITH OTHER-CONCERN

Affirming your own worth means being concerned with yourself and your own well-being. But even the ancients knew that ultimately a person cannot remain self-focused and continue to grow. There is an old Persian legend about a father who went on a long journey and left a mirror with his son. When he returned, he discovered that the boy had starved to death looking at himself. The wholly self-focused life is a self-destructive life.

In other words, you can be too concerned as well as too unconcerned about your own well-being. You can spend too much time and energy absorbed in your own problems. That will hurt you and your relationships. People who are depressed, for instance, can deepen their depression by mulling over their feelings too much. And those who are more self-focused are likely to have poorer interpersonal relationships, including marital ones, than are those who are more oriented toward others. You can only maximize the value of experiences by maintaining a healthy balance between self-concern and other-concern.

Unfortunately, an unexpected crisis not only tends to attack our self-esteem but also tends to hurl us into self-absorption. Some people get so enmeshed in their own problems that they hardly listen to others, much less express any concern for them. Other people find that other-concern is the means of surviving their own difficulties and that it enables them to turn their situation into a positive growth experience. This is what happened to Katie, a personnel administrator for a General Motors subsidiary.

Now in her thirties, Katie was stunned by her parents' divorce when she was a teenager. She recalls her feelings of grief, and her confusion and frustration when her mother asked her which parent she wanted to live with. "I didn't understand what happened between my parents," she said, her southern accent stressing the word "understand." "I was afraid that my mother was going to leave us. I cried for whole days. I went to school but couldn't study. I felt abandoned."

Katie's worst fear came true. She came home from school one day and found that her mother had left. Katie and her brothers and sisters waited for their father to come home, all of them crying as they waited. They begged him to bring her back. But the mother had disappeared. Neither relatives nor close friends knew her whereabouts. Days and weeks passed with no word from her.

Katie's father grew increasingly depressed. The family was fragmented and directionless, a leaderless, troubled group. Katie was grief-stricken. But she looked at her family and realized what was happening. She could not afford to nurse her own grief. Someone had to hold the family together. Katie assumed that responsibility.

"I chose to be a parental child," she recalled. "I became not only my father's daughter, but his closest friend, his housekeeper, and his secretary. I was not only the older sister, but also a friend, a counselor, and a teacher for my brothers and sisters.''

Katie was able to bring the family together again, and to continue her own education. But it was not easy for her. After a few years, the mother renewed contact with the family. She wanted to see her children. But Katie's father objected. He pressured the children not to see the mother. Her abandonment was proof, he said, that she did not care about them. And their desire to see her made him wonder about their love for him.

None of the children wanted to hurt the father. But they wanted to see their mother. Katie was caught in the middle: ''I was very frustrated. I wanted to comfort my brothers and sisters and also please my father. For the most part, I think I succeeded. I made arrangements for an occasional visit with my mother when my father was at work.'' Her father knew the children had some contact with their mother. But it was easier for him to accept if he didn't know exactly when and if all the children reassured him frequently of their love and appreciation for him.

Although her mother left eighteen years ago, there is still tension with her father over the extent to which Katie and her siblings see their mother. Her father's unwillingness to put his loss behind him is distressful to Katie. Still, she sees the experience as ''a valuable thing in my life. It made me stronger, more mature, and proud of myself.'' By refusing to become mired in self-concern, by maintaining her concern for others, Katie grew instead of shrinking into self-pity as her father had.

4. FIND AND USE AVAILABLE RESOURCES

When the tide of adversity sweeps over us, it tends to leave a disturbing feeling of aloneness in its wake. That aloneness signifies a certain helplessness, a sense of being without the resources necessary to meet the challenge. It is important to keep in mind that there are always options because there are always resources available. One of the resources used by Keith, the dentist, in dealing with his crisis of values was an article by psychologist Carl Rogers. Keith does not remember the title or where he read it. But he does remember its significance in helping him through his crisis.

Rogers discussed the fact that we each have two sets of values. One set is external. These are the values that we acquire throughout our lives. We get them from various sources—church, parents, government, laws, advertising, movies. Rogers said we simply accept these values, internalize them without questioning them, and act in accord with their instructions. The other set is internal. These are the things we actually believe, if we examine our feelings.

But we tend to act on the external values, because so many people advocate them that we think they must be right. It's possible to live for years without even realizing which values are dominant in our lives. But if something happens to bring the two sets into conflict with each other, we might begin to get in touch with what our internal values are. And that is exactly what happened to me.

The article not only clarified his experience, but helped him to work through it and grow.

Kimberly, a housewife, told us about a different kind of resource. A watershed occurred in her life when she tried to deal with the temper tantrums of her infant son. Kimberly had interrupted her career in television production to raise him. She and her husband, the chief financial officer for a manufacturing firm, agreed that she should stay at home for about three to four years before returning to work. Kimberly anticipated halcyon days of intimacy, a kind of extended vacation in which she and her son would experience richness of life and growth. But the first thing she discovered was that an infant is total demand at one end and total irresponsibility at the other. The moments of quiet intimacy were far less frequent than the moments of harried response to demands.

Worse, the fretfulness of the newborn gradually gave way to the temper tantrums of the growing infant. Her response was to spank the child. But that did not stop the tantrums. Kimberly was increasingly frustrated with her inability to change her son's behavior. In the midst of her bewilderment, a friend suggested a class on how to be a successful parent. The friend had found it very helpful.

Kimberly started attending. She talked with the instructor,

who was a professional counselor, and came to realize that her son's behavior was an extension of her own. She hadn't recognized that she was communicating her own frustration and tension to her son. She didn't realize how much she resented the break in her career. And she had not admitted to herself that she, an educated and successful woman, had doubts about her ability to raise a child. She began to see the counselor regularly. Eventually, she learned to accept her decision to forgo her career temporarily; and she discovered how to think before acting, how to avoid self-defeating thoughts, and how to feel confident about her abilities as a parent.

Kimberly's access to the needed resources began with a friend. It is hardly possible to overstate the significance of our relationships as resources. One man who had lived a fruitful and happy life explained his success in four words: "I had a friend." His "friend" was his wife. A meaningful marital relationship is one of the most important resources any of us has. A quality marriage is one of the best predictors of mental health in people. Friends and close relatives are also strong resources. They are a part of the social support network that enables us not merely to cope with but to master the problems of life.

5. LEARN THE ART OF REFRAMING

There is an old story about a man who wrote to the department of agriculture in his state to find out how to cope with the crabgrass that was spoiling his lawn. The department responded with a number of suggestions. The man tried them all, but he could not completely eliminate the crabgrass. Exasperated, he wrote the department again, noting that every method they had suggested had failed. His yard was still riddled with crabgrass. He got back a short reply: "We suggest you learn to love it."

That is the art of reframing, redefining something so that it is no longer as problematic. It isn't the situation that is changed, of course; it is your perspective on the situation. You learn to look at something that you had defined as troublesome for you and redefine it as adaptive and useful. The technique is useful for overcoming a variety of problems.

For example, a group of depressed and lonely college students met in groups to try to overcome their loneliness. One group was given instructions in reframing—on how to experience loneliness in a more positive way. The students were told that <u>loneliness can be a way of learning a new mode of life, of learning to be more adaptable and creative.</u> The other group was encouraged to try to overcome loneliness by such things as continuing efforts to meet new people. People in both groups became less lonely over time, but those who had learned to reframe had a more significant reduction in depression than those in the other group.

Reframing is not an exercise in self-deception. It is not a denial of your feelings. The technique is based on the fact that people can look at any situation in various ways. You can curse loneliness as a blight on your life, or you can view it as a transitional period that you can use to your benefit. You can see a crisis as an intruder that robbed you of a measure of happiness and peace, or you can define the crisis as an obstacle that led to your growth as you overcame it. Interestingly, your definition is not merely based on the outcome; rather, the outcome depends on your definition.

Vicky, a thirty-five-year-old accountant for a large brewery, learned to reframe when she felt that her home was being turned into an international hotel. What started out as an odious intrusion turned into an exciting adventure.

Five years ago, everything was going well with us. My husband Jed and I both had good jobs. We had a nice, large home. We had a daughter who had just started school. Then Jed came home one day and made an announcement that changed our lives. His boss was active in an international-friendship group and had asked if we would allow a foreign student to stay in our home for a year.

Now Jed didn't come home and ask me what I thought. If he had, I would have told him right then that it was the worst idea I had heard in years. I don't like people living in my house. I don't even like to have close relatives visit for more than a few days. You know the old saying? Fish and company stink after three days? That's exactly the way

I felt. But Jed didn't ask me. He *told* me that we were going to have a foreigner live with us for a year.

We had quite an argument that night. I absolutely refused. He said we had no choice. It was, after all, his boss who had asked him. I told him he didn't have to baby-sit for his boss. He said it wasn't like baby-sitting, it was more like reaching out and touching someone. I told him to forget the commercials and go tell his boss the answer was no. He told me the date that the student would arrive.

Vicky lost the argument and gained a houseguest. He was a young man from Sweden. After one week, she confronted Jed with the fact that she had been right: they had lost control of their lives. They no longer felt free to do whatever they pleased in their own house. Jed only shrugged and pointed out how much his boss obviously appreciated their willingness to participate in the program.

It turned out that Jed wasn't too happy about our guest either. Then one night as we were all watching television, I really looked at this stranger in our midst. He was sitting on the couch, sort of drawn up into himself. Like he was trying to keep separate from the rest of us. And I suddenly felt queasy, like I had been a child abuser. He knew how we felt, even though we had tried to appear friendly and interested in him.

That night, Jed and I talked a long time. I told him we had to do something. I didn't want someone in my house, but I wasn't going to let that boy go on feeling like he was some kind of a wart. I told Jed that we simply had to make the best of the situation. I suggested we accept the fact that he would be with us for nearly a year, but that we agree not to take in any more students after he was gone. That way, I could cope with it. I also suggested that we work on making him really feel wanted in our home.

Vicky knew that the only way she could make the young Swede feel welcome was to change her own feelings. Simply knowing that he would be the last foreign student in her home wasn't enough. Then it struck her that they knew very little about Sweden. Now they had a chance. "Let's look at this as a learning opportunity," Vicky suggested. "Let's find out what Sweden and the Swedes are really like."

Vicky reframed the situation from an intrusion to an opportunity. And the result was something unexpected: she and Jed so enjoyed their guest that they have continued in the program. Over the past five years, they have had students from twenty different countries in their home for varying amounts of time.

> Our family's life has changed. We are so much more aware of people, world events, customs, and even our own behavior. We've learned to love people of all kinds. It's been great for our daughter as well as for us. We've been to Europe once and are looking forward to traveling abroad more and more. Do you know that the sun never sets on our friends? We have them everywhere!

6. PRACTICE "SILVER-LINING" THINKING

Reframing suggests putting a whole new perspective on a situation or event. In some cases, you may not be able to completely recast an experience in a new light. But you can still practice "silver-lining" thinking, which is looking for the positive in an otherwise undesirable situation. For instance: Todd moved to a job in a new state, but quickly felt he had erred. After a number of years on the job, he still believed that the move was a mistake, but he found a way to deal with it.

> If I focus on the things that bother me about the job, I get depressed. Instead, I keep reminding myself of the good things I've gotten from it. And there really are some good things. I like where I live now. I've made some new friends. The job requires me to train others and I get a lot of gratification from that.
>
> My mother used to sing a song about looking for the silver lining. "There's always a silver lining," she would say, "no matter how black the clouds are." I believe that.

So I try to look for the silver lining. And that's where I focus my thoughts instead of on the black clouds.

Silver-lining thinking doesn't mean denying problems. It simply reflects the fact that there are nearly always some positive aspects, or some positive gains, in a situation. This is what you should concentrate on, particularly when you cannot change the negative aspects.

Silver-lining thinking is healthy. In a study of people whose homes were damaged or destroyed by fire, psychologist Suzanne Thompson reported that those who found positive meaning in the event coped better and were less likely to blame others. They found positive meaning in various ways. Some talked about such side benefits as bringing the family closer together. Some compared themselves with people who had had worse things happen to them. Some were grateful that there wasn't an even worse outcome, like someone in the family getting seriously hurt or killed in the fire. And others simply shrugged off the incident and got on with their lives.

Positive thinking helps us to cope better by enhancing our sense of well-being. Negative thinking about events and experiences diminishes our well-being. Moreover, negative thinking seems to have a subtle, long-term effect. For some unknown reason, people who have negative thoughts have a lower sense of well-being not only while holding the thoughts but also after the thoughts are no longer in their minds.

Still, can you control your thinking? Can you thrust out the negative thoughts and substitute the positive? You can if you practice. Begin by reminding yourself each day that you want to focus on the positive. Then whenever you catch yourself in a negative train of thought, say to yourself, *Stop!* Imagine that you are commanding yourself in a firm voice. Then consciously start looking for the positive to fill the void. You can also use other methods as reminders, such as snapping your finger against your cheek or arm as a signal to stop the negative thinking. These methods will not prevent any negative thoughts from entering your mind, but they will bring them quickly to an end when they do appear, and will allow you to get back to the positive.

For example, suppose that your boss berates you for a mistake or asks you to work overtime when you prefer to be doing other things. If you keep rehashing in your mind the interaction you had with your boss, thinking of what you said and what you wished you had said, you will only keep reexperiencing a negative event. But you can learn to say stop to yourself as soon as your thoughts turn to the interaction, and you can start thinking instead about something positive, such as a forthcoming vacation. Better yet, you can focus on the positive aspects of the encounter, such as how you will use it to improve your relationship with your boss and perform better on the job.

7. PERSEVERE WITHIN REASON

The history of human achievement is filled with stories of perseverance. Artists and scientists may struggle for years without any apparent progress or reward before they finally succeed. Similarly, you can miss out on a growth experience by giving up too quickly. ''Giving up'' may mean not working at a relationship long enough, or not searching hard enough for the positive in some traumatic experience, or not thinking long enough about an important decision, or not staying long enough at a new location. Again and again, people have told us about the positive consequences of persevering, of refusing to give up in the quest for meaning and growth.

Dr. Milton Erickson was a major figure in the development of modern clinical hypnosis. When he was seventeen, he fell victim to polio and was left completely paralyzed. He had to have a full-time nurse to care for him. But Erickson would not surrender to what seemed to be an inevitable fate. One day he was alone for a short time, tied securely to a kind of rocking chair. He wanted to look out of a window, but could not do so because of the position of the chair. Then he noted with surprise that his chair was rocking slightly. He realized that he must have made some movement with his body to cause the chair to rock.

Erickson began to concentrate on the ways in which he had moved his body before he got sick. He practiced making movements in his mind and tried to translate that to his body. Eventually, he was able to make some small, uncoordinated movements. He also watched his baby sister, who was just then learning how to walk. He observed her every movement until he knew the patterns that he would need if he were ever to walk again. As he continued to practice, he eventually regained conscious control over the movement of various parts of his body. Ultimately, he recovered most of his motor abilities. With the aid of a cane, he even walked again.

Erickson's remarkable recovery underscores the importance of perseverance. We would not want to be misleading, however. We are not suggesting that anyone can overcome any kind of illness or disease by exercising the power of the mind. That is why we say to persevere "within reason." Perseverance does not always yield positive results. As we write this, we are watching a bird on a neighboring house. The bird keeps flying into a glass window, bouncing off, peering at the window for a moment, then flying back into it again. For some reason, it seems to want to get in. It also seems willing to persevere. But we know that its perseverance is in vain. It will never gain entrance.

Perseverance is not always healthy. There are people who remain in an abusive marriage for decades. There are people who remain for years in a job that wrings all the vitality out of their lives. There are people who refuse to take the risk of a new location, choosing instead to persevere in a known and safer situation.

So it is important to distinguish between an unhealthy or unproductive perseverance and one that will yield beneficial results. The key is whether any progress is being made. The bird's futile efforts changed nothing. We know a physical therapist who is dissatisfied with his position, has been offered another that would require him to move to a different city, but remains where he is. He perseveres in the hope that his situation will improve. He has been waiting at least seven years, with no sign of progress.

In contrast, Erickson could see his efforts slowly yielding results. Similarly, Marianne, a television director, told us that she worked through a five-year period of difficulty in her marriage and now has a strong, supportive relationship with her husband.

There were times when I just wanted to chuck the whole thing. We were both getting our careers going and it caused a lot of trouble. Some problems, like who was going to do what around the house, took a long time to work out. We solved others with relative ease. For instance, we agreed early on that we would have to allow each other to work at odd hours, which meant we wouldn't always be able to have dinner together. If it weren't for those small gains we made from time to time, we would probably not be married today. And that would have been a real loss for both of us.

Reasonable perseverance, like that of Erickson and Marianne, pays off richly. It is a necessary ingredient in the transforming of mediocrity into excellence.

8. LOWER YOUR AWARENESS THRESHOLD

It is said that someone once asked Helen Keller to identify the worst thing that could happen to a person. The worst thing, she replied, is to have vision and not see. The person who looks at the world but never sees any of the marvels of life is a deprived individual. The person who listens to the sounds of the world but never hears anything exquisite or deeply meaningful is a deprived individual.

You can miss a watershed experience simply because your awareness threshold is too high. It may be too high because you are preoccupied with your own thoughts rather than engaged with the world around you. It may be too high because you are not interested in what is going on around you. It may be too high because you simply haven't put the effort into absorbing as much as possible of your environment. In other words, lowering your threshold means actively listening and actively seeing. And that means engaging with your environment, putting energy into seeing and listening so that you take in as much as possible, and reflecting upon what you have seen and heard.

Calvin, an ophthalmologist, learned the value of a lowered awareness threshold in an encounter with a "stranger" who turned out not to be a stranger at all. The son of a physician, Calvin knew from an early age that, like his father, he would pursue medicine as a career. A tall man with an easygoing manner, Calvin had always meshed comfortably with his world. Then, at the age of forty-two, when he was highly involved with his profession, satisfied with his ten-year-old marriage, and delighted with his two children, Calvin received the first serious setback of his life: his wife told him that she wanted a trial separation.

"I was stunned," he confessed. "I regarded this woman as a combination of Aphrodite and Hera, an exemplar and protector of love, beauty, marriage, and motherhood. I thought she was proud of me and my success and that she found fulfillment in caring for the family."

But Calvin's wife was restless. She wanted to explore her own potential. She wanted the freedom to discover herself. There was no other man, she assured him. And she would allow him to retain custody of the children. Calvin reluctantly agreed to the separation. "I thought she would soon realize what she had left and return home," he explained. "But she didn't. After a year, she filed for divorce, and went off to conquer the world."

After the divorce, Calvin began to take greater note of his environment. Previously, he had not paid much attention to other people. He was usually engrossed in his own thoughts about his work. But now he started watching couples to see if they appeared happy. He watched children to see how they related to their parents. "I began to be more observant about everything in an effort to understand a world that had become perplexing to me for the first time in my life," Calvin said. It was this greater awareness that led to his watershed. It occurred on a day that he went to a tennis club to pick up the children after a weekend with their mother.

As usual, I dreaded seeing my ex-wife. Every time I saw her, I relived the pain of the divorce. I decided to sit on a bench just outside the club and wait for her. I watched the people as they walked by. Among others, I noticed a middle-aged, slightly overweight, female tennis player coming toward me. She was neither attractive to me nor attention-getting in any way. She was just an average-looking, middle-aged woman, slightly overweight. There was really nothing to distinguish her from the thousands of unnoticed females one might see on the street every day.

As she walked closer, I also noticed the rather odd, almost masculine way she carried herself. And then, when she was within a few feet of me and spoke, I realized that this was my ex-wife. My Aphrodite! I suddenly realized that I had not been rejected by a goddess, but by an ordinary woman, not really distinguishable from thousands of other women in the world.

Calvin had been married to a fantasy. His wife had been an idealized projection of the kind of woman he desired for a mate. To be discarded by such beauty and virtue was a shock to his self-confidence. To see her in a new light was liberating.

I wonder now why I saw her so idealistically in the past. At any rate, that experience set me free. I saw her as she is, just another human with all the frailties and shortcomings of the rest of us. Since that day, I have been free to continue on with my own life. And it's a much different life. I don't think I will ever again go through a day so wrapped up in my own thoughts that I am oblivious of the world and all of its diverse people.

Active seeing and active listening require energy. You can't engage in them all of the time. Sometimes the mind lies fallow, and that is refreshing and renewing. But the mind that is always fallow will walk listlessly through a bland world. The energy required to lower your awareness threshold will pay rich and interesting dividends.

9. PERIODICALLY RESTRUCTURE YOUR LIFE

You can't teach an old dog new tricks? Don't believe it. We have seen example after example of people who used a crisis or a meaningful experience of some kind to restructure their lives in some way. We have encountered people who gained a new perspective on what is important or who changed some aspect of their personality or who made a decision to pursue a new direction in their lives.

Restructuring does not necessarily mean revolution. Gaining a new perspective, for instance, may seem to an outsider to be a minor change. But it can add a dimension of richness to an individual's entire life, as it has for Jesse, an insurance broker whose firm is in Philadelphia. He does not seem now to have the stubbornness of character that led to his watershed.

Jesse's experience occurred some six years ago when he was traveling in Europe with his wife and daughter. They were in France and decided to drive on into Italy. Jesse looked at the map. He felt they had plenty of gas to make the trip, even though his wife objected to taking a chance on running out. Jesse, however, didn't want to change any more dollars into francs. It was not a wise decision on his part.

My interpretation of the map turned out to be a little off, and by the time it was nightfall we had reached some mountains between France and Italy. At that point my wife was very upset. Our gas tank was getting empty and she started complaining about my stubbornness. She told me that I was just like my father—pigheaded. She had told me that before. But this time, for the first time, I knew she was right and I knew we could be in trouble because of it. We began the climb over the mountains. A red warning light came on to indicate that the gas level was down to about one liter. We passed through a town but it was a tiny village with no gas station.

This was the point that my watershed really began. We were suddenly in a pea-soup fog and I couldn't see forward or backward more than a few feet. I tried to follow the lines in the middle of the road. Eventually the lines disappeared. By then, we were in actual trouble. We had very little gas, no visibility, no lines to follow, and the certainty that there was a drop straight down somewhere nearby. That's not all. Things actually got worse. Trucks coming into France suddenly started passing us. They came out of nowhere. You could hear them before you could see them, but I didn't know whether I was on the right side of the road. I almost peed in my pants.

After what seemed like an interminable amount of time, they made it to the border crossing and slept there in their car for the rest of the night. The next day they drove into Italy. Once the fear and irritation subsided, Jesse reflected on the experience. He says he became "much more conscious of how much my wife and daughter mean to me." He still talks about the experience with a shudder: "It scares me even now when I think about what could have happened." He also feels that he is less "hardheaded" now. The restructuring is not radical, but it is meaningful. Jesse has discovered at a relatively early age that he can modify himself to improve the quality of his life.

10. DEVELOP HARDINESS IN YOUR PERSONALITY

One of the ways to restructure your life is to change some aspects of your personality, and one of the most important aspects of personality for dealing with unexpected crises is hardiness. Hardiness is a concept developed by psychologist Suzanne Kobasa. She studied a group of executives who had been exposed to similar demands over a three-year period. Some of the executives became ill as a result of the stresses while others did not. She termed the latter the "hardy" executives and raised the question of what differentiated them from those who succumbed to illness.

In essence, Kobasa found three personality dispositions that the hardy executives possessed: commitment, control, and challenge. Commitment involves an engagement with life. The committed individual confronts life and actively engages it rather than facing it passively or trying to avoid it.

Control is a sense of having some power or influence over the situations and experiences we face. It means that the individual does not feel helpless in the face of massive external forces but recognizes that he or she always has some options and some influence over outcomes. We never have complete control, of course. But that isn't necessary. We only need to recognize that we are not pawns that are being moved about by forces over which we have no influence.

Challenge is an acceptance of the fact that change rather than stability is the essence of life and that, therefore, we should look at change with anticipation rather than as a threat. Challenge means that the individual looks at change as stimulating, as an opportunity to grow. Growing people do not put their energies into protecting and conserving what is; they are ready for change and for the zest that change brings to life. This does not mean an abandonment of the past. We never change totally. Neither can we totally preserve. Challenge means to be ready to change in part and to preserve in part, and to recognize that both the change and the preservation can increase our well-being.

Kobasa found that executives who had a large number of stressful events but comparatively little illness had a greater degree of commitment, control, and challenge than those executives with a large number of stressful events and a good deal of illness. The hardy personality is a buffer between your well-being and the stress of unexpected crises or heavy demands. In a later study, Kobasa and S. R. Maddi found that hardiness can be developed in people. You can learn to have a greater degree of commitment, challenge, and control.

One way to develop hardiness is to recognize and practice its essentials. For example, if you recognize that you tend to hold back from your environment, you can make a conscious decision to become more engaged and to behave accordingly. If you are unable to do this (keep in mind that it takes time to develop this ability), you may need help from someone else. Psychiatrist Richard Formica argues that all patients are, at bottom, terrified of committing themselves to life and that they try to avoid commitment to their experiences. Unless you suffer from some deep-rooted problem requiring therapy, however, you should be able to practice and acquire the dispositions of commitment, control, and challenge.

Consider a simple example. Rachel, a buyer for a department store, is in her early thirties. She looks like a living advertisement for the well-dressed woman. Her watershed experience occurred when she was twenty-six. Rachel grew up with protective parents.

I was an only child. My parents loved me dearly, but they were probably overly protective. After I graduated from college, I got a job in another city. My parents didn't want me to leave home, and they were afraid for me to live by myself. But my best friend, Maxine, with whom I had been inseparable since the sixth grade, also found a job near mine. We decided to move into an apartment together, and my parents felt comfortable with that.

We both dated, but nothing serious seemed to develop until Maxine met this one guy. She really fell for him. We had been living together about four years then. But she decided to go to Europe with him for the summer. When she left, I felt afraid and lost. It was the first time I had been on my own. I didn't have any other relationship to fall back on. It was a really novel situation. For a while I was just afraid and lonely.

Instead of letting the experience become an episode of pain in her life, however, Rachel turned it into a positive watershed by exhibiting the qualities of hardiness. As she assessed her situation, she came to see that she faced a challenge, a challenge to redeem the situation and turn the change into something positive for herself. She realized that she was not a helpless victim in the situation. She was deprived of her best friend, but she was not deprived of all control. It was up to her to identify her options and decide what to do about the situation. Although she had been committed to Maxine, the friendship had limited her. She decided it was time for a change.

The first thing I did was to try to make friends at work. I had worked with some of those people for four years but had never done anything socially with them. I was surprised to find that I made friends rather easily, and I think they were surprised that I suddenly seemed interested. When I was with Maxine, I only made decisions jointly with her. In fact, I usually went along with her decisions, even when I disagreed. Now I began to make day-to-day decisions on the basis of what I felt *I* wanted to do.

Before long I had broadened my interests and felt more

independent and secure. So the consequence of the undesirable separation was that I formed other friendships for the first time in my life and greatly expanded my horizons. A scary and, at the time, negative experience had turned into an opportunity for me.

The hardy person can take the most negative experience and the most severe stresses, neutralize them, and even turn them into positive watersheds.

Here, then, are ten principles that form a powerful set of tools for the mastery of life:

1. Take responsibility for yourself.
2. Affirm your own worth.
3. Balance self-concern with other-concern.
4. Find and use available resources.
5. Learn the art of reframing.
6. Practice "silver-lining" thinking.
7. Persevere within reason.
8. Lower your awareness threshold.
9. Periodically restructure your life.
10. Develop hardiness in your personality.

The challenge is to move from knowledge of these principles to action. We heard a man teach a useful course on conflict resolution and admit that it was easier to teach than to practice. "I have to remind myself to use these principles in my own conflict situations," he said. "In the heat of controversy, I have sometimes realized that I was violating or ignoring all of the things I teach in this class."

In general, people don't automatically incorporate good ideas into their lives. We tend to continue on in the patterns to which we are habituated. That means that you consciously will have to remind yourself to employ the principles of mastery. You have been introduced to them. Take the next step and begin to use these principles in both the commonplace and the unexpected situations you face.

A woman who had a cherished gift from an old friend, a rather expensive silk handkerchief, accidentally got a blot of ink on it. She showed it sorrowfully to an artist friend one day, telling the artist that the handkerchief was now ruined. The artist asked if he could take it home. A few weeks later, he sent it back to the woman. He had used the blot as a starting point and had drawn a strikingly attractive design in india ink. The handkerchief was more beautiful than when the woman first received it.

The artist took the skills he had and turned what appeared to be a disaster into an object of exceptional charm. He refused to allow an accident to mar his friend's mood. He was an indomitable person—not because he was inherently stronger than the rest of us, but because he made use of the necessary skills. Indomitable people are made, not born. They are made as they learn and put into action the principles we have discussed. These ten principles enable you to seize the various opportunities that come your way, confront the unpredictable crises of life, and master them all in a way that will bring you the joy of growth.

Selected Readings

Allport, Gordon W. *Becoming*. New Haven: Yale University Press, 1955.

Baltes, Paul B., and Orville G. Brim, Jr., eds. *Life-Span Development and Behavior*. Vol. 2. New York: Academic Press, 1979.

Baruch, Grace, Rosalind Barnett, and Caryl Rivers. *Lifeprints: New Patterns of Love and Work for Today's Women*. New York: McGraw-Hill, 1983.

Bergen, Candace. *Knock Wood*. New York: Linden Press, 1984.

Berger, Peter L., and Thomas Luckmann. *The Social Construction of Reality*. New York: Anchor Press, 1966.

Borg, Bjorn. *My Life and Game*. New York: Simon and Schuster, 1980.

Campanella, Roy. *Good to Be Alive*. Boston: Little, Brown and Company, 1959.

Cheever, Susan. *Home before Dark*. Boston: Houghton Mifflin Company, 1984.

Colson, Charles W. *Born Again*. Old Tappan, N.J.: Chosen Books, 1976.

Ford, Betty, and Chris Chase. *The Times of My Life*. New York: Harper and Row, 1978.

Foyt, A. J., and William Neely. *A. J.* New York: Times Books, 1983.

Iacocca, Lee, with William Novak. *Iacocca: An Autobiography*. New York: Bantam Books, 1984.

Irwin, James B., and William A. Emerson, Jr. *To Rule the Night*. Philadelphia: A. J. Holman Company, 1973.

James, William. *The Varieties of Religious Experience*. New York: Modern Library, 1902.

Jordan, Barbara. *Barbara Jordan: A Self-Portrait*. Garden City, N.Y.: Doubleday and Company, 1979.

Klausner, Lawrence D. *Son of Sam*. New York: McGraw-Hill, 1981.

Lauer, Jeanette C., and Robert H. Lauer. *'Til Death Do Us Part: How Couples Stay Together*. New York: Haworth Press, 1986.

Lauer, Robert H. *Social Problems and the Quality of Life*. 3d ed. Dubuque, Iowa: William C. Brown, 1986.

Lauer, Robert H., and Warren H. Handel. *Social Psychology: The Theory and Application of Symbolic Interactionism*. Englewood Cliffs, N.J.: Prentice-Hall, 1983.

Maddi, S. R., and Suzanne C. Kobasa. *The Hardy Executive*. Homewood, Ill.: Dow Jones–Irwin, 1984.

Magruder, Jeb Stuart. *An American Life: One Man's Road to Watergate*. New York: Atheneum, 1974.

Marris, Peter. *Loss and Change*. New York: Anchor Books, 1975.

Martin, Mary. *My Heart Belongs*. New York: Quill, 1984.

Maslow, Abraham, H. *Toward a Psychology of Being*. 2d ed. New York: Van Nostrand, 1968.

Mills, Hilary. *Mailer: A Biography*. New York: Empire Books, 1982.

Moos, Rudolf H., ed. *Human Adaptation: Coping with Life Crises*. Lexington, Mass.: D. C. Heath, 1976.

Moustakas, Clark E. *Turning Points*. Englewood Cliffs, N.J.: Prentice-Hall, 1977.

Parkes, Colin Murray, and Robert S. Weiss. *Recovery from Bereavement*. New York: Basic Books, 1983.

Peck, M. Scott. *The Road Less Traveled*. New York: Simon and Schuster, 1978.

Reynolds, Barbara A. *Jesse Jackson: America's David*. Washington, D.C.: JFJ Associates, 1975.

Russell, Diana E. H. *The Secret Trauma: Incest in the Lives of Girls and Women*. New York: Basic Books, 1986.

Ryff, Carol D. ''Personality Development from the Inside: The Subjective Experience of Change in Adulthood and Aging.'' In *Life-Span Development and Behavior*, edited by Paul B. Baltes and Orville G. Brim, vol. 6. New York: Academic Press, 1984.

Scherer, Klaus R., Harald G. Wallbott, and Angela B. Summerfield. *Experiencing Emotion*. London: Cambridge University Press, 1986.

Schwarz, Ted. *The Hillside Strangler: A Murderer's Mind*. Garden City, N.Y.: Doubleday and Company, 1981.

Scott, Willard. *The Joy of Living*. New York: Coward, McCann and Geoghegan, 1982.

Seligman, M. E. P. *Helplessness: On Depression, Development, and Death*. San Francisco: W. H. Freeman, 1975.

Sheehy, Gail. *Passages: Predictable Crises of Adult Life*. New York: Bantam Books, 1976.

Steinbeck, John. *Travels with Charley*. New York: Penguin Books, 1962.

Tournier, Paul. *The Meaning of Persons*. New York: Harper and Row, 1957.

Turner, Jeffrey S., and Donald B. Helms. *Contemporary Adulthood*. 3d ed. New York: Holt, Rinehart and Winston, 1986.

Wheelis, Allen. *How People Change*. New York: Harper and Row, 1973.

Whitehead, Alfred North. *Process and Reality*. New York: Free Press, 1929.

Yankelovich, Daniel. *New Rules: Searching for Self-Fulfillment in a World Turned Upside Down*. New York: Bantam, 1981.

About the Authors

Widely published authors Robert and Jeanette Lauer hold doctorates in sociology and history, respectively, are married, and have four children. *Watersheds* is the fourth book they have written together. Currently they reside in San Diego, where Robert Lauer is a university dean and Jeanette Lauer is a professor of history.